Chinese Students Encounter America

Chinese Students Encounter America

QIAN NING

Translated by T. K. Chu

UNIVERSITY OF WASHINGTON PRESS

Seattle and London

Library of Congress Cataloging-in-Publication Data
Qian, Ning.
[Liu xue Meiguo. English]
Chinese students encounter America / Qian Ning ;
Translated by T.K. Chu.
p. cm.
Includes index.
ISBN 0-295-98180-6 (alk. paper)
ISBN 0-295-98181-4 (pbk. : alk. paper)
1. Chinese students—United States.
I. Chu, T.K. II. Title.
LC3071.Q2513 2002 378.1′9829′951073—dc21 2001044415

The paper used in this publication is acid free and recycled from 10 percent post-consumer and at least 50 percent pre-consumer waste. It meets the minimum requirements of the American National Standard for Information Sciences—Permanence of Paper for Printed Library Materials, ANSI Z39.48–1984. ∞ ♻

CONTENTS

TRANSLATOR'S PREFACE

On January 1, 1979, the United States and the People's Republic of China established diplomatic relations, three decades after the founding of the People's Republic. Five days before the diplomatic exchange, fifty Chinese students arrived in America to begin their studies in its universities. By 1995 more than 220,000 Chinese students had gone abroad, mostly to America, to study. In 1999 about 40,000 Chinese students were enrolled in American colleges and universities, and Chinese students were the highest percentage of international students on many American campuses.[1] Given these students' sheer numbers, their acquired skills, and the social consequences of their immersion in the American environment, the question of how America has influenced these students is of enormous importance to China and, to a lesser degree, to America as well.

Qian Ning attended People's University in Beijing, studying classical Chinese literature in his undergraduate years and Song dynasty poetry in his graduate program before joining *People's Daily* as a cultural reporter in 1986. In September 1989 Qian enrolled in the Journalism Fellowship Program at the University of Michigan and the following year began teaching Chinese literature there. After five years of teaching and interviewing Chinese students about their American experiences, he returned to China in May 1995, and his book about these experiences, *Liuxue Meiguo* (literally, *Studying in America*), was published in August 1996.[2]

Since China began its intense interaction with the West as European and American religion, trade, and military power entered China in the mid-nineteenth century, America—known in Chinese as Meiguo, the "Beautiful Country"—has loomed large in the Chinese people's consciousness of the foreign world. But the juxtaposition of the century-long humiliation dealt to China by foreign powers and the even longer period of China's self-designation as the "Central Kingdom"[3] has led some Chinese to view the West with arrogant ignorance or an inferiority complex, or both. In the summer of 1996 the best-selling book *China Can Say No* (Zhongguo keyi shuo bu), by five writers who had not been to America, denounced America and promoted China as a giant among nations.

Qian Ning's book, released at about the same time, became an instant bestseller. Its authorized and five pirated editions have together sold more than three hundred thousand copies, not counting separate editions in Taiwan and Hong Kong. After the book was published, the public learned that the author's father was Qian Qichen, then China's foreign minister (currently a deputy premier), and that the book was recommended reading for senior Chinese officials.[4]

This English edition allows American readers to see America through a Chinese lens and to reflect on their own society while learning about China. The author's approach is empirical, rather than the black-and-white, moralistic one often found in Chinese publications. America is portrayed as a country with many niceties as well as flaws, and Americans as real people who lead lives quite different from those of Chinese.

In describing China, the book discusses the basis for Chinese views of the West, the confines and harms brought to the Chinese people by the "work unit" system in China's socialistic economy, the hardships and injuries suffered by the people during the violent campaigns in China's three decades of isolation following the Communist revolution in 1949, and other issues.[5] This frankness is exemplified in the deathbed lamentation of a student's father: "I have kept faith with the Communist Party, but the Communist Party has let me down." But life's brutality is exposed always with deep feeling for the victim and never with condescension toward the perpetrator, who, in turn, is recognized as a victim.

Chinese Students Encounter America describes changes in the social behavior of people transplanted to an alien cultural environment. The interviews, though fragmented and without follow-up, include stories of the joys and sorrows of a struggling life in a new land. Present in many episodes are both dark shadows of China's three decades of destruction of human emotional bonds following 1949 and, at times, the sweetness of forgiveness and reconciliation.[6]

EARLIER CHINESE STUDENTS IN AMERICA

The First Dispatch, 1872

In 1872, the year that the Qing court sent its first dispatch of thirty teenage students to America, China had been left behind by the Industrial Revolution by more than a century. Its population had been increasing and the Chinese had become steadily poorer; China's per capita cultivated land, hence real wages, had declined slowly since the twelfth century and rapidly since the mid-seventeenth century.[7] For millennia, China's political and social system had used hierarchical human relations emphasizing benevolence and loyalty to promote social harmony; benevolence was expected from superiors, and loyalty was demanded from subordinates. This institutionalized Confucianism offered no practical means, except execution, for the removal of a ruler (or his power) when he had "outraged his proper benevolence."[8]

It was China's defeats by Great Britain in the First Opium War (1839–42) and by Britain and France in the Second Opium War (1857–60)—wars that also concerned America because of U.S. merchants' interest in the opium trade—that stimulated China's quest for modern knowledge from the West. Two people channeled that quest mostly to America, in spite of a vastly stronger British economic presence in China at that time and Britain's willingness to accept Chinese students. The first was Yung Wing, who went to America to study in 1847 at the age of eighteen and returned to China in 1854 after graduating from Yale University. While still at Yale, he concluded that the way to revitalize China was to send its youth abroad for a Western education such as the one he was receiving. After his return, he tried repeatedly to find supporters of this idea. Yung Wing was the first Chinese to recognize that China was the country lacking in knowledge: it had been ignorant of the outside world and had an unrealistic view of itself.[9]

On the American side, Anson Burlingame (U.S. minister to China from 1861 to 1867) opened the doors of American schools to Chinese students. Following the Second Opium War, there appeared a window of opportunity for a more open China and for more equal trade and state-to-state relations between China and the West.[10] After leaving his ministerial post, Burlingame became China's ambassador-at-large, lobbying in the West (and Russia) for China. In America, through his effort, the two countries signed the Burlingame Treaty of 1868, Article 7 of which stated, "Chinese subjects shall enjoy all the privileges of the public educational institutions under the control of the government of the United States" and provided reciprocal privileges for American citizens.[11] In 1871 Viceroys Zeng Guofan and Li Hongzhang memorialized to Emperor Tongzhi, "Article 7 of the new peace treaty with America states that from now on Chinese who wish to study in [American] government-controlled schools and colleges will be treated the same as citizens from the most favored nation.... For these reasons, your ministers are seeking approval to establish a bureau in Shanghai, to recruit bright young boys from coastal provinces, at the rate of thirty per year, and a total of 120 in four years."[12] Thus China launched its first-ever study-abroad project. Yung Wing became the deputy commissioner of the Chinese Educational Commission. He chose Hartford, Connecticut, as the city for its headquarters.[13] The average age of the students was twelve and a half.

The project met an extraordinary reception in America. The decade that followed the ending of the Civil War in 1865 saw legislations of healing between North and South and tolerance toward minorities. Hartford, besides being in a state experiencing frenzied postwar business expansion, was also an intellectual center in New England. Immigrants were accepted, if not embraced. The project was supported with conviction by clergymen, political leaders, intellectuals, and activists and policy makers in education. The call by Birdsey Northrop, secretary of the Connecticut State Board of Education, for homes to care for the first thirty Chinese students, at two to three per home, drew responses from 122 families in Connecticut and Massachusetts.[14] But the project, slated to continue for twenty years, lasted only nine.

The political climate began to change in the late 1870s. On the Chinese side, the new commissioner and his predecessor, both traditional Chinese scholars, asked Li Hongzhang to disband the commission because they believed the students had abandoned Chinese traditions, acquired foreign (bad) habits, and learned nothing useful to China. Yung Wing wrote to Li in defense of the commission. In America, he tried to secure admission for several Chinese students to the military academies at West Point and Annapolis, so as to meet China's practical needs and win the Qing court's support for the commission. In December 1880 Ulysses S. Grant, urged by Samuel Clemens (Mark Twain) and the Reverend Joseph Twichell of Asylum Hill Congregational Church in Hartford, both supporters of the commission, also wrote to Viceroy Li, advising continuance of the commission.[15]

But the project had also begun to lose its timeliness in America. In 1876 Rutherford Hayes was nominated as the presidential candidate of the Republican Party, thus making Grant a lame-duck president. The sudden drop of the labor market after the completion of the transcontinental railroad led American workers to revolt against immigrant Chinese mining and railroad laborers in Western states. An anti-Chinese sentiment, exploited by both Democrats and Republicans, then swept the nation.[16] The subsequent erosion of liberal disposition toward foreigners and minorities led to the military academies' refusal to admit the Chinese students.[17] The refusal was taken by Li as a violation of the Burlingame Treaty, and the students were recalled in 1881.

American educators protested strongly to the Chinese government. In a letter to China's Ministry of Foreign Affairs, Yale president Noah Porter and several others wrote about educators' anguish, love, and hope:

> The undersigned . . . exceedingly regret that these young men have been withdrawn from the country, and that the Educational Commission has been dissolved. . . . The studies of which they have been deprived by their removal, would have been the bright flower and the ripened fruit of the roots and stems which have been slowly reared under patient watering and tillage. We have given to them the same knowledge and culture that we give to our own children and citizens. . . . In view of . . . the injury and loss which have fallen upon the young men whom we have learned to respect and love, we would respectfully urge that the reason for this sudden decision should be reconsidered.[18]

At the time of the recall, only two students had graduated from Yale. Twenty others were studying at Yale, four at Columbia, seven at the Massachusetts Institute of Technology, and five at Rensselaer Polytechnic Institute; and about sixty students were in preparatory schools.[19] Not until 1909, after China's defeat in the Sino-Japanese War in 1894 and Beijing's occupation by the Eight-Country Allied Force in 1900 (amid other defeats and territorial losses), did the Qing court again send students to America.

China, after its earlier defeats by both the individual and the joint forces of Britain and France, had retained its traditional contemptuous attitude toward Japan, but its devastating defeat by Japan shocked the nation into an awareness of the need to learn from the modern world, both West and East.[20] Because of restrictive U.S. immigration laws and the expenses involved, few Chinese students went to America.[21] Japan, however, besides using Chinese characters as a basis for its written language and thus being easier to adjust to linguistically, was closer geographically and was eager to receive Chinese students.[22] By 1906 the number of Chinese students in Japan had exceeded twelve thousand.[23]

The Boxer Indemnity's Educational Legacy

The event that both enabled and forced China to send students again to America was the United States' agreement in 1908, upon China's prodding, to remit the part of the indemnity resulting from the Boxer Rebellion that was in excess of America's actual incurred losses.[24] The indemnity had been fixed by the Boxer Protocol of 1901 which ended the occupation of Beijing begun in 1900 by the foreign powers.[25]

Before the negotiation among the powers on the indemnity began, Secretary of State John Hay had instructed the American delegation to submit a claim of $25 million against China and to negotiate with the treaty powers for a combined total claim not to exceed $150 million. Hay had inflated the American claim by a factor of two over the country's actual incurred losses, intending to use a reduction of the claim as a bargaining chip to ask that other treaty powers scale down their claims and to secure trade privileges from China. The bargaining with the treaty powers, however, failed, and China was left holding the debt.

The remission was preceded by two related events in U.S.-China relations: initiation of the American Open Door policy toward China in 1899–1901 and the anti-American boycott in China in 1905. William Rockhill, a diplomat and China scholar, formulated the Open Door policy and the response to the boycott. Rockhill had studied Chinese in France, served at the U.S. legations in Beijing and Korea, and resigned from diplomatic service to travel in Tibet and Mongolia before returning to the service in 1893. He was also a special assistant in the American delegation during the Beijing talks on indemnity, and was among the first to question the validity of Hay's claim.

In the 1890s each of the European powers and Japan had carved out its "sphere of influence" in China.[26] In 1899, the year before the siege of the Legation Quarter in Beijing by the Boxers, Hay, urged by Rockhill, asked other treaty powers to adhere to a policy of equal tariff, collected by the Chinese government, on vessels of other nationalities at port cities under each power's sphere of influence.[27] During the siege, sensing that the powers would soon divide China, he expanded this policy to include the preservation of China's territorial and administrative integrity.[28] But the powers' replies were evasive, and the policy was eventually abandoned.[29] Rockhill was disgusted by the stance of the powers, concluded that the policy was poorly thought out, and felt pessimistic about China's ability to reform.[30]

In 1905 Rockhill was named the U.S. minister to China. The pressing issue that awaited him upon his arrival in May was the Chinese boycott of American goods in port cities—the first ever by China of foreign goods. The boycott was a protest against the U.S. policy on Chinese immigrants, the violence against the Chinese in America, and U.S. courts' and state governments' condoning of the violence.[31] Immediately after he assumed his post, Rockhill met with the Chinese merchant guilds in Shanghai that organized the boycott and then warned the Chinese government that it would be held responsible for all losses incurred from disrupted trade and other causes. To the American government, he reported that beneath the boycott he sensed important changes in China for the first time: the voicing of public opinion, the emergence of a native press, and the budding of a patriotic spirit.[32]

In both his advocacy of the Open Door policy and his response to the Chinese boycott, Rockhill was guided by a belief that an orderly society in China was necessary to American interests in that country.[33] It was against these background events that Liang Cheng, China's minister to Washington (1903–7), prodded the American government to return a part of the Boxer indemnity.

Back in 1875, Liang Cheng, an eleven-year old, was a fourth (and last)–dispatch student of the Chinese Educational Commission. He was tutored in Greek by professors at Amherst College before he attended Phillips Andover Academy, where he was a star slugger and pitcher on the school baseball team. The recall of the students in 1881 by the Qing court dashed his plans of attending Yale or Amherst in another year. After returning to China (and introducing baseball to the country), he worked in the Ministry of Foreign Affairs. In Europe he won recognition for his diplomatic skills.[34] During his tenure in Washington, he appeared to be received warmly by John Hay (who was known as an avowed friend of China) and President Theodore Roosevelt (who held the prevailing contemptuous attitude toward the Chinese).[35]

Liang, recognizing the United States as the legal owner of the money under the protocol, buttressed his negotiating position by trumpeting the justice of the remission in newspaper interviews, civic speeches, and discussions with high-level officials. He suggested to Hay that "perhaps a revision of the figures could be made by which the president would be enabled to obtain a clearer sense of the justice of the request my Government had made."[36] By degree, he arrived at a plan for a possible reduction, and Hay agreed to recommend the plan to the president. But the fulfillment of the plan was frustrated by the outbreak of the Russo-Japanese War in 1904 over Russia's demands and claims on China's Manchuria and on Korea, Roosevelt's involvement in the mediation of that war, and later, the death of Hay.

On May 13, 1905, shortly before Rockhill arrived in China to assume his ministerial post, China's Ministry of Foreign Affairs received a letter from Liang in which he stated that the prospect of a reduction of the indemnity payment to America had improved considerably and he had met with Rockhill to draw up an outline of the reduction. But during the meeting, Rockhill claimed that the president wished to know how the Chinese government would spend the money if it were returned. Liang answered that China would not make an advance declaration on a subject that was its internal affair. Sensing an intention on the American side to interfere, and fearful that the money would elude China's grasp, he advised the ministry to have an answer to Roosevelt's question ready when Rockhill called on the ministry as America's new minister. Liang also proposed an answer: the money would be used to establish schools and send students abroad. In his judgment this declaration would win the support of both America's government and its citizens, and the educational plan, if carried out, would be beneficial to China.[37]

On July 12, 1905, two months after his arrival in China and at the peak of the Chinese boycott, Rockhill wrote to Roosevelt, proposing remission of the Boxer Indemnity. He stated that the Chinese government had indicated to him that the money, if returned by the United States, would be used for education. Roosevelt's reply was strong on the issue of justice and ambiguous about what he intended to do.[38] Although the boycott was over by September 1905, he did not act on the remission in the next year and a half. A possible reason for the inaction was that Elihu Root, who succeeded Hay, wanted to postpone implementation until the United States had collected a "sufficient" amount.[39]

In early 1907 Liang Cheng revived his request to the president through Secretary of Interior James Garfield and Secretary of Commerce and Labor Oscar Straus, and Roosevelt agreed to act.[40] On June 15, 1907, Root notified Liang of the planned remission.[41] On December 3, 1907, the president asked Congress for authority to remit and cancel all claims upon China in excess of actual incurred losses. After the House of Representatives cut the president's request by $2 million, Congress authorized the $12 million remission on May 25, 1908.[42]

But the debate and the plot and counterplot on the use of the money had begun long before Congress authorized the remission, and lasted until 1909. Although Liang had first asked the Chinese Ministry of Foreign Affairs to make a declaration to Rockhill that the money would be used for education, both he and his successor, Wu Tingfang (who assumed the post early in the fall of 1907), and the Chinese government in Beijing resisted the interference of the American government in the use of the money. Yuan Shikai, the powerful commissioner of northern ports, wanted to use the money to build railways in Manchuria for defense against Japan and Russia, with the profit from the railway operation to be spent on education. But Rockhill thwarted all of China's diplomatic maneuvers to free the money from the educational plan.[43] In the end Rockhill prevailed on account of the strength of his ultimatum: accept the American proposal or risk losing the money. In the final agreement, the plan was included as an attachment and made no reference to the remission; the United States did not appear coercive, nor China subjugated. The remission won lavish public and private praise.[44] Thus China began sending students to America for the second time, with funding assured for thirty-one years. The remitted fund was also used to establish the Tsinghua School, which eventually would supply the students for study abroad. The first dispatch of fifty students began their studies in America in 1909.

American and Chinese Perspectives

In 1872 and in 1909 both Americans and Chinese viewed the issue of Chinese students in America from their own culture perspective. America's earnestness in accepting and educating the Chinese students was based on Christian missionary ideals and zeal: a Western education was considered necessary for China to become a civilized society, so that the Chinese could become patriotic, courageous, altruistic, intellectually clear-headed, and sincere—Christian attributes that they found lacking in the Chinese. Anson Burlingame, when serving as China's ambassador-at-large, promoted China by claiming that China was ripe for conversion to Christianity. Many of Yung Wing's supporters in Hartford were members of the Asylum Hill Congregational Church, and Yung Wing had as a teenager been taught in China and brought over to America by the Reverend Samuel Brown.

In 1890, a decade before the siege at Beijing, Arthur Smith, dean of the American missionary educators in China and one of the few China experts of his time, summarized his diagnosis of and cure for China:

> What they [the Chinese] do lack is Character and Conscience.... The forces which have developed character and conscience in the Anglo-Saxon race ... came with Christianity, and they grew with Christianity. ... What China needs is righteousness, and in order to attain it, it is absolutely necessary that she have a knowledge of God and a new conception of man, as well as of the relation of man to God.... The manifold needs of China ... will be met permanently, completely, only by Christian civilization.[45]

Smith met with Roosevelt on March 6, 1906, to press for the remission and the American educational plan, although he considered that the money was rightfully America's because it was a "*punitive* indemnity for a great criminal act" of the Chinese government against the American government. In the same year, Edwin James, the president of the University of Illinois, wrote to Roosevelt,

> The nation which succeeds in educating the young Chinese of the present generation will be the nation which for a given expenditure of effort will reap the largest possible returns in moral, intellectual, and commercial influence.... The extension of such moral influence ... would mean a larger return for a given outlay than could be obtained in any other manner. Trade follows moral and spiritual domination far more inevitably than it follows the flag.[46]

On China's side, the purpose of sending students to America was to acquire knowledge of machinery. With strong battleships at sea and powerful cannons in its forts, China could then ward off "ocean people's" invasion of its territory and treasury and their encroachment on its cultural ideal of benevolence. Two millennia ago a similar need to ward off land invaders had led to construction of the first segments of the Great Wall. In the late 1870s the commissioner of the Chinese Educational Commission and his predecessor, both of whom had been nurtured as classics scholars in China, were the most resolute opponents of the commission; they perceived that American education had eroded in the students China's cultural ideals, which they believed the students must retain. The influential viceroy Zhang Zhidong had defined the acceptable use of Western knowledge: Chinese learning was the essence, and Western learning was for practical development. In 1901 he and Viceroy Liu Kunyi advised the throne to send students to Japan because "there is no school in Europe and America that does not teach Western religion concurrently, and no school in Japan that does not teach harmonious human relations concurrently."[47] Western religion was seen as spearheading the threat to Chinese learning. (Zhang succeeded in preventing the State Department's appointment of an American as superintendent of the remission educational plan.)

The American side also viewed the recall in 1881 as a missed opportunity for exerting its influence and wanted a second chance. In the same letter to Roosevelt on the American educational plan in 1906, James wrote, "If the United States had succeeded thirty five years ago, as it looked at one time as if it might, in turning the current of Chinese students to this country, and had succeeded in keep[ing] that current large, we should to-day be controlling the development of China in that most satisfactory and subtle of all ways,—through the intellectual and spiritual domination of its leaders."[48] America wanted the Chinese students to acquire its moral, spiritual, and intellectual learning. China wanted the students to learn America's technological know-how. Education as a means to understand the cause of poverty and seek deliverance from it was not a stated goal. China had felt pain and humiliation in the stranglehold of foreign powers, but it had remained ignorant as to the Chinese people's progressive impoverishment.

The Republic Years between 1911–1949

Between 1909 and 1911, the last years of the Qing's reign, three detachments totaling 179 students were sent to America.[49] After the founding of the Republic of China, the students supported by the remission money were selected from the Tsinghua School. Between 1912 and 1925 a total of 852 students, including forty-three women, were sent to America.[50] In 1928 the Tsinghua School became a full-curriculum university and the remission fund became available to a nationwide pool of students. Although in subsequent years the fund supported an increasingly smaller percentage of students studying in America when other avenues opened, it continued to attract the brightest students in China.[51] In 1936, the year before China's War of Resistance against Japan began, 1,002 Chinese students went to America to study. During the war years, 1937–1945, the number dropped to less than a hundred per year. After the People's Republic of China was founded in 1949, no students from mainland China went to America for thirty years. After the breakout of the Korean War in June 1950, the United States blocked Chinese students from returning to China, a subject that Qian Ning addresses in this book.

THE INFLUENCE OF FOREIGN-EDUCATED STUDENTS IN CHINA

What did the American education of these students accomplish? Many of the teenage students who returned to China in 1881, in spite of the abrupt termination of their studies in America, later became outstanding achievers in engineering, industry, banking, the military, and civil services. Very few became revolutionaries.[52] This was also true, as Qian Ning discusses in this book, in the twentieth century of those who were supported by the remitted Boxer Indemnity Fund. It was the work of the largest group of returned students—those from America—that formed the foundation of China's progress. By comparison, many of the students who went to Japan at the turn of the century returned to China to participate in overthrowing the Qing dynasty, and many who went to France in the decade around World War I became prominent Communist revolutionaries.

Numerous factors contributed to these distinctions, such as the age of the students at their return and their fields of study while abroad. But the most important factor was the stability of the educational experience. The students who went to America, England, and Germany (and to the Soviet Union in the 1950s) experienced structured study and few distractions. The studies of many of those who went to Japan and France, however, were frequently interrupted by lack of funds and by distractions such as upheavals back home and difficulties in state-to-state relations between China and the host country. Becoming a revolutionary requires accepting a belief in a doctrine. After years of education in an environment conducive to learning, a student quite naturally becomes a builder.

The history of education in Taiwan illustrates the effect of stable education. At the end of World War II, Taiwan was more prosperous than mainland China because of the five decades of warless development it had enjoyed as a colony of Japan.[53] But, like mainland China, it had a rapidly rising population and an agrarian economy (which, by itself, would send ever more people into ever deeper poverty), no systematic legislation that would encourage wealth creation through commercial and industrial expansion, and was under rigid, one-party rule by the Nationalists (Guomindang). On February 28, 1947, two years before the full retreat of the Nationalists to the island, a protest by citizens against corruption and authoritarian rule broke out into antigovernment riots. The government reacted by arresting and executing thousands of prominent intellectuals and civilian leaders. The pattern of development and suppression evident in the February 28 Incident was to be repeated forty-two years later in Tiananmen Square. These convulsions resulted from the clash between the twin legacies of China's millennia-old civilization: the unyielding reality of national poverty and weakness, and the undying desire for prosperity at home and equality with other nations.

Taiwan held its first study-abroad examination in 1953, and 233 students passed. By 1975 the number had increased to 1,514; in the intervening twenty-two years a total of 23,540 students had passed.[54] Within some four decades following 1949, guardians of the old ideology died off one by one, the new generation was raised in an evolving new ideology, the economy changed from agrarian to commercial, and the political system from authoritarian to democratic. The younger generation that had received a stable education at home and abroad and had grown up in an environment without blood-spilling, social turmoil, and war brought about a transformation from ignorance to knowledge.[55]

Education itself is a millennia-old Confucian tradition. The cherished thought of study in America, although a recent development, is rooted in the Chinese people's respect and trust in the quality and openness of

American education. This respect and trust—which began when Yung Wing started his study in America in 1847 and can be neither enforced by treaties nor destroyed by legislation or war—remain intact today.

ACKNOWLEDGMENTS

I thank Sam Cohen, Harry Mynick, and Hironori Takahashi for their encouragement during my translation of *Chinese Students Encounter America*; Hong-yee Chiu for valuable comments on this preface, and Nancy Chapman on the endnote; and Lorri Hagman for her relentless pursuit of clarity in the edited text. I am grateful to my family, whose unfailing support has been essential to the completion of this work.

T. K. CHU
Princeton, New Jersey
June 30, 2000

AUTHOR'S PREFACE

On an April morning in 1988, I boarded a No. 320 express bus in the vicinity of Muxidi, Beijing, destined for Yiheyuan. I was going to the western district to do some errands whose precise nature I can no longer recall. It was early spring. The sun shone warmly, and the boughs of the trees lining both sides of the street had just begun to wear a new green. The fresh air seemed to purify my mind and body. I rested my head on the windowpane during the rickety ride and began to daydream. At that moment the idea of writing a book leaped out: "I'll go overseas to interview the students who have gone abroad to study, and I'll write down their experiences and feelings ..."

I was then a reporter in the literature department of *People's Daily*: youthful, passionate, and full of dreams. My initial idea was quite romantic. First, I would go to America. With a knapsack on my back, I would walk, hitchhike, or, better yet, cycle. I would travel on the majestic highways of Walt Whitman's poems. Along the way, between interviewing students, I would work at odd jobs. I would go to Europe, Japan, Australia ... And finally I would produce a kind of journalistic writing rich in feeling, overflowing with wisdom, and laden with tales of adventure. It would begin, "In the year nineteen hundred and ..."

In August 1989 I arrived in America.

Four years later, also on an April morning, sitting in the quiet graduate reading lounge at the University of Michigan, Ann Arbor, and listening to the chimes of the campus bell, I began to write this book. But by then many of my original ideas had changed. It dawned on me that four years before, the psychological distance between me and the topics I chose had been as great as the physical distance between me and America. In today's America, the sight of a traveler with a knapsack walking jauntily along an expressway is hard to imagine. The image would be far from romantic; perhaps it would be farcical, or even a little sad.

In fact, it was not only my ideas about writing the book that had changed. In the summer of 1993 I returned to China for a short visit. My mother, seeing her son apparently more or less the same after four years in America, was relieved, even elated. But I knew that deep in my heart I had changed. To change after studying abroad was perhaps quite natural. Had there been no change, the study would have been a wasted effort.

Obviously I was not the exception. In the last two decades, several hundred thousand Chinese students walked out the nation's "front door," which had been closed for a long, long time, and voyaged to more than seventy countries around the globe. Bombarded by alien cultures, their lives underwent a transformation that would not have been possible had they remained in China. Like their predecessors, they brought back science and technology as well as thoughts, ideas, and lifestyles that were radically different from those in China.

What were the changes that took place in a student? What were the implications of those changes for China? These were the questions I asked myself constantly while writing this book.

In my years in the United States, I studied and worked at the University of Michigan and traveled widely to interview Chinese students. In this book, I have attempted to sketch the historical and political background of China's study-abroad program and the magnitude of this tidal wave of Chinese students. In addition, a principal goal of the book was to reflect on the enormous impact of the rapid changes in cultural environment and in the social system on this generation of China's youth. I did so by recording their personal experiences, as they were vivid examples of how these changes had occurred.

This book is hence based on personal experiences—those of the people I interviewed and my own. Nowadays, although noteworthy scholarly research is usually based on statistical data, it is still individual experience that tells the poignancy of the story behind the data.

All of the people and events in this book are real. But in respect for their privacy, I have changed the names of the people interviewed and occasionally place names as well. Sources of information other than the interviews are given.

First, I wish to express my gratitude to Prof. Kenneth DeWoskin of the Department of East Asia Studies at the University of Michigan. Without his initial enthusiasm and his continuous support, I could not have completed the project so smoothly or presented the results in their present form. I also thank Prof. Charles Eisendrath and the Asia Foundation of America. Prof. Eisendrath, director of the Journalism Fellowship Program at the University of Michigan, not only helped me to gain an initial understanding of American society but also left me with many fond memories of my first year of student life in America. The Asia Foundation's grant in my first year made it financially possible for me to participate in the Michigan program and to conduct research for this book. In addition, my friends Yuhong, Jianhua, Wenhua, and Alice H. have given me their selfless help in conceptualizing the interview project and in writing this book. I thank them sincerely.

I also thank my wife, whom I have been able to count on for the most candid criticism.

Finally, I especially wish to thank those who took part in my interviews, engaged me in thoughtful discussions, and related to me their joys and sufferings. They have brought pride and honor to this fellow traveler.

QIAN NING
Ann Arbor, Michigan
May 6, 1995

Chinese Students
Encounter America

CHAPTER I

The Intermittent History

CHINA'S "FRONT DOOR"

China's door to the outside world is narrow.

In the early eighties, this statement was not only figurative, but also literal.

There is a street in the southern end of the Wangfu district in Beijing called Dongjiaomin Alley. In those days it was quiet and obscure. However, that little street had been anything but obscure in China's history; there, the Boxer rioters attacked the foreign establishments in 1900, an incident that led to the invasion of Beijing by the Eight-Country Allied Force.[1] At the western end of the street were two small, undistinguished doors covered with peeling red paint. A plate that hung on one of the doors read, "Visa Department, Bureau of Public Safety, City of Beijing." This was one of China's "front doors" at that time.

When I first saw this "front door," I was incredulous. How could it be? In a single decade, tens of thousands of Chinese students had managed to squeeze their way through these two narrow doors and walk into the world outside.

The door on the west side was the entrance to the First Visa Division, which accepted passport applications for travel to Europe, the United States, Canada, and Australia. The door on the east side was the entrance to the Second Visa Division—the route to Hong Kong, Macao, and Japan.

The morning of January 5, 1989, was cold. A light snow was falling.

I arrived sometime after eight o'clock to find out how to get an exit visa and passport. The office was not yet open, but already about thirty people were waiting in the street.

The doors opened promptly at nine o'clock. Moving with the throng, I entered the western "front door" for the first time.

The office consisted of two rooms. The anteroom was about twenty square meters. Numerous sheets of rules and regulations governing studying and visits abroad were posted on the right-hand wall. A registration book was placed on a table against the back wall that separated the two rooms.

The small room filled quickly. People came to pick up blank forms, to turn in completed forms, or to inquire about procedures. They elbowed their way to the table to register. Although it was cold and damp outside, a tense air of excitement and anxiety welled up in the room.

The door to the back room was shut, and nobody knew what the public-safety officers were doing behind the door. Someone impetuously walked up and knocked. Immediately, an officer came out, lectured the knocker on his rashness, returned to the back room, and slammed the door.

Everybody waited patiently now. Some were pacing, and some bowed their heads in thought. Still others rested with their eyes closed or asked every conceivable question of their neighbors.

It has been said that a prerequisite for studying abroad is patience. This wisdom was acquired from experience; the process of applying for an exit visa and passport was the training ground for that patience.

As the waiting continued, an "information-exchange center for studying abroad" quickly formed. Encouraging and discouraging information was exchanged, freely and quickly:

> "The new policy from the Education Commission no longer allows graduate students to go abroad."

> "The 300 or so students applying for an American visa just before Christmas had expected it to be easy. But no one got a visa."

> "Canadian visas are much easier to get these days. That's the reason for the huge crowd outside the Canadian Embassy every day."

There, freedom of speech was practiced liberally. The speakers would not be held responsible for what they said, and the listeners would not take seriously what they heard. The multitude of people, although from different social backgrounds, shared a common aspiration. There they would say freely what they would not say to their supervisors, colleagues, friends, or relatives, since they would not be investigated for their remarks.[2]

Finally there was a stir in the inner room. Public-safety officers called names. Each time, they admitted two or three people and then slammed the door. Witnessing that the bureaucratic machinery of the state had begun to grind, everybody settled down again with even greater patience.

"A classmate of mine left yesterday. She did not take the Graduate Record Examination (GRE) or Test of English as a Foreign Language (TOEFL), but they gave her a visa. It looked impossible at first, but it turned out all right. You just have to be bold," said a girl in her twenties. She wanted to study education in America, although her major in college was history. She, too, had not taken the GRE or TOEFL. She listed on her application form an American as her financial guarantor and claimed the American was her cousin, but she was concerned about convincing the public-safety officer of their relationship.

An hour passed, then two hours. The wait seemed interminable. The air in the room became suffocating.

"This is like torture," someone complained.

Most of the people came for their own visas, but a middle-aged man who looked like a Chinese Communist Party (CCP) cadre came to get a passport for the secretary-general of the Party branch of his work unit.[3] His patience was wearing thin.

"Next time, let the secretary-general come himself so he will know how it feels to wait like this," he grumbled.

At that time, an old man walked in and signed the registration book. He came to air grievances to an official of the Supreme Court. Someone good-naturedly told him that this was the bureau issuing exit visas and passports for studying abroad. The old man exploded, "You can go to whichever country you wish! It has nothing to do with me! All that's needed is for them to receive me. You can go your own way!"[4]

Everybody was silent. The reception center for people presenting grievances to the Supreme Court was in another building on the same street, and that place was connected to another facet of China.[5]

When I was finally called into the back room, it was past noon. In contrast to the air of boredom in the anteroom, the back room was alive and busy. It was smaller and held three desks, behind each of which sat an officer. In any given morning they interviewed about fifty applicants; they had no idle moments. The officers reviewed the applications expertly. Their answers to the applicants' questions were crisp, and delivered in a manner not unlike judges announcing sentencing in a trial. But if an applicant took too long asking a question or seemed unconvinced by their answers, the officers would immediately begin a lecture that was not delivered with the same precision.

Some of those who returned from the inner room were excited, some were dejected, and still others could hardly hide their anger. But most just left quietly. An exception was a middle-aged man who came to turn in his forms. As we left the room together, he commented, "There's been some improvement in their manners."

That simple statement gave hope to those who still waited.

"I've heard that a passport can be issued in just a month and a half."

"Some people have received theirs in twenty days."

The hoped-for ease of getting a passport, however, did not materialize. Six months later, the June Fourth Incident erupted at Tiananmen Square.[6] It shook Beijing, made the rest of China tremble, and sent shock waves throughout the world. Immediately, people began to suspect that the narrow, recently opened "front door" would be shut again. For a brief period, Beijing's Bureau of Public Safety rejected all passport applications. On July 10, 1989, it began accepting them again but with new rules. One was that people who already had a passport were required to procure a new exit visa. There were also changes in the Visa Department: the First Division issued forms and the Second Division processed them.

A year later the processing center for passport applications moved to a place near Yuanen Temple. The issuance of application forms and passports, however, remained in the Dongjiaomin Alley office. The requirement of a new exit visa was abolished soon afterward.

Four years later, when I returned to Beijing in the summer of 1993, I could no longer find the two narrow doors. The Visa Department of Beijing's Bureau of Public Safety had become the Office of Non-Official Entry and Exit Visas for Chinese Citizens, processing civilian applications only. Its modern service hall was spacious, clean, and comfortable. The application process had also been standardized.

The Dongjiaomin Alley had also changed; it had lost its quiet charm. Automobiles, pedestrians, and the farm-produce peddlers born of the free-market economy brought city noise and congestion to the place.

Recalling its old days, I could hardly picture it as the place I knew.

FRANK PRESS'S VISIT AND DENG XIAOPING: REOPENING THE FRONT DOOR

Whether they were aware of it or not, the people who waited so patiently in the small, stuffy room in the Visa Department of the Bureau of Public Safety were the fortunate beneficiaries of fairly recent developments in the U.S.–China relationship.

In the early eighties, although China's "front door" was narrow, it was nevertheless open. China had severed its ties with the West thirty years before, and with the Soviet Union and Eastern Europe more than twenty years before. During the following decades, no one in China would even have dreamed of taking a peek at a foreign country, let alone studying in one.

The opening of China's "front door" was one of the historical changes that took place in the late seventies. These changes would have an impact on China for many years to come.

On July 7, 1978, Beijing hosted the Double-Emulation Conference on Finance and Trade, which discussed how the country's industry and commerce could learn from Daqing and how agriculture could learn from Dazhai.[7] At the conference, Hua Guofeng, the chairman of the Chinese Communist Party, said China's economic development must follow the exemplary progress shown in those two places; that is, its economic policy must be guided by a continuing revolution under the dictatorship of the proletariat to implement economic development, assure supply, and carry the ideology of Marxism-Leninism into politics and production, and to the masses. The audience received Chairman Hua's speech enthusiastically; after the speech "the roaring applause continued for a long time."[8]

On that same day, Fang Yi, chairman of China's Science and Technology Committee, met Frank Press, the U.S. presidential adviser on science and technology, and his delegation, which had arrived in Beijing on July 6. The little-noticed news was published on page 4 of *People's Daily*:

> *U.S. Science and Technology Delegation Arrives in Beijing*
> July 6, Xinhua News Agency. Frank Press, the U.S. presidential adviser on science and technology and director of the Office of Science and Technology Policy, arrived in Beijing this afternoon by plane with a fourteen-person delegation specializing in science and technology. The delegation includes scientists and high-level officials from the National Science Foundation and government agencies for space flight, agriculture, health, geology, energy, commerce, and other programs.
>
> Welcoming the delegates at the airport were Jiang Nanxiang, deputy chairman of the National Science Commission; Zhou Peiyuan, vice-president of the Academy of Sciences and acting chairman of the Science Planning Committee; and several renowned scientists and leaders of various bureaus: Ren Xinmin, Huang Jiasi, Gu Gongxu, Luo Yuru, Zhu Qizhen, and others.
>
> Leonard Woodcock, director of the U.S. Liaison Office in China, and other officials of that office were also at the airport to welcome the delegates.[9]

The focal point of the discussion between Fang Yi and the American delegation was the exchange of information about science and technology between the two countries. To push forward its modernization plan, China acutely needed the advanced science and technology of developed countries. At the welcoming banquet, Fang Yi spoke of "a bigger step, a wider road." The United States recognized that a strong and stable China was important in maintaining global equilibrium and was also in the U.S. national interest. Hence it was also eager to strengthen and broaden that exchange. In his response, Frank Press said he hoped that "the scientific communities of the two countries will have an opportunity to develop new ties and advance mutual understanding" and that the two countries "can contribute mutually in agriculture, medicine, bioscience, energy, climatology, prospecting for natural resources, space exploration, and other fields."

The meeting lasted three days. Press described the meeting as "constructive," and Fang Yi said, "It was a good beginning."[10]

In those three days China and the United States achieved a breakthrough of historical proportions. As attested by later events, it not only changed the fortunes of many of China's youth, but also had a deep impact on China's course of modernization.

The breakthrough was China's agreement to send students to study in America. The negotiations were dramatic.

Mr. Leonard Woodcock, who later became the first U.S. ambassador to China, participated in the negotiations. On a winter day in 1991, this elderly gentleman, then more than eighty years old, recalled vividly for me the scene at the 1978 negotiations.

He said that China's agreeing to send students to America was a "pleasant surprise." Before the meeting, the American delegation had been prepared to make the exchange of students a part of the overall collaboration on science and technology. But the Americans had little hope that the proposition would be accepted; it was considered just a bargaining chip. In a morning meeting, not expecting a positive and speedy reply, the American delegation proposed that the two countries exchange students. That afternoon, the Chinese delegation said, "Yes, how many students could you accept?"

"This was completely beyond our expectations," Mr. Woodcock recalled. "Everybody was excited. But at that time we had only an idea, not a detailed program."

The American delegation huddled in an emergency discussion session. Delegates from the various disciplines estimated the number of Chinese students they could absorb in their own fields. After the session, the American delegation returned to ask, "How many would you like to send?"

The Chinese answered immediately, "How about five hundred?"[11]

Professor Michel Oksenberg verified what Mr. Woodcock described as China's unexpected stance on the exchange of students. Oksenberg was an adviser to the National Security Council of the Carter Administration and a member of the delegation. While teaching at the University of Michigan, he told me of a conversation he had had with a Chinese delegate during the welcoming banquet before the meeting. He was probing the delegate, in Chinese, on the issue of exchange students. The official said clearly, "We agree that it's a good idea." Professor Oksenberg passed along the information to his colleagues. But they were skeptical and asked him to ask again. He did so and the Chinese delegate responded, "Oh, yes."[12]

The American side obviously viewed China's concurrence on the exchange of students as the biggest breakthrough of the visit. Historically, Americans have always believed cultural exchange is the most effective means for expanding American influence abroad: "The nation which succeeds in educating the young Chinese of the present generation will be the nation which for a given expenditure of effort will reap the largest possible returns in moral, intellectual, and commercial influence."[13] The Americans did not wish to see a future in which the throng in Beijing's Wangfu district[14] would be fuming with anti-American sentiment.

To China, the move was not impulsive, but carefully planned. Although in the Double-Emulation Conference Hua Guofeng had repeatedly emphasized China's self-reliance in economic development, he had also mentioned learning advanced science and technology from other countries.[15] Sending students abroad to study was one of the most effective means of narrowing the science and technology gap between China and the developed countries. In fact, in March 1978, the Chinese government had held a screening examination in several universities to select candidates for study in Western Europe, Canada, Australia, and Japan. Twenty-three students were chosen, and at the time of Press's visit they were already receiving language training at Beijing Language School.[16]

Mr. Woodcock recalled only a minor disagreement on the exchange of students. He proposed that the Chinese students should consider studying not only at the most prestigious universities, but also at colleges of different standing, including community colleges. He reasoned that because the Cultural Revolution[17] had set higher education back ten years, China might not be ready for the most advanced technology. The Chinese side reacted with bravado and confidence: the Chinese students would study only at the best universities and learn only the most advanced technology.

On the evening of July 9, Frank Press hosted a farewell dinner in the Great Hall of the People. During a toast he mentioned the exchange of students for the first time in public: "This visit enables me to see that in the near future there will be a wide range of collaboration in science and technology between the two countries: information sharing, high-level workshops, research collaboration, student exchange, advanced training, and establishment of trade relations in technology."[18]

On the morning of July 10, Deng Xiaoping, then China's deputy premier, met Press and the other delegates. According to Xinhua News Agency, Deng Xiaoping said to the American visitors, "We want to learn advanced science and technology from other countries, including America."[19] On the same day, the *New York Times* reported that Deng and Press "agreed that an exchange of technological information could lead to increased U.S.–Chinese trade."[20] There was no mention of discussion of student exchanges.

But there should be no doubt that Deng Xiaoping, who in his youth had been a diligent and hard-working student in France, was the chief architect of China's reform and opening-up policy. As early as May 24, 1977, he admitted candidly,

> It appears that our science, technology, and education, when compared to those of developed countries, lag by twenty years. The United States has 1.2 million scientists and engineers. The Soviet Union has 900,000. We have just a bit more than 200,000, and that includes those whose technical knowledge is obsolete. The number of people who can actually function is far less.[21]

On August 8, 1977, in a workshop on science and education, he mentioned study abroad for students for the first time: "To send students abroad to study is also a concrete step."[22] The meeting with Frank Press also demonstrated that Deng was the principal decision maker for the Sino-American exchange program in science and technology.

Thus, the Press delegation returned to Washington with the news that China was ready to open its door.

On December 16, 1978, China and the United States announced simultaneously in Beijing and Washington that the two countries would establish diplomatic relations on January 1, 1979, and that Deng Xiaoping would visit the United States on January 29. On December 18, 1978, the Third Plenum of the Eleventh Central Committee of the Chinese Communist Party convened in Beijing and formally endorsed China's policy of reform and opening up. On December 26, just days before the establishment of formal Sino–U.S. diplomatic relations, the first wave of fifty Chinese students boarded a plane for America.[23]

Thus China opened its "front door" to let its students study in the West. It was the first among socialistic countries that dared to send a large number of students to the West. But to China, it was merely a continuation of an interrupted history.

YUNG WING, THE PIONEER

On January 4, 1847, more than 130 years before Chinese students left for America in December 1978, a Chinese youth, not yet nineteen, boarded the ship *Huntress* at Huangpu Harbor in Guangzhou (Canton), bound for America. It was a land that to this day still inspires awe, mystery, and wonder in China's youth. After sailing for ninety-eight days, he arrived in New York City, then a metropolis with a population of less than 300,000. Three years later, this youth was admitted to Yale University, from which he graduated in 1854. The youth was Yung Wing.[24]

Yung Wing was born on November 17, 1828, in Nanpingzhen, Guangdong. The town was not far from Macao, and hence it had early contact with missionaries from the West.[25] When Yung Wing was six years old, he studied with Mrs. Gutzlaff, the wife of an English missionary. But his studies were interrupted by the closing of the school, his father's death, and his family's poverty. At twelve, he went to Macao and resumed his study at the Morrison School.

The Morrison School was founded on November 1, 1839, to commemorate Dr. Robert Morrison, an English missionary. After the beginning of the Opium War in 1840,[26] the school moved to Hong Kong and was put under the direction of the Rev. S. R. Brown, an American and a member of the Yale class of 1832. Yung Wing recalled that Mr. Brown was an outstanding teacher. He was

> cool in nature, versatile in the adaptation of means to ends, gentlemanly and agreeable and somewhat optimistic. He found no difficulty in endearing himself to his pupils, because he sympathized with them in their efforts to master their studies, and entered heart and soul into his work. He had an innate faculty of making things clear to the pupils and conveying to them his understanding of a subject without circumlocution, and with great directness and facility.[27]

Yung Wing was the sixth student, and the youngest. The children studied mathematics, geography, and English in the morning, and Chinese in the afternoon. He was there for six years.

One day in August 1846, he made a decision that changed his life. On that day, Mr. Brown told the class that he had to return to America for health reasons. He said he would like to bring a few students with him so that they could complete their education there. Whoever wished to go with him could indicate so by standing up.

First, there was dead silence. Then Yung Wing stood up. He was followed by a boy named Wong Shing and then a boy named Wong Foon.

That evening, Yung Wing told his mother about his decision. She wept. To let her son go to America might mean that they would never see each other again. But she agreed that he should go. Four months later, Yung Wing, Wong Shing, and Wong Foon all boarded the *Huntress* and sailed to the New World. None had an inkling that they were writing a new page of history.

In the fall of 1848, Wong Shing returned to China because of illness. In 1850 Wong Foon went to Scotland to study medicine, and Yung Wing stayed in America to attend Yale University.[28] In the winter of 1854, Yung Wing returned to China. He carried back not just a diploma from Yale, but also a dream that would affect, to this day, the destiny of Chinese youth and China's course of development.

"Before the close of my last year in college," Yung Wing recalled in his later years, "I had already sketched out what I should do. I was determined that the rising generation in China should enjoy the same educational advantages that I had enjoyed; that through Western education China might be regenerated, become enlightened and powerful. To accomplish that object became the guiding star of my ambition. Toward such a goal, I directed all my mental resources and energy."[29]

With that dream, Yung Wing returned to his motherland, which was overrun by war, poverty, and ignorance. For his entire life he struggled to make his dream real.

In 1863 Yung Wing met Viceroy[30] Zeng Guofan, who was at the time the most powerful and visionary official in the Qing court. He earned Zeng's trust after he successfully completed the assignment of building a machinery factory. He then took the opportunity to lobby for his dream of sending students to America to receive a Western education.

Zeng acted in 1871. In a memorial to the throne written jointly with another viceroy, he sought and received approval for the project. A year later, Zeng died. In a life full of contradiction and complexity, sending students to America was his last achievement.

The plan was to send 120 students, between ten and fifteen years of age, over a period of four years, at a rate of thirty per year. Each would return after studying for up to fifteen years.

Yung Wing was appointed deputy commissioner of the Chinese Educational Commission[31] and was responsible for selecting the first group of students. At that time, a journey to America was a daring and dangerous adventure. It was hard to find applicants, especially from the inland region. Most students were recruited along the coastal area, which had earlier exposure to development. Twenty-five of the thirty boys in the first group were from Guangdong. The parents of each student were required to sign an agreement to "accept the will of destiny should the child become ill or die" during the study.[32]

After the selection, Yung Wing went to America first, to arrange the students' housing and education.

On August 11, 1872, thirty Chinese boys boarded a postal ship in Shanghai to cross the oceans to America. In the following three years, three more groups of Chinese boys went to America. This was the historically renowned Early-Teen Youth Studying in America Project, a miracle in China's history brought about by the single-minded effort of Yung Wing.

The Chinese Educational Commission was first located in Springfield, Massachusetts, and later moved to Hartford, Connecticut. There, Yung Wing saw his lifelong dream realized and then dashed to pieces. In 1912, after completing his memoir, *My Life in China and America,* in 1909, he died in Hartford, Connecticut.[33]

On a winter day in early 1995, after considerable effort, I finally located Yung Wing's grave in a quiet, snow-covered cemetery outside Hartford.[34] It was marked by a plain headstone on which was engraved his family name in English: Yung. At the foot of the headstone was a tablet on which was engraved, in Chinese, a brief biography. The two caretakers, though obviously knowing little of China and modern Chinese history, were familiar with this particular grave. They mentioned that others had come to visit it.

Today's Chinese know the names of many powerful politicians, nobles, valorous generals, and fiery revolutionary leaders in China's turbulent history of the last 160 years. But few recognize the name of this trailblazer who quietly devoted his entire life to open a door for Chinese youth to see the world outside. Yet only a few people in modern China could claim to have had a comparable impact on China.

Yung Wing was China's Columbus. He "discovered" America so that for the first time the Chinese could see the world outside the "Central Kingdom" with neither arrogant ignorance nor an inferiority complex. In addition, he found a "new world" for the Chinese people: there existed other cultures that nurtured brilliant human thought outside of traditional Chinese culture.

Yung Wing's work affected generations of China's youth, who in turn affected China's history.

A STORMY HISTORY

The ship that took Yung Wing to America crossed the Indian Ocean, looped around the Cape of Good Hope, and then crossed the Atlantic. On some days the sea was tranquil and the sun was warm. Other days there were gusty winds, torrential rains, and towering waves. At times the ship was in danger of capsizing. Yung Wing's project of sending Chinese students to study in America also encountered stormy weather.

In the fall of 1872, the first group of Chinese students arrived in America. When these young teenage boys in their Chinese clothing and their hair in queues first appeared on the streets of American cities, they were mistaken for girls. Americans would follow the boys and shout, "Look! Chinese girls!" The boys were embarrassed.[35]

But these bright boys, whose minds had not been completely numbed by exclusive studying of the Four Books and Five Classics, quickly adapted to the American way of life.[36] They lived with different American families. The free and independent spirit of this foreign country rapidly reinvigorated their long-suppressed young spirits. They changed to American clothing, and some were bold enough to cut their queues. They learned to play baseball and football, and to skate and cycle. Some even got into fist fights.

This change of behavior quickly aroused a bitter dispute between Yung Wing and Chen Lanbin, the commissioner of the Chinese Educational Commission and a Hanlin scholar.[37] Yung Wing was sympathetic to the boys, realizing that change was inevitable, even desirable, because one of the purposes of education was to nourish a spirit of independence and free thinking. But Chen believed that this education was polluting the youths' minds and blamed Yung Wing for spoiling them. From his vantage point, any boisterousness was an act of untamed rudeness. He believed that preventive measures must be taken, or else the Chinese boys would themselves become "foreign ghosts."[38]

Chen Lanbin's concern was typical among Chinese who, deep in their psyches, feared losing their Chinese identity. This fear was rooted in the ingrained notion of a Chinese race and was strengthened by the nationalist fervor that resulted from China's repeated humiliating capitulation to foreign powers in the nineteenth century. The fear strangled their spirit and clouded their judgment.

In 1875 Chen Lanbin was named China's minister to the United States.[39] Replacing him as commissioner was Wu Jiashan, also a Hanlin scholar. Twenty years before, Yung Wing had met Wu once in Shanghai and thought he was a crank. After working together on the Chinese Educational Commission for a few years, Yung Wing thought Wu should be relegated to "a cell in an insane asylum or to an institution for imbeciles."[40] Wu was in fact a staunch opponent of the project during its formative days.

Wu Jiashan exploded into a fury as soon as he assumed office. He was incensed when the students did not greet him by kowtowing, as they would have done in China. He accused Yung Wing of spoiling them. He and Chen Lanbin eventually wrote to the Qing court that the students "played more than they studied . . . , would soon lose their love of their country . . . , and would be good for nothing or worse than nothing."[41] They proposed to dissolve the commission and declared, "The sooner this educational enterprise is broken up and all the students recalled, the better it would be for China."[42]

September 6, 1881, was a day of immense sadness and anger for the Chinese students in America. The Qing court recalled them all.[43] The college studies of more than sixty students were disrupted, and many were still in high school. Only two of the 120 students had completed their college education. Thus ended China's first attempt to send students to study abroad.

In spite of the abrupt termination of their studies in America, many of those teenage students later became China's outstanding achievers. Among them were Zhan Tianyou, who surveyed and built the Beijing–Zhangjiakou railroad; Wu Yangzeng, who surveyed and built the coal-mining facilities in Tangshan-Kaiping; Tang Yuankang, a director of the Bureau of Telegraphs; Tang Shaoyi, the first premier of the Republic of China, founded by the Nationalists in 1911; and Liang Dunyan, a minister of the Ministry of Foreign Affairs.[44]

Before the recall of the students in America, students were also sent to Europe. Among them were more than forty who went to Britain, France, and Germany to study naval sciences and shipbuilding between 1875 and 1879. From these students emerged China's first naval leaders, many of whom died in the Sino-Japanese naval battle in 1894. They included Lin Zengtai, commander of the heavy cruiser *Zhenyuan* of the Northern Fleet; Liu Buzhan, commander of the heavy cruiser *Dingyuan*; Lin Yongsheng, commander of the armored battleship *Jingyuan*; and Huang Jianxun, commander of the rapid-deployment cruiser *Chaoyun*.[45] The best known was Yan Fu, the chief instructor of the Naval Academy in Tianjin, who today is best remembered for his translation of Thomas Huxley's *Evolution and Ethics.* Its publication laid the cornerstone for China's modern Enlightenment Movement.[46]

The recall of the teenage students interrupted the study-abroad program, but the opened door to the outside world could not be shut. After the recall, inspection study trips by government officials became fashionable. In 1887 (the thirteenth year of Guangxu's reign), the Ministry of Foreign Affairs issued fourteen rules governing foreign travel.[47] An official with a civil-service grade of the fifth rank or higher would be reimbursed the expense of transportation and of engaging an interpreter and a servant, in addition to a monthly stipend of two hundred taels.[48] The duration of an inspection trip was limited to three years.

Inspection-trip privileges, especially of those who were financed by provincial governments, quickly were abused. In 1902 (the twenty-eighth year of Guangxu's reign), the Ministry of Foreign Affairs reported to the emperor, "Many of the students who went abroad in recent years neither learned the foreign language nor took up any studies.... No other program is more wasteful in time and resources."[49] The result of this memorial to the throne is not recorded.

In about 1896 Chinese students began to go to Japan. This was a result of a proposal by Zhang Zhidong, viceroy of the Huguang district and an enlightened person for his time. In his *Essays on the Importance of Education,* he advocated studying in the East (Japan):

> As to which country to study in, the East is better than the West: the distance is shorter and hence more students can be sent for the same resources; it is closer to China and hence supervision is easier; the language is easier to learn; the writings of the West are quite complex, but the part that is irrelevant [to China's needs] has already been pruned or revised when they were translated and used in the East. The conditions and customs in China and the East are similar, and hence learning from and emulating the East are easier. Studying in the East achieves twice the result at half the cost.[50]

At that time, the Foreign Adaptation Movement[51] advanced by Zeng Guofan and Li Hongzhang went bankrupt because of the devastating defeat suffered by the Chinese Navy in the Sino-Japanese War.[52] The reform program advanced by Liang Qichao and Kang Youwei also failed to gain ground because of the failure of the 1898 Reform Movement.[53]

These humiliating events nurtured a passionate sentiment among the students to save their country from decimation. Among them were many revolutionaries of politics and literature: Qiu Jin, Zou Rong, Chen Tianhua, Huang Xing, Song Jiaoren, Liao Zhongkai, Hu Hanmin, Wang Jingwei, Yu Youren, Chen Duxiu, Li Dazhao, Lu Xun, and Zhou Zouren. Most of them participated in two of the most important political events in modern China: the 1911 Revolution and the May Fourth New Culture Movement.[54] The former overthrew the Qing dynasty; the latter liberated the spirit of the Chinese people that had been confined by traditional Chinese culture for thousands of years.

The second wave of government-sponsored students sent to study in America came at the turn of the century. The program was financed through a contribution by the United States from the surplus money it received from the Boxer Indemnity Fund.[55]

In 1900, the twenty-sixth year of the Guangxu reign, the Boxer Rebellion broke out in Beijing. About one hundred thousand people of the Boxer sect, claiming to be invincible to bullets, surrounded and attacked the foreign establishments in the city. Soon afterward the Eight-Country Allied Force attacked and occupied Beijing, and the empress dowager fled the capital.

In 1901 Li Hongzhang was forced to sign the humiliating Boxer Protocol,[56] under which China agreed to pay an indemnity totaling 450 million taels to fourteen countries over thirty-nine years. This was the historically infamous Genzi Indemnity.[57]

In 1908 the U.S. Congress passed legislation empowering President Theodore Roosevelt to return to China the excess money above the loss actually incurred by the United States; the money was to be spent for building schools in China and for financing students to study in America. The two governments agreed to establish the Tsinghua School and, beginning in 1909, to send one hundred Chinese students per year to America.[58] Thus, China resumed sending students to America under the Genzi Indemnity Fund Project.

In 1909, 1910, and 1911 examinations were held in Beijing for candidates drawn from a nationwide student pool. The applicants were required to know Chinese and English and to possess "good health, an upright character, no defects in physical appearance, and an unblemished background."[59]

The first examination for 630 students took place in August 1909. The preliminary examination tested Chinese language, English language, and Chinese history and geography. Sixty-eight students passed. The final examination tested physics, chemistry, natural science, algebra, geometry, trigonometry, world history, and world geography. The preliminary and final examinations together lasted seven to eight days. Forty-seven students were selected.

In October this first group of fifty Genzi Indemnity Fund students (the group included three additional students who were children of court officials) went to America. They studied chemical engineering, mechanical engineering, civil engineering, mining, agriculture, and commerce. Among the students was Mei Yiqi, future president of Tsinghua University.

In August 1910 the second examination took place, also in two stages. The first examined Chinese and English language and included writing essays on assigned topics. The title of the essay to be written in Chinese had a classical charm: "Without Compasses and Rulers, There Would Be No Circles and Squares." The title of the essay to be written in English was quite modern for its time: "The Pros and Cons of Issuing International Bonds for Building Domestic Railroads." In the second stage of the examination, the students were examined in European and American history, botany, zoology, general science, geometry, and world geography. More than four hundred students took the examination, and seventy were selected.

Among the second group was the renowned scholar Hu Shi, who ranked fifty-fifth out of seventy. The renowned linguist Zhao Yuanren and the meteorologist Zhu Kezhen were also on the roster.

One year later, in 1911, the third examination was held. That year marked the last group of Genzi Indemnity Fund students.[60] The program nurtured many outstanding scientists for China and provided the talent pool for the creation and development of many branches of studies in contemporary China's academic institutions.

On October 10, 1911, the 1911 Revolution (Xinhai Geming) broke out, and soon afterward China became a republic.[61] But the country was thrown into chaos and fragmentation because of infighting among the regional warlords.[62] Thus the second movement to send students abroad met its demise because of the violent turmoil.

The yearning of China's youth to study abroad, however, could not be quashed. In 1911 the Tsinghua School was established. Over the next decade it alone sent 566 students to America.[63]

Beginning in 1912, study in France also attracted enthusiastic followers. The Association for Work and Study in France was organized by Wu Jingheng, Cai Yuanpei, Wang Jingwei, and others. Taking advantage of the acute labor shortage in France caused by World War I, the association made arrangements for China's youth to work and study there. By 1920 there were about two thousand Chinese students in France.

But the project soon encountered difficulties. First, the organizers could not administer all the logistics for the ever-increasing number of participants. Frequently a shipload of Chinese students arrived while arrangements for the previous group had yet to be completed. In 1921 the Ministry of Education had no choice but to declare a moratorium on the project. The second problem was financing. The organizers declared abruptly that they had no financial responsibility for the students and discontinued the payment of the stipends they had promised. On September 21, 1921, about eight hundred students demonstrated angrily in Paris and later occupied Lyon University. The French government quickly expelled them and on October 13 deported 104 students.

Similar to the revolutionaries who emerged among the students who went to Japan, the hardship-weathered students in the Association for Work and Study in France also nurtured numerous illustrious revolutionaries, including Cai Hesen, Zhao Shiyan, Zhou Enlai, Chen Yi, Nie Rongzou, and Deng Xiaoping.

Between the mid-twenties and the end of the thirties, after nearly a hundred years of war and chaos, China enjoyed a period of relative peace. The success of the Northern Expedition established the power base of the Nationalist government.[64] The regional warlords had to agree, at least temporarily, that the country was united under the leadership of the government in Nanjing. Political stability allowed a brief respite during which the country quickly developed its economy. In the humanities, after the storm of the May Fourth New Culture Movement, intellectuals began to rebuild China's culture on a new foundation.

Of course, the civil war continued. The April Twelfth Incident in 1927 led to an open split between the Nationalists and the Communists.[65] The wound would not heal. Chiang Kai-shek initiated five campaigns to rout out the Red Army, and Mao Zedong led the Red Army on the Long March, retreating from the Ruijing region in Jiangxi to the remote and impoverished hinterland of northern Shaanxi.[66]

But the relative stability allowed China to resume sending students to study overseas. On August 17, 1928, the Tsinghua School was renamed Tsinghua University, and Luo Jialun was named its president. That year the examination for the government-financed study-abroad program began. In 1933 the examination for Genzi Indemnity Fund students to study in Britain also began.

But the tranquility did not last long. On July 7, 1937, gunshots rang across the Marco Polo Bridge outside Beijing.[67]

The breakout of the War of Resistance against Japan once more dealt a serious blow to the study-abroad project. The data on the number of students studying abroad in the 1930s and early 1940s reveals the extent of the setback:

Year	*Number of Students*
1932	567
1933	621
1934	859
1935	1,033
1936	1,002
1937	266
1938	92
1939	65
1940	86
1941	57

The number of students studying abroad increased steadily from 1932 to more than one thousand in 1935 and 1936. After the breakout of the War of Resistance against Japan, the government announced an interim policy on studying abroad. The number dropped sharply. In 1941 it reached a low of fifty-seven students.

In 1945 Japan surrendered, and the War of Resistance against Japan ended. In July 1946 a nationwide examination for the government-sponsored study-abroad program drew 4,463 applicants. In that year the number of students studying abroad rose to 730.

But violent turmoil followed.[68] A new era began as an old one came to an end.

One can only feel grieved by China's history of studying abroad. Yung Wing's project of sending teenagers to America was abruptly ended by the ignorance and ineptitude of the Qing court; studies of the Genzi Indemnity Fund students were interrupted by the breakout of revolution in the Republic; and the program in the thirties was assaulted by the breakout of another war. In those hundred years, days of tranquility were rare.

But the history of the study-abroad program paralleled that of China for the last hundred and fifty years. Since the First Opium War (1839–42), fighting had broken out nearly every decade, tearing the country to shreds: peasant rebellions, foreign invasions, military coups, civil wars, revolutions. We Chinese hardly ever had a period of peace that lasted more than ten years so that we could seriously and persistently pursue a meaningful task.

THE MARCH TO ISOLATION

At Tiananmen Square on October 1, 1949, Chairman Mao Zedong solemnly declared to the world on behalf of the new China, "From now on, the Chinese people have stood up!" But those who stood up discovered quickly that they could stand only on their own soil; they could go nowhere else.

After the breakout of the Korean War in June 1950, the United States imposed a blockade on China. Because of its sharply opposing ideology, the United States became China's number-one enemy. Except in the battlefield and across the negotiation table, the two countries—which had a century-long history of cultural intercourse—severed nearly all ties. The Chinese people once again could not cross the Pacific Ocean.

China completely stopped sending students to the United States and other Western countries. But another problem—the detention of Chinese students in America wishing to return to China—surfaced.

After the breakout of the Korean War, many of the Chinese students in America—about five thousand of them—hoping to contribute their skills to the development of the new China, applied for permission to return. The U.S. Immigration and Naturalization Service denied their request on the grounds that their scientific and technical skills would aid the Communist regime in mainland China. The notices forbidding their repatriation carried a warning: those who tried to leave without permission would be subjected to a fine of $5,000 or imprisonment of three to five years.[69]

At that time, mainland Chinese media published one article after another charging the U.S. government with unjustifiable detention of the Chinese students. Some of the published stories, including their exaggerated phrasing for propaganda purposes, would be inconceivable to today's Chinese and Americans alike:

The Encounter of a Chinese Student in America

There are more than 3,000 Chinese students in the United States. This past summer more than 1,300 of them applied to leave the country, which is ruled by the claws of the Fascists.... A recently returned student told this reporter, in fury, his story. On September 17, carrying two suitcases and in good spirits, he left Oberlin College and boarded a bus to Chicago, from which he and some other students planned to return to China together. On the bus, an American man seated next to him initiated a friendly conversation. When the Chinese student woke up from a nap, he saw his neighbor rifling through his suitcases, as in a highway robbery depicted in the movies. Before he could call for help, this seasoned American bandit flashed his certificate of immunity: a badge of the Federal Bureau of Investigation, an espionage organization of the U.S. government. The man told him to stay quiet. In the evening, the bus arrived at a small station in Toledo. To avoid further nonsensical entangling, the Chinese student hurried onto another bus. But he was immediately stopped by the demon's claws: "So you think you can get away?" The student then claimed he needed to urinate. In the washroom he changed to women's clothing, which he had borrowed earlier from a girl for acting in a skit. He hurriedly left the station and walked to the busy street outside. Two special agents, like police hounds, ran after him. They nabbed him and held his arms. The seasoned American bandit, under the brilliant streetlight of this "land of freedom," held a gun to his back and forced him to the local police station. There he was locked in a dark room.[70]

If the above story seems like a clipping from a cops-and-robbers movie, the following episode is like a Kafka fantasy:

Huang Baotong Unjustifiably Imprisoned by U.S. Authority after Applying for Permit to Return to China

[August] 19, Xinhua News Agency. Chinese student Huang Baotong described his 116-day detention by the U.S. Immigration and Naturalization Service after he applied for permission to return to China. Huang Baotong first applied for the permit four years ago.... On the day after he filed his request, he was arrested by that U.S. authority on the charge that his permit of stay had expired. Huang Baotong repeatedly pointed out that he had filed an application for renewal one month before the expiration date. The immigration office ignored his explanation and

> jailed him in the detention center on Ellis Island just outside New York harbor. He was not allowed to post bond.... Finally on September 17, 1951, after being imprisoned for 116 days, the immigration office released him after he posted a bond of $2,000 and agreed to other conditions: Each Monday he had to report to the local immigration office; he could not leave the area under the jurisdiction of the New York Regional Immigration Office; he could not attend any group gatherings.... Huang Baotong continued applying for permission to return to China but received no reply. Then in the summer of 1954, a letter from the Immigration and Naturalization Service informed him that if he continued applying for the permit to return to China, he could receive a maximum fine of $1,000, a maximum jail sentence of one year, or both.[71]

When viewed from today's vantage point, some occurrences in those days seem even humorous, though dark. At that time the immigration office persistently asked the Chinese students to apply for permanent residence or political asylum. This, to today's Chinese students who have tried so hard to obtain a Green Card, is utterly inconceivable:

> *Fifteen Recently Returned Students Describe How U.S. Government Obstructed Their Return*
>
> [August] 19, Xinhua News Agency. Recently, fifteen students returned to China from the United States. They described the method used by the U.S. government to obstruct their return in the last several years.... Tong Shibai, who studied electrical engineering at the University of Illinois, said one method used by the government was to intimidate the students by summoning them repeatedly for interrogation. If a slight discrepancy appeared in their answers, they would be framed for charges of perjury and sentenced. He and other students have repeatedly received these summons.
>
> Tong Shibai went on to say that the U.S. Immigration and Naturalization Service also confiscated the students' passports without cause and then forced them to apply for permanent residence or political asylum.
>
> Guan Yingqian, who at one time studied chemistry at the University of Chicago, said, "For several years I repeatedly applied for a permit to return to China. But each time the reply was an application form for political asylum."[72]

In September 1955, about two years after the end of the Korean

War, the two countries reached an agreement at a Sino-American ambassadorial-level meeting in Geneva. Before the agreement, the U.S. government also declared that it would no longer block the Chinese students' return.

But the propaganda war continued. China's Foreign Ministry charged that the U.S. government continued its obstruction of the students' return and refused to disclose the number and names of the imprisoned students.[73] The U.S. State Department declared that the charges were groundless, as not a single Chinese student had been denied departure; anyone who knew of someone who wished to leave the country and had been blocked could notify the State Department at once.[74]

Actually, the number returning to China in the fifties was only a small fraction of the more than five thousand Chinese students then in America. Most of them remained there for one reason or another.

Near the end of the decade, following the return of the last group of Chinese students, China and the United States severed all ties. For the next twenty years or so, there was no more contention between the two countries on China's students in America.

While the door between China and the West was shut, the door to Moscow in the North was wide open. In the fifties, China modeled itself after the Soviet Union without reservation, in politics, economy, and culture. China received massive economic aid from the Soviet Union and sent many students to that country. In that period, there were about ten thousand Chinese students in the Soviet Union and Eastern European countries.[75] Many of China's leaders today in politics, science, technology, and art who are around the age of sixty received their education in the Soviet Union.

Although the Soviet model draws much reproach today, it cannot be denied that in that period the Soviet Union was far more advanced than China in science and technology, in art and literature, and even in studies of Marxism-Leninism.

In 1961, after a bitter battle over ideology, China and the Soviet Union openly split.[76] The Soviet Union withdrew all of its advisers and experts, and China withdrew most of its students.[77] The last door to the outside world was shut. Thereafter, China stopped sending students abroad altogether, except for a few students who were sent to study foreign languages.

In 1966 China fell into the decade-long frenzy and chaos of the Cultural Revolution. Albania, a beacon for European socialism, was the only loyal friend to China. Chairman Mao once used a Tang dynasty poem to describe the relationship between China and Albania:

> In the wide world there exists still one truthful friend;
> Though he is at the most remote corner of the earth,
> I feel he is my neighbor next door.[78]

The words "exists still" and "feel" accurately describe China's isolation at that time.

Little by little, the outside world faded from China's consciousness and China faded from the world's consciousness.

In 1978, when Deng Xiaoping opened China's "front door," China had isolated itself from the outside world, especially from the West, for nearly thirty years. It was as if the Chinese people were awakened from a deep, stupefying slumber. They opened their eyes. They saw a brand-new world outside.

CHAPTER 2

The Road to Studying Abroad

THE STIRRING POLICY OF PERMITTING PERSONALLY ARRANGED OVERSEAS STUDIES

When the news of the first wave of students going to America appeared in newspapers near the end of 1978, few Chinese grasped its historical significance and its far-reaching impact on their lives. At that time, the thought of studying abroad was outside their consciousness. A country overseas, as far from China as heaven and hell, was irrelevant.

When I first heard the news, I paid little attention to it. I was then in a small, remote city in China's southwest. Daily, public loudspeakers broadcast songs such as "The Embroidered Golden Banner," "The Hills and Waters of Jiao County," and "Horse, Tread Slowly."

Most youth then were preoccupied with finding a city job, struggling to prepare for their college entrance examination, or shedding tears for Liu Xinwu's novel *Love's Status.* Nobody was concerned about studying abroad.

At that time a few people began to leave.

At first, all students were chosen by the government, and nearly all were also financed by the government. Most went as visiting scholars and only a few as graduate or undergraduate students. For most visiting scholars, being selected to go abroad was similar to other events in their lives that were arranged by their work units. Many were selected because they had high scores, especially in a foreign language, on their entrance examinations for colleges or graduate schools.

The process left little room for individual choice, as people were accustomed to "submitting to the Party's arrangements in all things." A thirty-year-old student who returned from Tokyo University with a Ph.D. said that he did not really expect to study abroad when he took the graduate study examination. But there was a quota of two people in his field, and he did well in the examination, especially in English. In addition, on the application form he put a checkmark on the question "Are you taking the examination for studying abroad?" He was sent to Dalian Foreign Language School to study Japanese and later was sent to Japan. When he returned, his fluent American English had been replaced by fluent Japanese.

In the early eighties, news of students being sent abroad began to appear more and more frequently in the media. Still, few people dreamed of going abroad; that opportunity was available to only a few well-known scientists and high achievers in prestigious colleges.

What stirred society and excited the people was the policy of permitting students with private financial means to study abroad. On January 14, 1981, the Office of the Premier approved a plan drafted by the Ministry of Education and six other ministries in their "Request for Instruction Regarding Studying Abroad with Private Financial Means"[1] and issued the "Interim Regulations on Studying Abroad with Private Financial Means." This was the boldest step taken by the Chinese government in its opening-up policy.

An unverified report stated that some privately financed students were among the first group of students that went to America in 1978.[2] In 1979 the U.S. Embassy in China issued 523 F-1 visas.[3] The Chinese ministries also acknowledged in their drafted request that "the number of students applying for studying abroad with private financial means increased markedly since last year." According to *China Education Almanac*, there were between three thousand and four thousand such applicants in 1980 alone.[4] Nevertheless, before 1981, obtaining permission to study abroad with private financial means required making frequent trips to Beijing to solicit help from government leaders.

The policy of permitting overseas study with private financial means opened the "front door" for everyone. Many youths discovered that for the first time in their life they could dream of studying abroad and could work toward the realization of that dream.

One day, before the "Interim Regulations" were announced, a neighbor came to my house. She was the mother of a five-year-old and had been recently transferred to Beijing from a petroleum refinery in nearby Fangshan. She asked loudly as soon as she walked in, "Why aren't you applying for studying abroad? Lots of people have."

"How do you apply?" I was totally unenlightened then.

"You must initiate contact with foreign universities!"

"What do you mean? Besides, I don't have the money to pay the tuition."

"Maybe they'll give you a scholarship."

At that time, those words were like passages from Tales of the Arabian Nights. *How could anybody study abroad without going through the Ministry of Education?*

She left after some chatting. I have not seen her since, nor do I know if she has gone abroad. But I did hear that she had borrowed an English typewriter from a friend and started teaching her five-year-old to type. She showed uncanny foresight.

Later events proved my neighbor was right.

Most people probably felt somewhat envious upon reading that others were leaving for advanced studies overseas but did not give it another thought. Then their parents would tell them that the son of a colleague or the daughter of a neighbor living five blocks away was going to America to study. Some began to wonder, "Really?" Then the news would come that a college classmate in another department or a friend in a higher class of the same department was leaving for New York or Paris. They could not help wondering, now with a pang of jealousy, "How did he do it? Does he have an uncle there?" Then one day, a classmate or best friend would break the news: "I'll be leaving the day after tomorrow." They would be stunned. Then suddenly they would have a rude awakening: "If they can do it, why can't I?"

Understanding the issue of studying abroad was like understanding the revolution as expounded by Mr. Sun Yat-sen: there were those who understood it quickly, those who understood slowly, and those who would never understand.

A twenty-eight-year-old graduate student at Northwestern University in Evanston, Illinois, recalled that she had never considered studying abroad; the opportunity simply was thrust on her.

She and her boyfriend graduated from a prestigious college in Beijing. They began dating their junior year. She recalled their busy college life with nostalgia: classes, examinations, seminars, sports, partying. The even busier life while they dated made them dizzy. In 1985, after finishing graduate school, they were assigned to the same research institute. They rode bicycles side by side to and from work. The work at the institute was neither leisurely nor busy; there was always time available for chatting or sneaking away to do some shopping. They began to plan their wedding. Should the wedding banquet be held at the Beijing Hotel or the Imperial Kitchen in Beihai Park? Should they go to Huangshan or Hangzhou for their honeymoon?

In their junior year, two of their classmates, who were both student cadres of the Chinese Communist Party, had been sent abroad by the government. While having a high opinion of the event, they paid little attention. But by the time of their graduation, about one-third of the class of thirty had left China. A year later only five or six classmates remained, and they were trying feverishly to go abroad.

The woman could no longer sit still. One day, she said, "I want to go abroad."

Her mother responded, "How can you *do it?"*

Her boyfriend neither supported her nor objected: "Go ahead and give it a try. If you succeed, you can do some exploration for me, too."

So she started reviewing her English. Six months later she passed the Test of English as a Foreign Language (TOEFL), and soon afterward she passed the Graduate Record Examination (GRE) with a high score.

A year later the couple separately received letters of admission from two American universities. About a month before the June Fourth Incident, they boarded the same plane for America.

On the day of their departure, only one person in their class remained in China, forever; he was diagnosed with leukemia and died soon after he took the TOEFL.

Reflecting on the past, she said thoughtfully that it was fortunate that she decided to go to America. Perhaps because they had left China, she and her boyfriend parted ways two years later. But she had no strong regrets.

With an ever-increasing awareness of the opportunity, going abroad to study started like a ripple in a pond and grew to be a wave in an ocean. In 1983 there were only about one thousand privately financed students. In 1986 the number exceeded ten thousand. In 1987 it broke one hundred thousand.[5] Suddenly, male and female, old and young, with or without a foreign connection or a yearning for more education, were all seriously considering studying abroad.

If the generation of the Cultural Revolution was hardened by one "movement" after another, the subsequent generation grew to maturity in an environment of one "craze" after another. First there was the literature craze. This was followed by the politics craze, the business craze, the campaign craze, the aesthetics craze, the culture craze, the petition craze. . . . One fad waxed while another waned. The studying-abroad craze, however, persisted unabated. To China's youth, studying abroad was a challenge filled with adventure, a search for personal values, and an opportunity that could change one's life.

Chinese society at that time left little room for the younger generation to grow. There were no motivating agendas in politics, no wealth to seek, no battlefield for the spirit to roam, and also no private life that was worth defending against outside intrusion. To survive, people simply sat and waited. For what, nobody had a clue.

Greetings between the young always included these two sentences:

"How are you?"

"Down in the dumps."

Thus, going abroad became a big event in a life that was otherwise ordinary, languid, and colorless. The yearning might eventually turn from a sweet dream to a nightmare,[6] but doubtless it had brought boundless hope and a lust for life to China's youth by giving them the freedom to choose their own path.

The motivation for studying abroad varied. Some students went because they had lofty aspirations or sought an opportunity for their talent; others left for higher pay or to escape an unsatisfying marriage. Going abroad meant different things to different people. Some did it to earn honor for their country or to pursue personal growth, wealth, or freedom of speech. Some left simply to bear another child. But regardless of what one sought, the best approach was always going abroad. Even when one had no goals, the process was worthwhile in itself. A friend, unwilling to drift, said to me with deep feeling, "No matter how you look at it, going abroad is at least *something*."

Once the decision was made, life changed abruptly from lethargy to tension, from boredom to excitement. There was no time to worry about the destiny of the country or one's fellow countrymen, to criticize the government, to verbalize endless grievances, to complain about the boss. The year-end bonus, the promotion, and colleagues' appraisals were no longer fussed over. One rose to the occasion, far above daily pettiness.

In the eighties, when two acquaintances met on a Beijing street, the most frequent dialogue was these two sentences:

"Hey, how goes it with your study-abroad project?"

"It's in progress!"

ENGLISH AS A WEAPON FOR SURVIVAL

The journey toward studying abroad was like the Long March.[7] There were turbulent waters, snowy mountains, and grasslands that had to be crossed. At times one was surrounded, hunted, cornered, intercepted. Some fell, some straggled behind, some gave up. Only the few people with a strong will unintimidated by the prospect of failure could reach their destination.

The first step of this long march was to study a foreign language.

"Foreign language is a weapon in life's struggle," wrote Karl Marx. People learned that maxim during the Cultural Revolution, but they probably understood its profound significance only in the late eighties.

All foreign language teaching was halted during the Cultural Revolution and was resumed only in its final days to fit China's political agenda. I was taught English in elementary school because of anti-imperialism, Russian in junior high because of anti-revisionism, and finally English again in high school. To this day I can recite the two English sentences that I learned in elementary school, but have not yet found an occasion for their use: "Chairman Mao is our Red commander" and "We are his little Red Guards."

In the early opening-up period in the eighties, students' proficiency in English was poor, as illustrated by the well-known campus anecdote about the girl leaving the cafeteria after dinner who pushed open the door, which struck the head of an incoming boy. Eager to practice her spoken English and to apologize, she said, "Thank you," leaving the confounded boy massaging the bump on his head. During English examinations for studying abroad, while the minutes and seconds were ticking toward zero hour, people outside the test room would tightly clasp their copies of *Learn with Broadcasting English* to hone their proficiency. In every social stratum and every corner of the country, the zeal for learning a foreign language rose spectacularly among the young. A colleague of mine said, "Don't use up all your energy at work—save some for expanding your English vocabulary at home."

China's market economy quickly responded to the study-abroad craze. Foreign-language dictionaries became and remained best sellers. *The New English-Chinese Dictionary* and *The English-Chinese Dual Explanation Dictionary* had numerous reprintings. New teaching material also appeared in the market. First there were *Lingaphone* and *Essential*; then there were *New Concepts* and *Learn with Me*; these were followed by guidebooks such as *A Brief Introduction to Foreign Institutions Accepting [Chinese] Students*, and *A Guidebook for Studying Abroad.*

The most spectacular sight in this cultural whirlwind was the mushrooming of continuing-education schools teaching foreign languages. On any given day in 1989, the *Beijing Evening News* (Beijing wanbao) would carry numerous advertisements such as the following:

> *Foreign Language School Accepting Applicants*
>
> Foreign teachers, computer facilities. TOEFL, GRE, career training. American dialogue, advanced English, business English, Xu Guozhang's *English, New Concept.* Teacher well-traveled in the United States. Beginners, intermediate, accelerated, full-time leave classes.[8] Register at XX elementary school.

In April 1989, before my departure for America, I signed up for an intensive TOEFL class in a continuing-education school named Guanghua. The class was held in a high school, on Tuesdays and Thursdays from seven to nine o'clock in the evening. The semester lasted two and a half months, and the tuition was ¥150.[9] Other concurrent classes were "Grammar Simplified," "Advanced Conversation," and "Business English." What attracted me in the advertisement was "Classes are taught by teachers with American M.A. degrees and by American citizens."

After completing a simple application and paying the fee, I was issued an attendance permit. Admission required no placement test, no letter of recommendation from one's work unit, and no review of one's political background. It was an educational system regulated by market economy alone.

Thus each Tuesday and Thursday I rode my bicycle to be drilled intensively in preparation for the TOEFL.

On the first day, there was a din of voices and a swarm of bicycles at the school. The entire administration was run by an elderly man who by day was the custodian of the high school. First he served as the school doorman, then as the bouncer, checking attendance permits from one classroom to another.

There were more than twenty students in my class. No one seemed to know anybody else, nor did anyone seem to care. Everyone appeared to be aware that, though we came from different places, we were on this journey together because we wanted to study abroad.

The teacher, a smart-looking young man, walked in. He was known to have received a master's degree in English in America and had a day job at an international trading company. He immediately declared that he was not going to follow the textbook required by the school; that would be used for homework only. He would teach the salient points in grammar from his own notes.

Thus we set our textbooks aside and opened our notebooks. He began with some general considerations on how to study English, then discussed the special usages of articles, special forms of certain nouns, and irregular verbs. After two classes and three pages of notes, the school administrator declared that the teacher would be replaced; Mr. Huang's contract had expired and an American would replace him.

The new teacher was a young American named Bill, with blond hair and blue eyes. He looked younger than twenty and came from Michigan. Like many other American youths, after graduation he traveled around the world and earned his living by teaching English.

The new teacher, of course, had a full command of English. But he seemed unfamiliar with the TOEFL.

The first day, he sat at the teacher's desk and told the class that he was going to teach some real English. Nobody doubted his ability to do so. But it was Bill's comments about China that were more interesting. One morning, while riding a bicycle across Dongda Bridge, he saw a woman sitting on the pavement, sobbing. Many spectators surrounded her. Why were there many onlookers but not a single person who asked what the problem was and if she needed help? He said this could not possibly happen in America. If you were concerned, you would offer to help; if you weren't, you would leave.[10]

About a month and a half later, my intensive learning abruptly ended because of the June Fourth Incident.

Surprisingly, in early July, soon after some order returned to public places, the foreign-language continuing-education schools stubbornly returned to life. Not a single foreign news reporter noticed this earliest indication that China would remain on track with its reform and opening-up policy.

I became busily occupied with the formalities of going abroad and stopped attending the class.

The first hurdle in the journey to studying abroad is the TOEFL: "In this section of the test, you will have an opportunity to demonstrate your ability to understand spoken English. There are three parts to this section, with special directions for each part." I imagine that many students who are abroad now would feel nostalgic upon hearing this explanatory statement of the TOEFL. It would remind them of a distant past, like a familiar song from childhood.

Tuofu, the phonetic transliteration of TOEFL in Chinese, became a household word with a Hong Kong flavor.[11] The TOEFL is administered by America's Educational Testing Service. It tests the English proficiency of foreign students whose native language is not English. American and Canadian universities frequently use TOEFL scores as one of the considerations in admitting foreign students.

In the early eighties the supply of Chinese students for the New World was quite limited, and many American colleges gave "most-favored-nation" treatment to Chinese applicants, in admission as well as scholarship awards. Generally speaking, American colleges required a TOEFL score of 500 for undergraduates and 550 for graduate students. In America, however, every business deal can be negotiated, and the TOEFL score is no exception; there is no absolute admission standard.

To standardize the study-abroad process, the Chinese government agreed to the American proposal of setting up TOEFL test centers in China. On December 11, 1981, the first TOEFL tests in China were held in Beijing, Shanghai, and Guangzhou.

The number of TOEFL centers quickly expanded to eight cities, and in 1987 to fifteen cities and twenty-nine examination sites. Even this rapid expansion could not satiate the ever-growing demand.

The TOEFL test fee was $26 in 1986; two years later it was raised to $29. In 1996 it was between $38 and $45. To a Chinese whose average monthly income was only a couple hundred yuan, twenty-some dollars was a sizable sum.[12] But the cost never appeared to dampen the enthusiasm of TOEFL test-takers.

As the number of test-takers increased, matters beyond knowledge of the English language contributed to the difficulty of passing the test. In 1986 it was relatively easy to register for the TOEFL test in Beijing. But in 1988 and 1989 it became as hard as getting a ticket for a sleeping berth on a train. The would-be test-takers queued up all night, and numbers were issued and swapped. Some students organized teams to take turns in the queue. Probably the only other spectacle of comparable magnitude was the crowd waiting outside the Shenzhen Security Exchange to buy stock.

Although it was a real struggle to register for the TOEFL test in China, the test facilities were first-rate. In Beijing the test-site colleges made available their language laboratories, and before the test, the facilities were thoroughly checked. But in America, facilities for the TOEFL were not as standardized. A student who took the TOEFL in Detroit said the examination was held in a terraced lecture hall for about a hundred test-takers. There were no earphones for the listening part; two loudspeakers that rumbled were placed on a lectern.

The rise in the number of test-takers was accompanied by a rise in scores. With a several-thousand-year tradition of taking examinations, the Chinese would not be outdone in tests. In the beginning, a score of 500 was considered respectable, and 550 won praise. In the nineties, a score below 600 was considered a failure, and perfect scores were frequent.

After mastering the TOEFL, students advanced to other tests, such as the GRE, and conquered them too. An example was published in *People's Daily* (overseas edition), November 3, 1992:

> *Zou Qiuzhen, Only 18, Leaves for the U.S. for Doctoral Studies*
>
> From our news service. Zou Qiuzhen, an eighteen-year-old who just graduated from the Department of Radio Engineering of Southeastern University, has been admitted to Stanford University. At this time, he is on his way to America to begin his doctoral studies.... In May, in the general examination for graduate students and the English proficiency examination for foreign students, both written and administered by an American testing agency, Zou Qiuzhen scored 2,130 in the GRE and 630 in the TOEFL. Based on these scores and the letters of recommendation from his college, several prestigious American colleges competed in offering him admission.

The story had been circulating that many departmental chairs in American colleges, faced with several Chinese applicants with equally high test scores, were hard pressed in their selections. These professors may have been impressed by the diligence and the intellect of the Chinese students, but it would have been difficult for them to understand that, to many Chinese students, the TOEFL was not simply a test of English proficiency but a means of winning a struggle for a new life.

EXPLORING AVENUES TO THE NEW WORLD

In China, life was pretty much set at birth. From kindergarten through high school, people had little choice about schools, textbooks, or clothing. The reason was simple: schools admitted only neighborhood children; stores were short of food for the body as well as for the mind. The resumption of a uniform college entrance examination allowed individuals opportunities, for the first time in their lives, to shape their futures. But once you entered college, your life resumed its predictability. You would be assigned to a certain class and a certain dormitory. During the day you would attend classes according to a fixed curriculum, and at night you would sleep in the same room with others who were unlikely to cherish the same ideas or follow the same path as you. After college, you would be assigned to your work unit. Thereafter, your life would be so straight that you could predict it until the very end: you would date, court, and marry according to socially acceptable norms; have one child according to the guidelines of the Neighborhood Planned Parenthood Committee; receive a housing allocation when you became thirty or so (if you had not committed political errors); be promoted at about forty; and retire at sixty. After retirement you would practice *qigong* in the morning or take a stroll after dinner, until you died.[13] Upon death you would be assured of a memorial gathering.

Most Chinese had become accustomed to this choiceless life and did not feel its terror. On the contrary, after being so conditioned, they became worry-free. Like tamed animals, they lost their wild nature and life force. They were overtaken by inertia.

But going abroad changed all that.

A thirty-nine-year-old student, who went to America in 1982, recalled that after he and others had endured the grueling examination, they were sent to Beijing Language School. There they received language training and instruction on foreign culture. At the conclusion of the training, they all waited patiently for their assignments to foreign colleges, just as they had after college graduation. Instead, they were told that they then had to apply to American colleges for admission and scholarships on their own; the Chinese government would fund only the travel cost and subsistence for the first year. The students were all shell-shocked.

China's socialist, planned educational system was thus spliced onto the American educational system of capitalist self-determination.

For those who went with private financial means, the process required a personal commitment, sometimes even some personal sacrifice. In that very process, China's youth understood for the first time the meaning of freedom.

When you walked into the reading room of the Beijing Library and opened guidebooks to American colleges, you saw the thousands of colleges listed alphabetically: their names, fields of study, admission standards, tuition, scholarship availability, addresses ... The reading made you dizzy with fantasy. Although you were still sitting in the room, your heart already reverberated with those calls. Maybe you could apply to Harvard, or Berkeley; yes, you could go to Hawaii, but also Alaska ... You were choosing your own destiny.

That distant, mysterious, and alluring New World thus became faintly visible from those densely printed volumes. This discovery of the New World was one of the most important events in China in the eighties. That generation of China's youth was no less passionate and courageous than Columbus.

Illustrating the newly gained initiative of Chinese students was the drastic change in funding sources within a short time. In 1979, 54 percent of the students who went to America were financed by the government or by their work units. In 1985 that percentage decreased to 17, while at the same time 57 percent found support from American colleges on their own.

Of course, to probe the New World required not only commitment and courage, but also strategies and techniques.

Tens of thousands of application letters left China and went to the several thousand American colleges, from the most prestigious to the unknown, from the Ivy League to community colleges, from language schools to seminaries.

Applicants were moved to find that the American colleges answered every inquiry and always enclosed a beautifully printed catalog or other document in their reply. In China, people had been conditioned not to expect a reply to their inquiries. So when youths living in back alleys in Beijing or Shanghai suddenly received letters from American colleges bearing the signatures of departmental chairs, they were overwhelmed by the seemingly undeserved flattery.

The admission process of American colleges required a lot of paperwork. Generally, the colleges required a completed application form, an original undergraduate transcript, two or three letters of recommendation from professors, the TOEFL and GRE (for applying for graduate studies) report, and proof of ability to pay or a financial guarantee. Several months of running around were required to assemble these documents.

To meet the hard-nosed American-style admission requirements, which are stringent but not rigid in terms of test scores and sources of funds, many Chinese quickly learned how to sell themselves. Some invented techniques with a Chinese flavor.

Admission application forms usually had a section called "Describe Yourself"; it asked about the applicant's motivation or research plan. The colleges took the answer seriously. A Chinese equivalent would be "Motivation for Joining the Party" in a CCP membership application. To many students, to go abroad was the end, and to study was only the means; it was a matter of seizing an opportunity in life, not just learning a special skill. Some strategic thinking was called for. To increase the chance of landing a scholarship, many students changed their field of study to an obscure one so that competition for scholarships would be less severe. Of course, you would never say so in "Describe Yourself." Instead, you would start with "Since early childhood I have had a passionate love of studying . . ." The essay would go on to describe your unyielding devotion in the past and your planned dedication to the subject in the future. The specialty could be education of disabled children, though you might have repeatedly resisted a teaching assignment after you graduated from your teachers college; it could be Sanskrit, although your knowledge about India and Buddhism might be limited to what you read in *The Journey to the West.*[14]

The college transcript was a realm allowing great individual creativity. Because of differences in educational systems, curriculum, grading systems, and language, a transcript, once translated, acquired a higher luster. "Selective Readings in Marxism-Leninism" became "Philosophy of the West," "International Communist Movements" became "International Politics," "Theory of Political Economy" became "Theory of Macroscopic Economy," and "Moral Education" became "Ethics," "Psychology," or "Anthropology." Even readings in political indoctrination, such as "The Thirteenth Congress of . . ." or the "The Fourteenth Congress of . . ." became "Theory of Political Science" or "A Study of Chinese Politics." As to the conversion of grades, from Excellent, Superior, Average, and Below Average to A, B, C, and D, each person had a personal conversion standard. There were other ingenious moves to promote a favorable perception. For example, to promote an impression of one's personal creativity, some people sent artwork that had nothing to do with the field of study, and others with confidence in their good looks enclosed a personal portrait. A friend of mine enclosed a chance photograph of herself with Zhao Ziyang, the ex–secretary general of the Chinese Communist Party. She received exceptional attention.

In China professors rarely wrote letters of recommendation. Even if a professor knew some English, it would be hard to write letter after letter for students. Thus letters of recommendation, though signed by the professors, were frequently composed and written by the students. It required talent and creativity to write three letters of praise that differed in content and style.

Preparation for the TOEFL and GRE required hard work, but there were also a few instances of people taking the tests for others.

Some complained that the application process was full of dirty tricks. A few went to the extreme. A woman who came from north China and enrolled at the University of California at Berkeley told me that the I-20 form she used for applying for her passport was forged.[15] She did not say how she received her visa. But then, I thought, if she could fool people as alert as the officers in the Chinese Bureau of Public Safety, she would have had no problem fooling the foreign officials.

Money was a decisive factor in the admission process. Except for the few students who were supported by the government, few people could afford the tuition. Thus, getting a scholarship or teaching assistantship became the key to success.

It was far easier for science and engineering students to receive financial support. The need for technical people in American college laboratories offered tremendous opportunities for Chinese students, who were capable, hard-working, and relatively inexpensive when they worked as laboratory technicians. Students from a reasonably good college in China, after persistent tries, usually had a good chance of being admitted to an American college and receiving financial aid. Many students used the opportunity of being the local guide for a visiting American professor to establish a personal contact. These contacts greatly enhanced the success rate of an applicant and were far more effective than dealing exclusively with the admissions office.

Humanities students were not so fortunate. There were far fewer scholarships and fellowships available, and the competition for them was keen. But persistence generally yielded results. In addition to searching for an obscure field of study, applicants first tried to find a financial guarantor to accomplish the task of getting to America. How to make a living would come after arrival.

Finding a financial guarantor required knowing someone in America. But not every Chinese had relatives in America. An "overseas connection," however, could be cultivated. Hence numerous comedies, tragedies, and cliff-hanging dramas unfolded.

In the early eighties, when I was still in college in China, the college administration notified students of the following story. A student got to know an American and asked him to be his financial guarantor. The American willingly obliged and expeditiously helped him with all the paperwork. When the student arrived in America, he went to the address of his financial guarantor. Behold, it was the address of an organization affiliated with the CIA! The authenticity of the story was not verified, but the school administration used it to serve warning to all students: stay vigilant in class struggle!

Of course, not every story was so scary. One story I heard in the language continuing-education school had a happy ending. A graduate of the Foreign Language School had dreamed for a long time of going to America. Unfortunately, a search of his family genealogy yielded not even a distant relative in America. By chance, however, he met an elderly American woman touring China, and he volunteered to be her guide for two days. After the American returned, he sent her audiotapes in which he called her "my American mother" and, making effective use of his language training, expressed an affectionate longing for her. The elderly woman was so moved by her "Chinese child" that she became his financial guarantor.

When I was in the United States, an American student told me about her experience in China. She said everybody was nice to her and she made quite a few friends. But one thing made her feel awkward: many people asked her discretely whether she could be their financial guarantor. She said, "I told them, 'I'm poor. I'm really poor.'" I know she was telling the truth; not every American can afford to be a financial guarantor. Many American students have to take out loans or work at odd jobs to finance their own education.

The search for new lands of opportunity first concentrated in America and Western Europe. Then it turned to Canada, Japan, Australia, and

New Zealand. Still later it spilled into Eastern Europe and Latin American countries, or any other country that would accept Chinese students.

The following statistics confirm that trend.

In 1978 twenty-eight countries hosted more than four hundred students sent by the Chinese government; in 1979, the number of countries increased to forty-one.[16] Four years later, it increased to fifty-four, and in 1984, to sixty-three.[17] On November 24, 1988, *Guangming Daily* reported that in the ten years after students were again being sent abroad, China had sent students to seventy-six countries.[18] By the beginning of 1993, according to *People's Daily*, Chinese students had set foot in more than one hundred countries.

In 1979, of the 1,200 students who had been sent abroad, about 500 went to the United States, 300 to Britain, 200 to West Germany and France, and only 100 to Japan.[19] The number of students going to Canada increased from 1,200 in 1986 to 3,250 in 1989.[20] In the same period, many more went to Japan and Australia. In Japan remedial students from Beijing, Shanghai, and other cities were studying Japanese language in preparation for regular attendance in a college. In 1983 Australia had just over seventy privately financed Chinese students but had 4,810 in 1987.[21] In 1989 the number exceeded 10,000. As a result, the Australian government tightened its requirements on the admission of foreign students.[22]

Then in the late eighties some language schools in foreign countries began accepting applications directly from China. This development triggered a rapid increase in the number of Chinese students in Canada, Japan, and Australia. The language schools provided an opportunity to study abroad for those who could not attend a regular college for one reason or another. Admission to these schools required no transcripts or TOEFL or GRE scores, but only tuition and plane fare. Thus, many people determined to go abroad went into debt, pawned their heirlooms, and left behind their spouses and children.

But problems quickly arose because of the sharp increase in applicants, the emergence of profit-oriented language schools, and the inadequate preparation of some of the students. Governments on both sides became concerned. In the fourth Sino-Japanese Civilian Conference, held in Beijing April 28–30, 1988, the issue of Chinese students in Japan was a topic of discussion. According to *People's Daily*, "Both sides expressed special concern about the rapid increase of privately financed Chinese students in Japan since 1985 and their academic and nonacademic problems. There are now problems that should not have occurred."[23] In Australia 50 percent of the Chinese students had only high school or even lower levels of education.[24] In addition, disputes arose over the return of the tuition money when visas were unobtainable or when language schools went bankrupt. These events led to diplomatic negotiations between the two countries.

Following the rapid saturation of the language-school market in Canada, Japan, and Australia, Chinese students started to find new countries for studying abroad, such as Hungary, New Zealand, and many countries in South America. In the nineties if you should meet a Chinese student in the Maldives, Belize, or Niue, don't be startled.

When studying abroad became only a means toward the goal of going abroad, methods to achieve that goal blossomed. The bureaucrats made use of their authority; the famous, their connections; the movie stars, their names and faces. Ordinary citizens had their own plots: some took the fast track of marrying a foreigner and emigrated; some, staking their lives, tried entry by having themselves smuggled. Meanwhile the concept of studying abroad became broader and more encompassing. Some practiced their culinary skills as devotedly as their English vocabularies, hoping to possess a talent that would never fail them; others took up English as a supplement to their *qigong* practice, aspiring to the lofty goal of rendering health benefits to the foreigners across the ocean.

In that tidal wave of going abroad in the eighties, the Chinese people witnessed many dramas, some comical, others sad. Many of them led to regrets and others were utterly deplorable. But one undeniable feature emerged: people began to shed their inertia and regain their life force. Going abroad reinvigorated the spirit of the Chinese people.

When the offspring in a family become dispirited, they stay put and fight tooth and nail for the family legacy no matter how meager it is. But if they have high aspirations, they walk out of the house to create their own future.

China was just such a family. In the eighties, thousands and thousands of China's youth met the challenge of going abroad to seek their fortunes elsewhere. Could this be foretelling the rise to prosperity of China in the next century?

THE OMNIPOTENT WORK UNIT

For many people the difficulty of going abroad lay not in being admitted to a university or obtaining a passport, but in obtaining permission from their work unit.

In China, the social structure consisted of the government and the family. The pivotal institution that supported the government above it and enlightened the family below it was a person's work unit. The government could be loved or scorned, the family could be ignored or fragmented, but one must not commit an offense against one's work unit. The work unit was omnipotent in dispensing all social benefits: it managed birth, aging, sickness, and death; it decided what one ate and drank and where one disposed of waste; it issued pay, allocated housing and holiday goods, and admitted children to kindergarten. Finally, it was the situs of everyone's dossier. Although nobody knew what was in that dossier, not knowing where it was would assuredly make people anxious.

After you had been admitted to a university and had received a financial guarantee, you had to obtain a letter of recommendation from your work unit before applying for a passport. Whether you could get such a letter depended on how enlightened the head of your work unit was, or the mood of the personnel administrator authorized to write such letters.

The Chinese language is flexible, hence rules and regulations written in it also are flexible. Furthermore, only the leadership and the administrators knew the rules. If the head of your unit or the personnel administrator wished to prevent you from leaving, they could accomplish their objective by praising you: "Such a talent cannot be allowed to drain out," "Indispensable." Sometimes they gave no reason.

To wear down the leadership required mastering the art of persuasion.

Some tried sincerity: "You see, I've never asked for special favors like joining the Party, bigger housing, or exemption from the one-child-per-family rule. I have only this one wish to go abroad. Please help me."

Some took a light-hearted approach: "You can view it as a sentence of ten-year banishment, executed overseas."

Some took a crude approach: "Boss, you can regard me as a fart—just let me go."

To deal with the human resources department, one had to be extra humble. I believe that everyone who went into the office of human resources to obtain a letter of recommendation was smiling, no matter how overbearing they might have been elsewhere. Sometimes civility in manners had to be supplemented by civility in substance. I met a student in Ohio, then over forty, who absolutely refused to return to China even though he had received his Ph.D. and had not found work. One of the reasons was the crushing humiliation dealt to him by his work unit when he was asking for permission to leave. He said, "I never want to go through that again."

Colleagues in the work unit could also be a problem. At times, their curiosity went beyond normal friendly concern. When the idea of going abroad was barely formulated, they would ask, "When are you leaving?" Before you had received your passport, they would ask, "Are you coming back?" A few days later they would say in astonishment, "What, you're still here!" A colleague who had no desire to go abroad himself said you should never publicize your intention before you leave; deny it vehemently until you receive your passport. Even if you are already abroad, make sure that when you call China, you say, "I haven't left yet." Although your colleagues have no authority to stop you from going, an unsolicited report from a colleague in a time of political sensitivity could destroy all your dreams.

The following is a rather ordinary story of the time:

A woman from Jiangsu majored in foreign languages and graduated in the class of 1984 from a reputable university in Shanghai. She is now a staff member in a well-known international organization.

In college, aside from her daily one-lap jog around the campus at four o'clock in the afternoon, she spent all her free time facing a wall to practice her spoken English. By the time she graduated, she was nearsighted and suffered from insomnia. Her command of English, however, far surpassed that of her classmates. She was admitted to graduate studies at a university in Beijing, specializing in oral translation of English. She became the first graduate student in the department ever to pass an international examination on English translation. Later she passed her second one, now in German, and became the only person in China who had passed both examinations. She was twenty-five.

After graduation she was retained to teach a twice-weekly English drill class. Other than that, she spent her time in political studies and on a campus beautification project.

Many of her classmates went abroad in this period. She knew very well that it would be impossible to improve skills further if she did not go abroad. Also, if she did not use these languages, her command of them would falter and fall behind her classmates. Besides, she was young; the glittering world outside was more attractive than her shared-room dormitory.[25] *She decided to study abroad.*

Several colleges in America, Canada, and Europe accepted her and gave her a scholarship or fellowship. After two years of teaching the English drill class, she requested permission from the department to study abroad. The departmental chair was also her former teacher. This woman, about 50, like many other middle-aged intellectuals, was formal, serious, and principled, but also stiff.

"It is not yet the time for you to go abroad," the chairperson explained to her in a simple, firm, nonnegotiable tone. "You're young. There will be plenty of opportunities for that later."

The young woman was speechless. She could not start a contentious argument, nor could she figure out the reason for the denial. Against school policy? Many others had left. Against departmental policy? But she was not assigned any serious work. In fact, she was not even certified to teach regular courses. Had she offended the departmental chair? No, they appeared to be getting along all right.

Actually, there was no reason other than that, in the view of the departmental chair, it was not the right time for her to leave. She made repeated visits, but the departmental chair would not budge. The young woman could not even get a copy of her transcript. Angrily, she announced her resignation. That was refused also: she would have to first reimburse the government ¥20,000 that it cost to educate her.[26] *She felt wronged and helpless. The only relief was to cry in her dormitory.*

Opportunities slipped away one after the other. The American universities agreed to hold her admission space and her scholarship for one more year, but they could not do it indefinitely. She turned twenty-six, twenty-seven, twenty-eight . . . She began avoiding the departmental chair, who now made her nervous and frightened. Although she was bitterly resentful, she knew her obstruction was not personal vengeance. Sometimes she wished that the departmental chair was simply wicked, in which case she could have been bribed.

The departmental Party secretary, however, was sympathetic. Privately he offered consolation and empty promises. Out of gratitude and a desire to maintain a good relationship, she frequently gave him presents from abroad, and once she gave him her allotment of imported goods and American dollars from attending an international conference.[27] *But the support of the Party secretary could not sway the departmental chair.*

Then in June 1989, events took a dramatic turn. One day, the departmental chair called the young woman in. "Go! You can all go!" This diligent woman was obviously agitated over all the people who wanted to go abroad.

So, after three years, the departmental chair approved her resignation.

Perhaps it is true that one reaps what one sows. At about the time of her departure for Europe, the departmental chair encountered similar troubles. She was to be transferred to a government office abroad when the June Fourth Incident broke out. Her departure was stopped at the last moment by the president of her university in Shanghai, who had received an unsolicited report disclosing some of her words and conduct before the June Fourth Incident. She had no choice but to stay, to respond to the allegations. That took a year and a half.

Three years later the two women met again at an international meeting in Brussels. Both then had long-term contracts with the same international organization. Time had passed and the scene had changed; neither brought up the old sores. They got together and made dumplings to celebrate their reunion.

When I met the first woman, she had already worked abroad for many years. After reflecting on the many wrongs she had endured in China, she complained about the lonely life abroad and the there-is-nothing-to-do work environment in her international organization. Then abruptly she remarked that she might have accomplished something in China had she stayed.

I said, "Then why don't you go back?"

She thought for a while and said, "It's better here—at least I am free."

I could understand that.

In contemporary China, the individual and the work unit, respectively the receiver and the dispenser of all benefits, have a subordinate-superior relationship. To a large extent, the degree of freedom an individual can enjoy depends on the unit and its leadership. Through the unit, political pressure can be gradually dissolved or infinitely intensified and personal freedom greatly expanded or sharply curtailed. Thus, political persecution often has been persecution by the work unit or a personal vendetta by its leadership. That was true during the Anti-Rightist Movement and also during the Cultural Revolution.[28]

I have often thought that if China should ever reform its political system, it should probably start with the abolishment of the omnipotent work unit.

In the eighties the National Education Commission began implementing an "agreement" system: people who wished to study abroad had to agree to return to their work units upon completing their studies. From these agreements, one could see the shadow of the subordinate-superior relationship. Like Faust, applicants exchanged their freedom in the future for the opportunity at hand. The unit, under the guise of national interest, maintained its control over the individual.

In China even the rule of law had never earned high respect, let alone an "agreement." But these agreements involved not only the political relationship between the individual and the work unit but also their monetary relationship. Mingling money and politics led to disputes. According to a newspaper report, one institution in Shanghai used the agreement to press a yet-to-return student for financial compensation. The charge and countercharge went to court, but the judgment is unknown. Another story is told about a student whose university sent him abroad and who repeatedly postponed his return. Armed with the agreement, the university sought compensation from the student's father, an elderly intellectual of high repute. But when high finances are at stake, civility is abandoned. The student's father pounded on the desk and shouted, "Money, I don't have! Life, I do! Come and take it!" The university controlled the damage by quietly withdrawing its demand.

Assaulted repeatedly by the tide of people going abroad, this subordinate-superior relationship showed signs of loosening. Around 1988 the Department of Labor, the National Science Commission, the Guanghua Company, and, it has been said, also the Ministry of National Security established many human-resource exchange centers. They served as the guardians of dossiers of people who had been denied permission from their work units to leave. These centers provided the documents that individuals needed to proceed with their applications. In exchange, the individuals paid a monthly dossier-storage fee. These centers were probably disciplined later, but at that time they helped those who were admitted by foreign universities but could not secure permission from their work unit to leave. What is not known is whether those who registered for dossier storage are still paying monthly storage fees today.

DASHED DREAMS AT THE AMERICAN EMBASSY

To many Chinese youth, China's "front door" was narrow, but the visa window of the various foreign consulate offices was narrower still.

In January 1990, six months after June Fourth Incident, a time when many people in China were eagerly seeking to go abroad, President George Bush issued an administrative order to "protect" Chinese students in America.[29] On January 26 the front page of the *New York Times* published an article from Beijing:

> Despite concern that China might stop allowing students to go to the United States, many Chinese students say the main obstacle to going abroad is the United States Embassy. Students who wish to go abroad must get approval from employers and security agencies. But for many students who have been accepted at American universities, rejection is more likely to come when they apply for an American visa.

In the article, *Times* reporter Nicholas Kristof said ironically, "Dreams are dashed each day at the United States Embassy."

Yes, reality is at times both laughable and cruel.

In the early eighties, when passports symbolized privileges, getting a visa was not difficult for officially sponsored and privately financed students alike; the world welcomed the students from long-isolated China with the same zeal it showed for giant pandas. In the mid-eighties, as China's policy on studying abroad relaxed and the number of students soared, the visa policy of many countries became increasingly rigid and the rate of refusal sharply increased. There had always been a subtle relationship between the width of China's "front door" and the narrowness of the visa windows in various consulates. But in general it became increasingly difficult to get a visa as years went by. This was especially so for privately financed students.

On the morning of May 12, 1989, I went to the American Embassy on Xiushui Street to find out how to get a visa. I knew many others who did the same: before you actually applied for a visa, you made on-site exploratory visits. Getting a visa, like a marriage, had an impact on your whole life and was not to be trifled with.

There was a crowd outside the embassy. Those who had turned in their applications were already in the courtyard. The people outside, other than those making their exploratory visits, were professional "observers" and "well-informed people." There, you could hear all the latest developments.

"It seems that they have stopped giving F-1 visas," a middle-aged woman stated. Her voice lacked conviction, indicating that she had heard this second-hand.

"Impossible. They only made it a little more strict," a young man in a tweed suit said authoritatively.

"You've got to show a receipt for the tuition payment before they give you a visa. This is a new practice implemented by the new ambassador," someone interjected.

"Nobody can predict the outcome," the man in the tweed suit said. "If they give, you get a visa. If they don't, you don't get a visa. A few days ago, a student from Tianjin came to apply. He was well equipped—he had a full scholarship for a J-1 visa. It looked like smooth sailing. But during the interview that kid talked too much. He said that he was doing important research at his school in China. So the American said, 'Well, if you are doing such important work here, you shouldn't leave.' He already had been given the yellow slip. Then suddenly everything fell through."

Everybody felt sorry for that young man.

"That consul must have had a fight with his wife the night before," someone commented.

"It would be nice to know somebody inside," the middle-aged woman lamented. Unexpectedly, the comment elicited another story from the young man in the tweed suit.

"A friend of mine knows the Chinese secretary quite well. One day the Chinese secretary called and asked him to turn in his application as soon as possible, since a consul's wife had just found out that she was pregnant."

"A lot of visas were granted during Bush's visit," someone else interjected.

In those days, on Monday through Friday mornings the embassy accepted applications for F-1 visas for privately financed students; on Monday, Wednesday, and Friday afternoons it accepted application for J-1 visas for government-financed students and visiting scholars.

On July 26, 1989, I went to apply for a visa. Finally, I was in the courtyard. Before being admitted to the building, I first completed an application handed out by a loquacious young Chinese man.

"Oh, a reporter! I guess you are not coming back." I said that of course I would come back. The young man, now with a broad smile, said, "No problem, you can tell me the truth. Certainly you're not coming back. Are you?" I kept quiet.

I turned in the application before I entered the building. Two Chinese secretaries made sure that all documents were in order. Then we were led inside. At one end of the room were several rows of chairs. A partition had been placed in the middle of the room. The work window for the consul's office was on the other side of the partition. More than thirty Chinese sat there silently, waiting for their turn to be called for the interview.

A story, which might incite a nationalistic indignation in some people, had been circulating. One day, the waiting compatriots had become impatient and started chatting. Some even stood up, peeking through the cracks of the partition to see what was going on. Suddenly, an annoyed woman consul burst into the waiting area, pointed her finger at several people and said, "You, you, and you. There will be no visa for you. You may leave now." They were stunned and then started to plead. Among them was a girl, who began to cry. The Chinese secretary returned their documents and said, "The American's upset. There's nothing I can do."

Some people who came out appeared light-hearted; obviously their applications had been approved. A middle-aged man who was interviewed before I was came out dejected; his financial guarantee, written by the Bank of China, was not acceptable. Another young man also had trouble. He had been studying in America and was planning to have his wife visit him. Then his wife was diagnosed with lung cancer and he rushed back. Now his wife had died and he wanted to resume his studies. The consul said his IAP-66 form would expire in a month and he needed a new one for his visa.[30] His sad story did not move the American consul.

Then it was my turn.

"Why are you going to the United States?"

"To attend a training program in journalism at the University of Michigan," I answered.

"How long do you plan to stay in the United States?"

"About a year," I said.

"Welcome," the woman consul said. "You can pick up your visa on August 2."

I sighed happily. It was so simple, so disappointingly simple. I had been expecting a tense and terrifying encounter.

The truly exciting scene occurred outside the embassy compound. As soon as I walked out the gate, a swarm of people surrounded me as if I were a movie star.

"You got it?"

"Did they speak to you in English or Chinese?"

"How much is your scholarship?"

People anxiously sought guidance from other people's experience, whether success or failure.

Generally speaking, it was not too hard to get a J-1 visa, as it carried a two-year stay limit, after which the visa holder had to return to China. Another reason was that the financial assistance for J-1 visa applicants was secured. The privately financed students applying for the F-1 visa, however, faced much tougher struggles.

Early each morning, many applicants queued up outside the American Embassy. Sometimes, because of the huge crowd, the embassy resorted to giving out numbers. The busiest time was just before the beginning of the fall semester in American colleges. I heard that the numbers handed out on January 26, 1989, were for visa interviews scheduled for mid-August. Some people queued for the visa interview numbers before they even had a passport.

If what went on outside the embassy compound was an endurance battle, what went on inside was a blitzkrieg. Sometimes a lifetime dream and several years of work were destroyed in those few minutes of conversation with the consul.

The American consuls could interview close to a hundred people each morning, but only those who were admitted to prestigious colleges and awarded full scholarships had a chance of getting a visa. Those who relied on friends or relatives as their financial guarantors were most likely refused a visa. The reasons varied. For example, a certain document did not meet the requirement, the amount of the financial guarantee was insufficient, the field of study and the applicant's background were mismatched, or the applicant was a single woman of marriageable age. Of course, "having an inclination to immigrate" was the most frequently cited reason.

The authority for granting a visa rested completely with the consuls. Each consul had his or her own criteria and hence each applicant had his or her own luck.

Two consuls were well known by their nicknames within the circle of applicants in Beijing. One was "Big Beard" and the other "Miss Taiwan." Big Beard, so the story went around, was muddle-headed and, when in a good mood, would approve numerous visa applications, while Miss Taiwan was picky and biased against mainland Chinese and would approve none. Those in the waiting crowd probably were all praying that they would be interviewed by Big Beard, not by the unlucky Miss Taiwan.

The feelings after having one's application denied were complex. First was the suffering: a dream embraced for several years was suddenly dashed. Some people had staked everything on the project: they had resigned from their work units, broken up their families, run around procuring the needed documents, and spent all their savings. Now they had to return to the same old reality. But the hardest to bear was the letdown of spirits. Many people wanted to go abroad because of the repeated disappointments in their own country; they rested their hope, be it the yearning for democracy or the pursuit of happiness, on that distant land of freedom. Now the land of freedom had declared, indifferently, "No."

Nobody knew how many dreams were dashed outside the American Embassy every day. But behind each broken dream was a small tragedy.

I still remember one scene clearly to this day. It was in early 1989. I passed the American Embassy and saw a young man in a suit standing motionless, head bowed, hands tightly gripping the railing outside the embassy. People looked at him curiously. The young man, perhaps suddenly aware that he was the center of attention, turned around, held up a package of documents, and said in a voice of pain and suffering, "My documents are all complete, all complete! Everything." Obviously he had just been denied his visa request.

Then there were those who would never give up.

A thirty-four-year-old woman was a graduate of a foreign-language school. She was not beautiful, but she had a clear head and boundless energy. After college she had been assigned to teach in a high school. Being single, she was not given housing, nor did she wish to live with her parents. Living out of a suitcase, she slept on any vacant bed that she could find in the dormitories of her friends. Although she led a colorless life, she had a colorful dream: to study abroad. For that dream she resigned from her high-school position and applied to study abroad on private financial means. She started with her Neighborhood Committee,[31] *worked her way up, and finally received her passport. But she was denied an American visa. Three months later she was denied again and was told not to reapply for one year. She was disappointed but not dissuaded. She earned her living by doing translation work for a foreign publisher. Then the thought of going to Europe began to take root. After all documents were in order, she was refused a British visa. After that, she tried Denmark, Belgium, and once again the United States. As of the summer of 1992, according to a friend of hers, she was still trying.*

The American consuls were keenly aware that they were the makers of the daily tragedies. A colleague whom I met at the University of Michigan worked in a consulate in China. He told me that he tried his best to give out visas. Sometimes when he had to deny an application, he was pained by the applicant's suffering. His older colleague, on the other hand, perhaps because he had gone through this for many years, was unsympathetic. He turned down applications frequently and justified refusals by saying, "Don't give them visas. Once they're in America, they'll never come back." These words were harsh but true.

As the difficulty of getting an American visa mounted, the applicants flooded the Canadian Embassy. Soon the refusal rate there rose also.

In 1985, because of the admission procedures of language schools in Japan and Australia, the consulates of these countries suddenly became busy. The bustle lasted until October 1988, when the Japanese government suddenly tightened its review of visa applications for Chinese students wishing to study Japanese in these language schools. In Shanghai alone, thirty-five thousand students with passports and admission notices could not begin their journeys because they lacked visas. On November 7, 1988, thousands of youths demonstrated outside the Japanese Consulate. They chanted, "Our broad swords land on the neck of these ghosts."[32] Several years later, the Australian government faced a diplomatic controversy on the issue of tuition refunds after Chinese students were refused visas. On August 30, 1989, it issued a new rule: beginning in 1990, all applicants had to first undergo a "qualification appraisal," and only those who met the requirements would be allowed to apply for a visa. The earlier incident outside the Japanese Consulate was now repeated outside the Australian Consulate. Beginning on October 6, 1989, several hundred Chinese students who had been refused visas demonstrated outside the Australian Consulate, protesting the new policy. They pounded on the sedans parked outside the office, shouting, "Cheaters! Cheaters!"

During that period, some embassies that rarely attracted visitors also became the focus of thousands of visa applicants, but they quickly recovered their calm after tightening requirements for visas.

The reality was simple: No country in the world could accept that many Chinese students. This reality could not be altered by one's love of freedom or by these countries' respect for human rights.

The going-abroad craze in the eighties has been described as the great triumphant runaway; the Chinese, who had suffered various disappointments in their land, longed to run away from that land. But they quickly discovered that there were few places they could go.

This is perhaps the sorrow of this generation of Chinese. We are Chinese, but we wish to leave China. Many years from now, perhaps after we have journeyed around the world, we may come to realize once more that our most precious possession is right under our feet: the land that we inherited from our ancestors, however impoverished or scarred it may be.

HOW MANY HAVE GONE ABROAD? WHO ARE THEY?

How many students have left since 1978? An accurate number is hard to come by.

In October 1988, Leo A. Orleans's book *Chinese Students in America: Policies, Issues and Numbers* was published in America. The author, a China specialist from the Library of Congress, wrote in the Introduction, "Neither the Chinese nor the Americans know precisely how many Chinese students and scholars are in the United States now or at any time since exchanges began in 1978."

We also do not know how many students are in other countries, nor do we know the number of students who went abroad in any given year, sponsored by government institutions or privately financed, as visiting scholars or graduate or undergraduate students. The problem is not lack of data, but rather contradictory data.

Let us use the first few years as an example.

In 1978, the first year in which students were sent abroad, the number was 480, according to *People's Daily*.[33] But an official count completed in August 1988 gave the number 314 (80 undergraduate, 5 graduate, 229 visiting scholars), a discrepancy of 166 people.[34] A possible explanation is that the former number includes students who went to countries in areas other than North America and Europe.

The number for 1979 also is problematic. According to *China Education Almanac*, the number was 1,750. Leo Orleans gives the number

2,700, which was provided by Xinhua News Agency, but the government figure was 1,277.[35] In addition, these numbers do not include those who left on private financial means.[36] According to *China Education Almanac* (1980), the number from September 1978 to the end of 1979 was 2,700, but this was changed to 3,480 in the 1981 edition of *China Encyclopedia Almanac*.[37]

The accurate number for 1980 is also unknown. According to *China Education Almanac* and *China Encyclopedia Almanac*, the number of students sponsored by government institutions was 2,124, China's official count completed in 1988 was 1,862, whereas Leo Orleans gave the number 5,192 (provided by Xinhua News Agency).[38] It is possible that the last number is a composite that includes students financed by private means, estimated at 3,000 to 4,000. The table in appendix 2 gives the numbers of students studying abroad from 1978 to 1988, according to the various sources.

We will never know exactly how many students have gone abroad since 1978. First, since China at that time lacked the technical knowledge for accurate recording and treatment of data, there were inevitable errors and omissions in the statistics. Second, there were many avenues out of China. For instance, someone who was publicly financed could have received funds from either the government or their work unit; and someone who was privately financed could have received funds from private sources with public sponsorship or from purely private sources. Also, many people first went abroad for family visits, on official travel, or as tourists and later changed to student status. If they were included in the count, the total number would far exceed the numbers given in the table.

Although the numbers vary and are at times contradictory, two call for special attention. At the end of 1988, in its Open Door annual report, the International Education Association stated that in 1987 and 1988 the country that sent the most students abroad was China, with a total of 42,481 study-abroad students, while Taiwan had the most students in America.[39] But in less than a year, the U.S. Information Agency reported in November 1989 that, according to a survey of American colleges for the 1989–90 academic year, the total number of students from the Chinese mainland was 29,040, exceeding the number of students from Taiwan for the first time.[40]

All sources agree that the number of Chinese students studying abroad increased every year from 1978 to 1989. In the decade before 1989, the total number of students abroad was 70,000; it reached

170,000 in 1991 and 190,000 in 1992. The latest number, for 1995, was 220,000.[41]

A question directly related to "How many?" is "Who?" This is perhaps even more important.

A favorite and frequent comment of the print media in Taiwan and Hong Kong was that most of these students were the children of highly placed officials; that is, sending children abroad was one of the privileges of the most privileged class in contemporary China.

Although numerous examples could be cited to support this argument, the statement was misleading, as it was not based on an analysis of the data. Overall, the selection process had been similar to that for college admission—fair and competitive. This is not to say that it was free of corruption and abuses by the specially privileged. As a government policy, whether in its initial formulation or in its later implementation, it treated everybody equally—a rather rare occurrence in China.

In March 1990 the Chinese Political-Science Students and Scholars Association of America administered a survey on issues related to China's politics. Questionnaires were sent to Chinese students at eighteen colleges, including Harvard, the University of California at Berkeley, and others. A report was written based on 360 replies. A result that interested me was an analysis of the background of the students and scholars: 52 percent were from big cities, 29.8 percent from medium-sized cities, 8.4 percent from small towns, and 8.8 percent from rural areas. As to their family backgrounds, 51.8 percent were from families of intellectuals, 24 percent from families in government services, 10 percent from working-class families, and 7.2 percent from peasant families. The author of the survey stated, "The majority of the students and scholars were male, came from a big city and an academic institution, were born in the sixties and raised in an intellectual family, did not join a political organization, and received a fairly high academic degree."[42]

These data and analyses may lack precision but should be fairly factual and do not support the criticism of rampant favoritism.

DIFFERENT POLITICAL CLIMATES, DIFFERENT POLICIES

The leadership of the Chinese Communist Party and Chinese government, when meeting with Chinese students or discussing policy on studying abroad, loved to say that the policy would not change.

On May 29, 1980, Hua Guofeng, the premier at that time, met about fifty Chinese students in Tokyo during his visit to Japan. This ex-chairman of the Chinese Communist Party, a person known for his repeated emphasis on China's self-reliance in its economic development, told the students warmly, "We should control our own destiny and be self-reliant, but we should not isolate ourselves. We must learn useful things from other countries, including advanced science and technology and management." He continued, "In the future China will send students to other countries to learn business administration. Our business administration is also behind that of other countries."[43] This was probably the first time that he, as the leader of the Party and the government, commented on China's policy of sending students abroad.

In November 1983, Hu Yaobang, the secretary-general of the Chinese Communist Party, visited Japan. In the atmosphere of "China and Japan being friends for generations to come," someone questioned him about China's Clean Up Spiritual Pollution Campaign.[44] Hu stated that the campaign would in fact advance, not slow, China's policy of opening up.[45] But from Tokyo to Kyoto, he could not disengage himself from the issue of cleaning up "spiritual pollution," so he stated repeatedly, "Ridding China of spiritual pollution will merely wipe the dust off our face. It will not obstruct our policy of opening up to the outside. It will in fact benefit the implementation of that policy."[46] The cleanup issue in fact did not affect the policy of opening up.

On December 3, 1988, Zhao Ziyang, who succeeded Hu as secretary-general of the Chinese Communist Party, met repatriated exemplary students in the Great Hall of the People and emphasized, "We must uphold our policy of sending students abroad."[47]

Six months later, the June Fourth Incident broke out. The new generation of leaders on the political stage stated, on a variety of occasions, that the policy "would not change." On October 6, 1989, Secretary-General Jiang Zemin and Premier Li Peng met with returned students in Huairen Hall in the Zhongnanhai compound. Like his predecessor, Jiang said, "To send students to study in other countries was part of our policy of reform and opening up. It remains so."[48]

In the decade since the mid-eighties there have been several political storms in China. Many students lived with the anxiety that the policy would be changed overnight and hence they would miss the last train. Many foreign observers also repeatedly predicted that the policy would once more die young. Facts have shown, however, that the policy was carried out with consistency, a rather rare occurrence in China's history.

For more than ten years after China's opening up in the late 1970s, its policy on allowing students to study abroad had varied according to domestic politics. The strange circular dance consisted of alternately relaxing and tightening the control of the individual by the government and the work unit.[49] Today, now that society has begun to revolve around the economy, perhaps the policy can finally shed the ritualized circular dance and instead reflect the privileges and obligations of China's citizens.

THE PARTING SCENE

A colleague studying oil painting told me that he had an idea for a painting. Its title would be *Parting*. The canvas would show the front of an automobile heading toward the airport. Through the windshield one would see a student dressed in a suit. He would soon bid farewell to his family, for he was leaving for another country to study. The student would look thoughtfully through the car window. My colleague said he would like to paint those eyes, for they would reveal extraordinarily complex emotions—excitement, anxiety, reluctance to leave, a feeling of something amiss.

I do not know if my colleague ever completed his creative piece. He has since left China. I also do not know how he felt at his moment of parting. Life is often complex but rarely that romantic.[50]

After all the work of getting their passports and visas, packing bags, and purchasing tickets, the departing students finally stood in line to have their tickets checked. The time had come to bid goodbye to family and friends. Soon they would leave their country behind and set foot in an unknown land in which they must battle for survival. What were they thinking?

"That was the most fulfilling moment of my life," said a twenty-eight-year-old student at the University of California at Berkeley. On that day his parents, two sisters, a brother-in-law, his uncle and aunt and their two children, and his girlfriend all came to say goodbye. He had a full scholarship to study physics at a

prestigious university. He knew that he was the pride of the family, and he had shaken up his classmates and the colleagues in his work unit. Everything happened so naturally that he could not say that it had been a battle or even a struggle. When he graduated from high school, the college entrance examination had been in use again for two years; he had not witnessed the sad, eerie sight of a desolate Peking University campus during the Cultural Revolution or experienced the idle passing of life in a commune. He simply sailed through the entrance examination and entered the University of Science and Technology. Four years later, he was admitted to Peking University as a graduate student. After completing his graduate studies, he worked in a research institute of the Chinese Academy of Sciences. Just when he was thinking of taking the TOEFL *and* GRE, *a professor from the University of California at Berkeley, who was interested in the same research field, visited the institute and showed strong interest in his work. A year later the professor made all the arrangements for him to come to Berkeley. "I wasn't nervous at all. I knew I would do all right. Look at my living quarters here, and my car. They're like those of a deputy minister in China," he said.*

"I knew then that perhaps it would be our last embrace," said a twenty-five-year-old woman who went to Australia to study at a language school. On the day of their parting, her husband went to the airport with her. They had experienced numerous separations during their three years of marriage. They had met at a party when she was working in an art unit and he was an actor in a Beijing troupe. A friend brought him to her work unit and hence into her life. They fell in love at first sight and were married half a year later. But life after marriage was no longer romantic. Like many other couples in China, they had to live apart.[51] *During those three years of marriage, she took trains and buses and got rides between Beijing and Tianjin. This time, however, she knew the separation would not be short. She was leaving not just for a paper diploma but for a change in life. She did not wish, in her own words, "to live the harsh and trivial life of a small-city person." Fate seemed to have taken good care of her to have arranged that change. On a fateful autumn day, walking on fallen leaves, she went to the post office to mail her visa application to the Australian Embassy in Beijing. When she arrived, the last postal clerk was just locking up the office for the coming long weekend. She did not wish to delay the mailing and pleaded for help. The kind-hearted clerk reopened the door and posted her registered mail. A few days later the Australian Embassy announced new, stiffer rules for visas, but her application arrived just before the old rules expired. She received her visa. She said that at the airport, "my husband felt the same way, but he was unwilling to acknowledge it." Four years later she and her husband, who was still in China, completed their divorce proceedings.*

"At the airport, I couldn't help but curse. I know that wasn't right, but I couldn't bear it any more. Were it not for his irresponsible agitation, why would I have gone to faraway New Zealand?" She was referring to a male colleague. This thirty-nine-year-old divorced woman was a straightforward person with straightforward opinions. Before she went to New Zealand, she had been a reporter at a Beijing newspaper and was content with her work and proud of her accomplishments as a reporter. Covering news, writing, turning in dispatches, soliciting advertisements, and attending news conferences kept her busy; there was no time to think about going abroad. But the tide of people going abroad finally lapped up to their office. A colleague, who had always enjoyed working on colorful broadcasts about political intrigue and who seemed to have busied himself in attending every political gathering, appeared to have suddenly refocused his attention. He brought in all kinds of agitating new ideas. Seemingly more concerned about her than she was about herself, he would say, "Hurry up and do something! This is the last chance to go abroad!" She would answer, "At my age, why should I bother?" And he would respond, "Many older people are doing that." With his encouragement, her heart stirred and her pulse quickened. First, she sold her books and furniture, gathering more than ¥10,000.[52] *Then she entrusted her four-year-old daughter to her mother, resigned from the newspaper, and devoted all her energy to going to New Zealand, the virgin land that had just opened up to Chinese students. At the airport she suddenly had doubts, but it was too late; there was no turning back.*

Two years later, in a letter to her colleagues at the newspaper, she said she was caring for an elderly person in a rich family and was well paid. But, she said, "The old man has cancer and may not live long. The family members all wish him to die, the sooner the better. That way they can each collect their share of the inheritance. I'm the only person who wishes the old man to live. When he dies, I become unemployed. I'll cry when the old man dies."

As for me, the parting was neither sad nor romantic. On the way to the airport, I began to worry about unforeseen problems with my passport, visa, plane ticket, or luggage. Perhaps I wouldn't be able to leave, and the whole dream of going abroad would be dashed at the last moment. These needless worries made me bid farewell hurriedly to my family. I then walked anxiously through the inspection hallway. After I passed passport and visa inspection, I sighed in relief. I turned back to look for my family at the other end of the hallway, but they had already left. At that instant, I felt I could no longer turn back. Passport, visa, and national boundaries, being so much more powerful than an individual, had led me away, for the first time, from friends and relatives, a familiar life, and a "motherland" of which I only had a vague concept learned from geography textbooks.[53]

The plane took off, but my mind could not settle down. The plane leaving Beijing still had to stop in Shanghai. I reminded myself incessantly, "No, you haven't left yet."

After a brief stop, the plane took off again. This time, it left the country; it crossed the ocean; it headed toward the far shore.

When I loosened the seat belt, my mind relaxed, too. I knew it: now I was truly going to America.

But I did not know what kind of world was awaiting me.

CHAPTER 3

The Shock Overseas

FIRST IMPRESSION

In 1978 the first group of Chinese students that went to America had to fly via Paris and change planes. The total trip took more than thirty hours.

Nowadays a direct flight to New York from Beijing or Shanghai takes about twenty hours. The time difference makes one feel as if it is only five or six hours. In the morning you say goodbye to your family and colleagues at Beijing Airport. Somehow it seems as if you have already arrived in America by three o'clock in the afternoon, carrying a big suitcase and feeling lost and lonesome among the stream of busy passengers at Kennedy Airport.

A strange feeling overwhelms you. The whole world, like the scene on a stage, has changed completely in the blink of an eye. Although you feel that only a few hours have passed, the true difference between China, a developing country, and America, a developed country, is as great as if you had time-traveled to a future century.

Geographically speaking, to fly from China to America was simply to travel from the eastern to the western hemisphere. But to a newly arrived Chinese who had grown up in a country that had a totally different culture and social customs and who had been immersed in an opposing ideology for an entire lifetime, this New World was novel, strange, and at times unreasonably odd.

I asked many students about their first impressions of America and got different answers.

A visiting scholar, forty-eight, who went to America in the early eighties, told me of his first impression. During the several months just before he left China, he was working in a small city in Anhui. Power outages often occurred at night, and the city would be thrown into darkness. On the day of his arrival in America, his plane had to stop at Los Angeles first. When the plane took off again, it was already dark. Through the window he saw the city below, sprinkled with millions of lights from horizon to horizon. At that instant, he thought, So this is the city of "the red lanterns and the green wine"[1]—a phrase used to describe the debauchery of capitalist society.

A twenty-one-year-old student who had gone to America even earlier said his first impression was of the vastness and emptiness of the expressways. He took a bus from the airport to his school and wondered all the way why there was not a single person on the road.

A twenty-eight-year-old woman who went to America in 1984 said she arrived in San Francisco on a sunny afternoon. White cumulus clouds drifted in the sky. "I'm not bashful in saying this," she said. "I was thinking, Wow, even the clouds in America are whiter!"[2]

Of course, some people had more complex first impressions.

A doctoral student from Nanjing University, jointly sponsored by China and the United States, went in 1986. He had only $50 when he landed. His adviser, who could not meet him at the airport, told him to take a taxi to the campus thirty miles away. "All the way, I was watching the fare meter intensely and my heart was racing," he said. The taxi quickly got to the small city. The driver, unfamiliar with the streets, could not find the campus and took him for a friendly tour. Sitting in the back seat, he watched helplessly as the meter jumped from $30 to $40, $45 . . . When the meter reached $49, he could bear it no longer. He shouted at the driver to stop at once and let him out, no matter where they were. He said, "First impression? My first impression was that the digital display of that meter was leaping too fast."

But the students who went in the nineties had less profound first impressions than the earlier arrivals.

A student who arrived in 1991 right after college said, after some serious efforts at recollection, "Really, nothing special." Then he added, as if to offer an excuse, "Perhaps I had already seen a great deal of America in movies and magazines."

As for me, the first impression of America was unforgettable.

I arrived on August 30, 1989. After flying twenty hours over the Pacific Ocean, the Northwest Airlines plane made a smooth landing at Detroit International Airport.

The local time was two o'clock in the afternoon. After getting off the plane and entering the waiting lounge, I saw brilliant sunshine on the tarmac and runway outside through a huge plate-glass window. The passengers dispersed quickly. The gigantic hall was quiet, even a little desolate.

"So this is America," I thought. But there was no impression to speak of yet.

My destination was the University of Michigan at Ann Arbor, forty miles away. After I completed the entry registration form and passed the customs inspection, I could not find my checked luggage. Also, I had not expected that Margaret, the secretary of the Journalism Fellowship Program at the university, would meet me at the airport. This kind-hearted elderly woman, who had worked at the program for more than a decade and would soon retire, had been waiting for two hours, holding a placard with my name on it. I felt embarrassed, for I had never been honored with such a serious reception. I hoped that someday Margaret could visit China so I could wait for her in the airport for two hours.

The car moved swiftly on the expressway. There was farmland on both sides. Buildings, big and small, were scattered about. About half an hour later, the car stopped in front of a white house well shaded by foliage. This was the prearranged place for my stay, the home of an elderly American woman.

Thus I left China and arrived in America. My surroundings changed completely in twenty hours. I was rather dazed, but there was no time to let my thoughts settle.

After some unpacking, I asked Mrs. Lewis, my landlady, where the campus was and whether it was far from her house. Mrs. Lewis pointed to a street and said, "No. It's not far—a ten-minute walk."

It was late in the afternoon. The sun was still brilliant but no longer scorching. I walked along the street toward the campus. I will always remember the scene.

Everywhere along the street, people were partying. Loud beats of music rippled through cool evening air that was permeated with the smell of barbecue. Fraternity brothers and sorority sisters, dressed in suits or short skirts, sang and laughed as they walked in groups, on their way to parties. In the city countless students in T-shirts and jeans crowded into small restaurants, coffee shops, bars, and ice-cream parlors, talking and laughing while drinking cans of beer or eating ice cream. The street was noisy. Standing in the middle of the street, I saw the campus through the arched gate: the ivy-covered classical architecture of the law school and, further on, the imposing clock tower bathed in the golden rays of the setting sun.

It was the week before the school session began. After a long summer, the returning students were enjoying their free time, realizing that there was not a moment to lose.

Facing this scene, I was shaken and awed. The reason was simple. Three months before, I had stood in Tiananmen Square. My mind recalled the indignation of the demonstrators, the students on hunger strike, the banners, the slogans, and the loudspeakers.

The world in front of me was so different from that of Tiananmen Square that it was almost impossible to reconcile the two. These worlds, although on the same globe, were so contrasting, so different, that I doubted they could ever comprehend each other, even with telephones, televisions, live satellite transmissions, and any other form of advanced communication technology.

Looking at the world in front of me, the scene at Tiananmen Square became so faint, almost unimaginable. And when I thought about Tiananmen Square, the scene in Michigan became unreal, an illusion, a dream. Which was real? I was confused. I suddenly felt as though my entire worldview had shattered. At that very moment I came to understand a simple truth: we Chinese, at least the younger generation, could lead a different kind of life. Those vacillations in policy, criticisms, denunciations, demonstrations, and exuberant mass displays of cheering, vengeance, and hatred should not become an entrenched lifestyle.

My first impression of America was unforgettable. But the cultural bombardment that followed was even more intense.

A MATERIALISTIC LIFE, ANN ARBOR, AND THE AMERICAN DREAM

This is a true story:

An outstanding young Chinese known for his study of Western civilization visited Hong Kong while on his way abroad. There he was invited to dine in a restaurant at the top floor of a luxury hotel near the airport. The dining room had an elegant decor, a soothing atmosphere, exquisitely prepared food, and courteous and unobtrusive service. Outside the plate-glass window was a pleasing view of the whole city. Our young man was deeply moved. Afterward, having not yet lost the traditional virtue of an Easterner, he said, "I vow that someday I will bring my wife to dine here."

In China, many people yearned for a life idealized by Western thought and culture. But upon arrival in the West, they would immediately feel a much more powerful lure: that of the materialism that is the pillar of Western thought and culture.

Years ago, a seasoned Chinese reporter went to Paris for a business trip and witnessed the bustle of the city. When asked about his impressions, he said, "It's like Beijing's Wangfu district, except there's no end to it!"[3] When I was in college, a professor talked about his visit to Japan. What most surprised him was that color televisions in Japanese stores were never sold out. In China at that time, color televisions were hard to come by.

Chinese students who had grown up poor were heavily bombarded in America by the lure of Western materialism.

The skyscrapers, the colorful displays in shop windows, the crisscross expressways, and the perpetual stream of automobiles of different designs made new arrivals dizzy. If you walked along Fifth Avenue in New York City, you would conclude that the main street in Beijing's Wangfu district was incomprehensibly short; if you visited Capitol Hill and the various museums in Washington, D.C., you would realize that Beijing's Great Hall of the People, though solemn, was not peerless in its grandiosity.[4]

But, in my first days in America, what most surprised me was not the hustle and bustle of the big cities but the suburbs where the middle class lived, and the peaceful, quiet life in some mid-sized and small cities.

Ann Arbor was a college town. The city and university were well integrated. More than half of the residents were directly or indirectly affiliated with the university. Each fall the local newspapers announced the return of the students. These students brought life to the city. They bustled about in the streets, the libraries, and the coffee shops until the next May. When the academic year ended, the students left, and the city once again looked half-empty. Thus as the year went by, the pace of the city alternately quickened and slackened.

Most people in Ann Arbor lived outside the city and drove to work. Their favorite pastimes were jogging and walking the family dog. On weekends, they would go cycling or picnicking in the lakeside park. Of course, when they turned on the television, they would see news about street murders in New York City, riots in Los Angeles, political storms in the Soviet Union, or civil wars in Yugoslavia. But the outside world would be forgotten as soon as the television was turned off. Ann Arbor had no argument with that world. One could live there peacefully and safely for a lifetime. There would be no revolution, no political mobilization, almost nothing at all that could make one's heart thump harder.

I have visited many cities in America with a similar design. There would be a main street serving as the city center. It would have a few fast-food restaurants and supermarket chains. A bit further away from the center would be churches, schools, and residential areas. These cities would leave you with similar impressions: clean, peaceful, and quiet.

In this environment, the most direct and immediate impression on the Chinese students was the abundance of food. The cost of food relative to one's income was at times unbelievably low. In America nothing was easier than getting fat from overeating, and many Americans were overweight. In China, to eat fried chicken at KFC might show intimacy with things foreign; but in America the rich frequently would not eat there. Those who had money or were health-conscious had no stomach for the grease in the three pieces of deep-fried chicken. American girls loved ice cream. However, after eating it they would work themselves to a sweat to get rid of the calories. The food in the supermarket was rich in variety, good in quality, and colorful and tempting in appearance; meat, eggs, fruits, vegetables, and dairy products were all appealingly fresh. The Chinese students, who had led a subsistence life on a monthly ration of two ounces of soy sauce and eight ounces of cooking oil, were overwhelmed. Two weeks after the June Fourth Incident in 1989, I received a letter from a friend in New York City that barely mentioned the event that had shaken the world. Instead, the two-page letter gave a detailed description of the fresh, lean meat sold in New York's Chinatown.

The shopping malls, which made their debut in the seventies, embodied the materialistic pull of the West. These centers of consumption integrated shopping, eating, and entertainment establishments under one roof. Some malls were a collection of individual retailers, while others were anchored by leading chain stores. Usually they were built in a large open area outside the city. Parking places were ample. Inside the mall the shoppers, shielded from the outdoor heat or cold, were immersed in a consumer's dreamland: superb displays of colorful merchandise, from food to clothing, from household items to transportation needs. Their abundance made you feel you could consume endlessly without exhausting the supply. As soon as you walked into these shopping centers, you felt enveloped, pressured, and charmed by goods. Shopping and window shopping in these malls were favorite pastimes for Chinese students during holidays.

The materialistic lure of the West seemed infinite. After essential needs were satisfied, one discovered things of even greater attraction: cars, houses, sailboats, jewelry, luxury hotels, country or beach homes.

On a fall day in 1989, Prof. Charles Eisendrath, director of the Journalism Fellowship Program at the University of Michigan, invited all of the participating journalists to spend a weekend at his farm in the Great Lakes area of northern Michigan. This farm had been in his family for generations. More than a hundred years ago, state homestead laws gave any registrant a piece of land for farming. Those days were long gone; Charles rented out the land to an agrarian corporation to grow cherries, and he kept the farmhouse as a family vacation retreat.

Charles's lakeside vacation home was far from the nearest city, and the surrounding countryside was sparsely populated. The region had primeval forests and was dotted with lakes large and small. The house was a typical old farmhouse, simple but comfortable. The top floor had a loft from which one could overlook the lake and distant fields.

In the house one could watch the fog rising from the lake and dispersing gradually into the woods, and hear the rain on the roof and windows and the crackling logs in the fireplace. A weekend at the farmhouse certainly relaxed one's body and mind.

The next day we visited Charles's neighbor, a businessman who owned several franchised retail stores in Indiana. We crossed a dense, damp forest devoid of humans. After walking for half an hour, the people in the lead shouted, "Here it is! Here it is!"

In front of us was not a small farmhouse, but a mansion whose exterior and interior were built with round logs. Even the bathtub was carved from a single log. The house was on the lakefront. Through the floor-to-ceiling plate-glass windows, one could see the mist and ripples of the vast lake.

Only the owner's granddaughter was there. The family came a few times a year and employed a year-round caretaker.

"You can see the difference between a businessman and a professor," Charles commented jokingly.

At times the materialistic lure was irresistible.

Not long after I arrived in America, I was chatting on the phone with a high-school classmate who was studying sociology at a college in Atlanta. We talked about politics in China and the whereabouts of other classmates. The conversation then turned to whether we would stay in America or return to China.

I said that I would like to return someday.

"You'll change," she said confidently. "When we first arrived, we also planned to return to China as soon as we finished our studies." Now, four years later, she and her husband were both applying for Green Cards.

I said my case might be different. Then we talked about China, its present and future. But neither could convince the other. Then I changed the subject and mentioned that I had bought a lot of bananas that morning. They were big, delicious, and cost only nineteen cents a pound. They were so cheap that I felt almost embarrassed to buy them.

"Of course there are advantages in going back to China," she returned to our original subject. "But if you go back, do you think you can eat bananas that are so big, delicious, and cheap?"

We laughed.

She had left China some time ago, and China today was no longer the same as that in her memory.

In truth, many Chinese students ultimately decided to stay in America not because they were attracted to democracy and the freedom of the West, but because of the materialistic pull of a developed country. This decision should not be regarded as a moral failure, even though traditional Chinese culture has always viewed materialism as morally corrosive. Confucius praised his disciple Yan Hui for being "content in poverty and joyful in truth." He also declared, "To me, wealth and fame are only passing clouds." These teachings had led the Chinese to believe that being a person of scanty means and remaining so is a moral high ground to which one should aspire.

In fact, the materialistic life has its own influence on our ethical behavior.

When I was in China, I once interviewed an elderly economist who had been a student of Mr. Wang Ya'nan, the translator of Marx's *Das Kapital.* The economist first criticized China's bureaucracy, then said that in a socialistic environment with an insufficient supply of goods, it is hard for people to develop any notion of democracy. When one goes shopping, one must have ration coupons, or wheedle goods out of the store clerk, or get them through the "back door."[5] These daily trading activities invisibly increase the dependence of the individual on the government and society and ingrain in him a slave mentality.

After arriving in America, I discovered that the economist's thesis could be verified from another angle. The materialistic abundance of the West ingrained in people a strong consciousness of choice. From daily merchandise to jobs, from lifestyle to political party to the vote, the privilege of choice was regarded as a birthright. That privilege was in fact the most basic component of democracy and freedom.

Let us take the example of the American dream. At its first stage, it is very materialistic: a house symbolizing family and including children, cars, and a family dog; and a stable job. But some American scholars also emphasize that such a materialistic dream embodies the American spirit: all people have the right to pursue happiness and, through their own efforts, to realize their dreams.

Hence, when confronted with the materialistic world of the West, Chinese students not only felt the attraction of worldly goods but also sensed the underlying American ethos.

MONEY CONSCIOUSNESS WHILE BEING POOR

My nephew left for America with his parents when he was six years old. He was put in the first grade. In the beginning he did not know what was going on in the classroom, so he played dumb. But once, in a composition assignment, he amazed his class by earning an "Excellent" on his essay titled "Rain." He wrote, "It is raining now. But I wish it were raining ten- and twenty-five-cent coins. Then, I would have lots of money to buy the many things that I want."

While in China my little nephew had no notion of money. He had a penny, but just as a toy. Within half a year after arriving America, he acquired money consciousness.

That was not unusual. Almost all Chinese students quickly acquired money consciousness in America.

One student had financial trouble soon after his arrival, so he asked for a loan from a classmate who had arrived a few years earlier. The classmate gave him a stern lecture: "This is America. How can you walk around and ask for a loan? Here nobody will lend you money simply because you're a friend." Then he calmed down and added, "Because we are old friends, the advice I just gave you is free."

When one was under the pressure of poverty, the importance of money quickly emerged in one's consciousness. The reason was simple. In Western society, in which freedom was abundant, a person with no money enjoyed little freedom. Although all people were equal, those with little money received little respect. In childhood we had learned the motto "Wealth does not necessarily bring happiness." In the West we learned its provocative counterpart: "Poverty certainly brings misery."

China had been a poor country, but since 1949 the Chinese had not felt deprived by their poverty. Because the whole country was uniformly poor, people felt equal to one another. But as soon as they set foot overseas, they began to realize how poor they were, how poor their country had been. In addition to the traits "hardworking" and "accepting challenges" that were usually ascribed to Chinese students, another one could be "poor."

Many privately financed students saved for years to buy a one-way airplane ticket, and they were practically penniless when they landed in America. Whether they were studying astrophysics or literature or art, they had to find a dishwashing job in a Chinese restaurant before assuming the role of a scholar with an inquiring mind in a classroom. Some reputable professors who went as visiting scholars had to put up with sleeping in a living room or buying used clothing at a flea market because of money problems; there would be no special treatment for being a full professor.

A forty-nine-year-old woman who was a visiting scholar at a college in New York had a toothache soon after arrival. She wished to have the aching tooth extracted, but her medical insurance did not cover dental services. Her friends advised her to live with it, as dental costs were exceedingly high in America. After two days, she could bear it no more. "I'll have this tooth extracted regardless of the cost," she said. So her friends drove her to the hospital. She held her cheek during the drive, moaning and groaning, and screamed each time the car hit a bump. Upon arrival, she was first told of the registration fee. She immediately asked to be taken home. Strangely enough, on the way home there were no complaints about the pain.

The newly arrived, even those with money, would not go on a spending spree. Even low-cost items could seem frighteningly expensive when the dollar amount was converted to *renminbi*.[6]

But there were abundant opportunities to pick up things from the curb: televisions, mattresses, tables and chairs, cooking utensils. With a little bit of luck you could pick up anything that you needed. Sometimes a good-hearted foreign friend would help you do that, too. A thirty-two-year-old student studying comparative literature in Canada told me that she had once invited a Canadian student to dinner. The friend arrived carrying many serving plates, explaining, "I just found these on the curb. I knew you could use them, and I also knew that you and your husband like the curbside treasure hunt."

Being poor made it necessary to economize, but for the poor, the available channels for cutting expenses were few. Many resorted to eating less.

In America, because food prices were low, a person spent about $100 a month on food. With care, that could be cut to $50 or $60. I was told of a girl studying in Miami who set a record of living on about $20 a month. Her method was simple: she bought only chicken thighs. Meat was cheaper than vegetables, and chicken thighs were the cheapest meat. For a couple of dollars one could buy several pounds of them. As for vegetables and fruits, she met her needs at dinner parties.

There were some tragic stories.

In Japan, a Chinese visiting scholar was found dead in his laboratory. An autopsy showed that he had died of starvation. The story was that to save money to buy some big-ticket items to bring home, he ate only instant noodles. Prolonged malnutrition and a heavy workload finally made him faint. Because he was working on a weekend, no one discovered him until it was too late.

The harsher the experience was of being poor, the stronger the consciousness became of the importance of money. But in a deeper sense, the emergence of a money consciousness was a result of the assault of American culture.

Before the nineties, China was a power-based society. The factors that determined the relationship between one person and another were the relative status and authoritative power of the individual in his family and in society. Money might make small things happen, but it might not be able to do so for big things.[7]

America is a truly money-based society. Money is the invisible hand that controls all events. It is a fluid society: there are no aristocrats or commoners, no upper class or lower class. In the consciousness of most people, the strongest index for classifying people seems to be wealth.

But those with a lot of money may gradually have less and less, and those with less money may eventually have a lot more.

In the summer of 1990 I attended a summer class on American politics and policies at the University of California at Berkeley. The students took a field trip to Washington, D.C. There, we visited a law office specializing in Congressional lobbying. Mr. Kutzwell, a principal partner of the firm, received us. During the panel discussion, this impeccably dressed professional lobbyist, teeming with energy, came straight to the point: "In America, all problems eventually become a dollar issue. Any change—whether the passing of legislation, the election of a Congressional member, or a court decision—always signifies the flow of dollars from one pocket to another."

How true. In America, money not only sets the course of policy and influences the economy; it is also a yardstick in value judgment. It even affects how Americans think and how they approach a problem.

In the early nineties, President George Bush declared a war on drugs in a nationwide televised speech. There were no slogans, no mass mobilization, but only a request for Congress to pass a budget of tens of millions of dollars to combat drug use. The scenario was similar to the satirical comments on the NBC television program *Saturday Night Live* about the 1992 presidential candidate Ross Perot: to solve the problem of racial violence in Los Angeles, the Texas billionaire would simply write a check to the city and then declare that the problem had been eradicated.

American society is like a giant machine in which money is continuously produced and simultaneously swallowed. Everybody—whether businessman, scholar, or politician—is spun around the swirling vortex, and nobody can get out.

A thirty-five-year-old man who went to America as a visiting scholar did neither teaching nor research after arrival. He spent all his time working to accumulate money. He said that at first his target was to save $10,000. But after making $10,000 he wanted $20,000, then $30,000, and eventually he simply did not know when to stop. He is still working and accumulating money.

A forty-two-year-old man, who went with his wife to America in 1984, was working at a computer company in California. Their combined annual income exceeded $100,000. Still he worked day and night, trying to earn as much overtime pay as he could. When his mother came to visit him, she found this behavior *incomprehensible. She said, "You have so much money already. Why do you feel that you still don't have enough?"*

In the early nineties, there were several bestsellers in China that told realistic stories about Chinese students in America. The characters in these stories had different career paths and lifestyles, but the single yardstick of their success was whether they had become rich.

Money, albeit capable of vulgarizing life, could also magically transform a person. In Western society, money not only expresses one's wealth and purchasing power but also signifies social status, personal dignity, self-value, and the extent of control over one's destiny.

A thirty-five-year-old woman went to America as a visiting scholar in 1984 and worked as a technical staff member in a chemistry laboratory at a university in New Jersey. She had gone on her own initiative, and after her arrival, she had always worked diligently. She got up at seven, arrived at the laboratory before eight, and began working before her boss, an American professor, arrived. She worked late. Frequently, it was two o'clock in the morning when she finished an experiment. She also worked some weekends.

Three months passed. The initial excitement quickly faded. The elusive dreamy glow of American life began to dim; life became dull and ordinary again. The work of a technical staff member was busy but routine: making reagents, heating, vibrating, observing, measuring, recording. Days passed without color, without a spark.

One day she received a letter. It said, "Congratulations to you, the new millionaire! You have already won $10 million!" It said that the $10 million would be paid to her in thirty years, at $333,333 per year. All she had to do was mail back the number of the certificate for confirmation. On the reverse side were portraits of the alleged winners in the past two years. Under the pictures were the names, addresses, and the amount of the awards. A blank space was left for a tenth photograph; to its side was written, "This place is reserved for you, the new millionaire."

Ten million dollars! She could not remember when she had mailed the forms for this particular drawing; she had mailed many of those forms before.

That night she completed the two easiest of her many plans. First, she bought two pounds of her favorite tomatoes, which formerly had seemed too expensive. Second, she slept late and, the next morning, did not arrive at work before her boss.

The next day, she followed the instructions and mailed in her number by registered express mail. Then she waited quietly for the miracle. Days and weeks passed. She received no answer. Two weeks later, she noticed that an American student in the same laboratory had also received a lottery notice.

"Ten million dollars? Garbage!" The student mindlessly trashed it.

She noticed that the announcement was exactly the same as hers. She felt tense. "Doesn't it say here that you've already won?" she asked.

"Don't believe them. This is just an advertisement."

"But it says here you've already *won," she said persistently.*

"That's just a trick. 'Already' means that they've already drawn the number. If your number is the same as that number, then you would have already won."

Now she understood. She asked no more questions. The next morning she went to work early as usual.

Two years later, when she was laughingly telling me this episode, she, with the help of her boss, had already received her H-1 visa and was applying for a Green Card.

THE BURDEN THAT COMES WITH FREEDOM

America is a free country.

There was an area of open space in front of the graduate library of the University of Michigan. It was often used as the staging area for exercising the freedom of speech, and was also the gathering place for students. There, anybody could deliver a speech on any subject. A young, handsome preacher was the most impressive among the speakers. Except on rainy days, he could be seen standing on a stone bench, holding the Bible and delivering eloquent praises of Jesus. During class breaks, some students lay on the lawn sunbathing and paid only casual attention to him. But occasionally they would ask some challenging questions.

Each April a nationwide meeting of drug users was held there. They gave impassioned speeches advocating freedom of drug use and the legalization of marijuana. Different organizations passed out pamphlets, from a beginner's guide to drug use to one on the formation of a union of prostitutes. There was no interference from the local police, who directed traffic and maintained order. But if anyone were to use drugs, the police would move in immediately and make arrests. Freedom of speech might be guaranteed by the Constitution, but drug use violated the law.

One frequently witnessed similar events that seemed strange to a foreigner. When I first arrived, the U.S. military had just invaded Panama. One day I saw several students holding placards and demonstrating outside the student-union building. But there were so few of them that they appeared comical, and they were puny when compared to demonstrators in Tiananmen Square. Two years later there was a gay and lesbian rally, but on a much more massive scale.

In May 1991 the university invited President George Bush to the commencement. During the ceremony, some students, protesting against the Gulf War, turned their backs to him.

Frequently there were people advocating socialism. The portraits of Marx, Engels, Lenin, and Stalin could be seen in numerous places. I read a pamphlet published by an organization called International Maoism claiming that a new member could read *Quotations from Chairman Mao* in Chinese. For that talent this member commanded great admiration from fellow members.

Ann Arbor is a fairly liberal city. But without a doubt, the source of the liberal tide in America is Berkeley, where a branch of the University of California is located. In the sixties, Americans used to say, the "revolution" began in Berkeley and was echoed in Ann Arbor.

In summer 1990 I lived in Berkeley. Berkeley is a pretty town, with hills at its back and water at its front. There is sunshine year-round, and the climate is comfortable. Since UC Berkeley is known for setting cultural trends, the town is noteworthy not only as an academic bastion but also as the birthplace of various new cultural movements, including the hippie culture of the sixties.

Berkeley in 1990 appeared to be quiet and relaxed. The stormy student movements of the past had become history, although each year there still were numerous student demonstrations. I asked Chancellor Chang-Lin Tien, a Chinese American, what issue gave him the most headaches. He answered without hesitation, "Student demonstrations."

The street scene in Berkeley was a colorful cultural kaleidoscope. There were many gaily attired young people. Grotesquely clothed singers and dancers displayed their artistic talent in the streets, making the little town burst with vitality. People's Park, which twenty years before had been the focal point of the clash between students, residents, and the National Guard, was now filled with homeless people from various places. They had their own culture, formed their own legislature, published their own newspaper, and even had their own poetry publications. Once I witnessed an unusual scene: a Chinese American with a flowing silvery beard, standing on a wooden crate, held a placard on which was written: "Protest the Invasion of the Yuanmingyuan by the Eight-Country Allied Force!"[8]

In 1993 the Naked Man appeared in Berkeley. Every day he carried his backpack and attended classes in the nude. His philosophy was simple: clothing, other than for warmth, was uncomfortable and unnecessary. He also considered not wearing clothing to be his personal freedom. But the university finally expelled him for "impeding the attention of other students during class."

In America, the event that best embodied the sense of freedom was perhaps long-distance highway driving. You rose early, prepared your food and packed clothes, grabbed a map, and you were ready. You could drive to New York City, to Washington, D.C., or to the Grand Canyon, or you could head south. No matter where you were heading, you could listen to folksy country music or rock and roll, stop at any gas station to fill up the tank, eat in any restaurant in any town, and spend the night in any motel. Nobody knew where you came from, and nobody paid attention to where you were going. During those moments you felt completely free.

Jack Kerouac, the representative writer of the escapist generation of the fifties, gave a stirring description of that feeling of abandon in *On the Road*: a generation of young people fled society, refused employment, escaped marriages, and drove fast on the highways to wherever they wanted. At that time, being on the road symbolized personal liberation and protest against traditional, mainstream America.

Americans place personal freedom above everything else. The concept is deeply ingrained. Once during a haircut the barber asked me where I came from. "China," I said. He said that he had never been to China and had heard that China was developing very fast. But, he said, how could the Chinese government suppress personal freedom at will? He could not understand because he was not brought up by China's "collective" education.

In America, freedom carries with it a certain weight. Not every mainland Chinese could bear that burden.

After arrival in America the Chinese students felt they were free from various confinements: no work unit, no Chinese Communist Party, no political studies, and no disciplinary talk from the leadership. One could live the way one chose. But one also had to decide one's own future.

A forty-eight-year-old visiting scholar who went to America in 1988 said, "Yes, America has freedom. Nobody bothers you, but nobody cares about you, either."

That was a realistic assessment.

The Chinese had led a life in China that relied heavily on their government, their work units, and their families. This acquired habit of dependence made them feel lost when they entered an environment of complete freedom.

In contrast, in America, where individual freedom is the most carefully guarded privilege, people are far less dependent for survival on government, workplace, and family. The less dependent, the freer they are.

Zhuangzi said that a truly free person must have no expectations; he is completely free from dependence.[9] In the real world, that was a lofty, unattainable goal. The life of a sparrow would always be easier.

The personal freedom of Western society is frequently haunted by the shadow of loneliness and helplessness. In Chinese society, you might frequently have felt that things were not going well, but you rarely felt depressed. After living in America for some time, you not only sensed depression but began to understand why so many Americans visited psychiatrists or took drugs to destroy a life that was so superior materialistically.

Chinese students, while they enjoyed their personal freedom, also felt lonely and helpless.

A thirty-five-year-old student studying biochemistry in a college in Connecticut told me about the depression he experienced at one point: "At first it was just loneliness. Every day it was work, work, work. There was nothing else in life and no one to talk to. Then it was depression: a loss of interest in everything, a loss of will to work.... The depression became unbearable after a while. I felt I was going crazy. Finally I decided to see a psychiatrist."

The loneliness was deepened by the students' separation from their country, families, friends, and relatives and by their marginalized status as foreigners.

A twenty-nine-year-old graduate student who went to America in 1982 said the most miserable times were weekends. Walking home carrying her backpack, she saw cars passing by, each one loaded with American students laughing and screaming on their way to parties or to vacation spots.

In America, when you stared at the skyscrapers in a big city, when speeding cars passed you, when you faced a crowd in which each person seemed to be walking purposefully to some destination, you would feel lonely and isolated. You would become aware that all the activity surrounding you was part of another life totally unrelated to yours, and you would realize that you might never be admitted. In that instant, you were free—you could do anything you wanted, say anything you wished—but nobody would pay attention to you, or care. Suddenly, you would feel that the world had forgotten you; your existence had become irrelevant.

To be happy, we need a sense of belonging. In America, Chinese students who were accustomed to a collective life and the care of their institutions turned to other groups to satisfy the need to belong. A classmate of mine who was very active in group activities in college and was a member of the Chinese Communist Party became a devoted Catholic after living in America for several years. Many Chinese students, because of religious faith or for other reasons, took up institutionalized religion in America.

This scenario was quite similar to that in the novel *Dangling Man* by the Jewish American writer Saul Bellow: A young man was called to serve in the military. While waiting to enlist, he resigned from his job and enjoyed his days of freedom to the utmost by window shopping and seeing movies. But the army recruitment office somehow overlooked him. Thus, after days and then months, he became a purposeless street-wanderer. Gradually, this freedom became an unbearable burden, and the young man eventually reported to the recruitment office voluntarily, demanding immediate enlistment for any available assignment.

People are always pursuing freedom, but freedom is not the only need in life.

THE PEDAGOGY OF WESTERN EDUCATION

When you first arrived in America, you felt kind of stupid, like a country bumpkin entering a city.

Upon arrival, I went to a bank to open a savings account. The bank clerk was very helpful, explaining to me the differences among the various kinds of accounts. I did not fully understand. After I had completed a form and turned in several hundred dollars, I was told that I could leave. Doubt arose: What do you mean, I can leave? Where is my passbook?

I left the bank, feeling unsettled. A few days later, the mail brought an ATM *card. I did not know how to use it; all those bank machines looked mysterious, even a bit intimidating.*

Actually, you felt not only like a country bumpkin, but like a healthy person who had suddenly become disabled.

First, your ears and mouth no longer functioned. Even though you had studied foreign language in China, once you were outside China you became half deaf and dumb. Other than "Hi" and "Bye," you could neither understand what was said nor know how to express yourself clearly.

Next, your legs became paralyzed. In that nation of cars, if you did not have a car or did not know how to drive one, it became exceedingly difficult to move about. Buying groceries could involve a walk of several miles. Even if you could manage to walk there, it would be impossible to walk back while carrying a heavy load of groceries.

But more serious was the discovery that the brain seemed to have stopped functioning. When faced with a computer, even those who had always prided themselves in being quick-witted did not know what to do.

In my first days at the University of Michigan, I wished to type a letter in English. But on the whole campus I could not find a typewriter. There were many computer centers in which hundreds of computers were available for students to do homework or write theses, but when I sat down and faced the computer, I felt that I had regressed to the first grade.

Computer technology had become widespread in America. Americans seemed no longer willing to use their brains for memorization. Whatever the question, they would hit the keyboard and find the answer on the computer. One wondered whether the society would become paralyzed should the computer system fail.

This total trust in computers has its origin in Americans' worship of machinery. Some American museums are devoted to exhibits of machines that were invented in America. The development of science and technology directly shaped American society. The emergence of automobiles in the past and that of computers today have twice changed the appearance of America and the life of its people.

The gap in science and technology between China and America could be easily observed. Chinese science and engineering students often had to take remedial courses. But the gap was not just technological; humanities students felt it as well.

A thirty-six-year-old man who received his Ph.D. in philosophy from Harvard in 1989 said that when he first started there, he felt that his whole academic world had collapsed. What he had learned in China was completely outdated, and he was unaware of the many new branches of his discipline. In America, statistical data and their analysis had become a routine method of research in social sciences, but in China verification through "pure theory" was still the norm; in America, cross-disciplinary research had become commonplace, but in China, research still meant the studying of a single book for a lifetime. The professor of one course would not permit this student to attend class because he had not had prerequisite courses in statistics and sociology. Fortunately he was quick to respond. He argued that his political studies in China could compensate for these deficiencies since they covered politics, sociology, philosophy, and even anthropology. He also emphasized that he was knowledgeable in Marxism-Leninism and study of the Soviet Union. He was thus allowed to attend.

The pedagogy of modern Western education presented another challenge.

Reading was the first problem. Sometimes the reading assignment was forty or fifty books and simply could not be completed. But this Harvard Ph.D. said that he soon discovered there was nothing to fear. Each book had only a few salient points. After thumbing through the table of contents and reading chapter summaries, he would be ready to participate volubly in the discussion. "After you finish your contribution," he added, "the professor looks at you, and you at him. But don't blink." He agreed that the training he received at Harvard was rigorous and serious. The books on the reading list were all first-rate. Once he mentioned several less scholarly books during a discussion. The professor removed his glasses and asked, "We have never studied the books you just mentioned. Why?" The student wished to explain, but the professor continued seriously, "Remember, Harvard does not discuss these books."

Another difficulty faced by Chinese students was writing. Some humanities students, although they had published research papers in China, discovered that they could not really write. A thirty-five-year-old student studying literary theory at Columbia University said that in the beginning the professor corrected his essays from start to finish. The problem was not his grammar but his method of expression.

Humanities education in China lacked basic training in writing. First, an essay was often filled with vague concepts without a well-defined context. Second, a hypothesis stated in a previous paragraph would suddenly become a theory without further discussion and verification.

But the hardest of all for Chinese students was the topical seminar, the quintessence of the Western education. That Harvard Ph.D. said with emotion that he was often confused in these classes. In seminars designed for upper-division students, the advanced topics were covered. During discussions, the professor encouraged the students to be creative and imaginative. Sometimes the professor would indulge in mumbling to himself—this was dubbed "conversing with God" at Harvard. If a student made some illuminating statement, the professor would look pointedly at the student. After class, they might continue the discussion in a bar.

The seminar I attended in the Journalism Fellowship Program at the University of Michigan met twice a week. At each meeting an expert on the subject was invited to give a lecture. The topic could be economic prospects, the status of AIDS, protection of the global environment, or the presidential election; it could also be techniques in television news coverage, the music culture of African Americans, or car sales. The speaker would talk for about twenty minutes; afterward there were questions and answers and a discussion. The atmosphere was always lively and casual, and there were refreshments. The speaker would inject some humor from time to time, and the students might even sit back and put their feet on the table.

These seminars provided an opportunity for students to be exposed to the latest developments in their research fields. The interaction between the speaker and the audience stimulated the mind.

By comparison, education in China placed too much emphasis on learning basic knowledge. Such learning could build a solid foundation for the student, but when carried to extremes, it could stifle creativity.

In the summer of 1990 I began to prepare to teach in the Department of Asian Languages and Cultures at the University of Michigan. Before the class started, I invited the director of instruction for coffee. I asked him for advice about how to teach. He thought for a moment and then said politely, "Speak less and let the students have a chance to talk." After some hesitation, he continued, "The problem with Chinese teachers is that they tend to teach too much."

A SOMEWHAT CASUAL ATTITUDE TOWARD SEX

Forty-second Street in New York City is well known. At its eastern end is the headquarters of the United Nations, and at its western end is the Office of the Consul General of China. Halfway between is Times Square. But 42nd Street is also well known because it was once the city's red-light district.

If you just stopped there and observed for a while, you would discover that 42nd Street revealed the absurdity of human life: at the UN headquarters, diplomats discussed world peace with the utmost seriousness; on the street, people streamed in and out of the various corporations and stores, solemnly and purposefully, and worried about the stock market, interest rates, and the latest sales figures of their companies; and at the same time, a sex shop tried to lure customers in to view a five-minute peep show for twenty-five cents. Inside the shop, cheap pornographic magazines, videotapes, and sex toys were on display. More prurient performances were said to be staged on the second floor. These parallel activities that never interfered with one another made up life in New York, symbolizing the internal contradiction of American culture.

It was hard to believe that the sex culture in America had always been conservative when compared to that of some European countries. This conservative attitude had its roots in the Puritan tradition of the early immigrants. Even today, prostitution is illegal in most states, and nudity is not shown in serious publications or on television, which also expunge many swear words.

But American society in the eighties and nineties was also flooded with pornography and sex businesses. Pornographic magazines could be bought in stores on practically any street corner. Sex videotapes of different varieties and for different inclinations could be rented easily. Striptease shows, massage parlors, and call-girl services openly advertised their business.

The widespread sex culture was directly related to the freedom of speech guaranteed by the First Amendment to the Constitution, which publishers of pornography used to legitimize their business. The public apparently felt that restrictions on freedom of speech would do more harm to society than would allowing pornographic publications; hence the public had a tolerant attitude.

Since the sixties, sexual liberation and the feminist movement had contributed to an even more liberal attitude toward sex. Automobiles also played an important role: many people completed their sexual revolution in the backseat of their cars.

Today on college campuses across America, dating is a generally accepted practice, and cohabitation is a normal lifestyle for a well-behaved student. Recently the AIDS epidemic has led school authorities to consider making condoms available to high-school students. The joking slogan for sex in the sixties was "Just do it!" and in the nineties was "Just wear condoms!"

This liberal sex culture created another kind of cultural impact on the Chinese students.

Perhaps because of a curiosity arising from having grown up in a society where pornography was banned, many Chinese students began reading pornographic magazines and viewing adult videos soon after they set foot in America. A student who went in 1983 to study anthropology at a college in Michigan said that at first he shared an apartment with several other Chinese students. One weekend, they rented and watched an adult video. The experience made their hearts race, and reminiscing about it years later made them laugh.

There was a copy of the Chinese edition of *The Plum in the Golden Vase* in the collection of the Asia Library at the University of Michigan.[10] Each fall, soon after the semester began, the book would quickly disappear from the stacks; it was checked out by newly arrived Chinese students.

Of course, some students went farther.

One twenty-eight-year-old who had studied in the same school with me in Beijing loved to see striptease shows. Afterward he liked to describe in vivid detail the provocative figure of the dancer and how she sat on his lap. At first, he went with several students from Taiwan, and later he became an expert at striptease watching: how to best view performances on tables, how to place tips on the dancers' thighs. He also loved to persuade other students to go with him; afterwards he would broadcast that so-and-so had gone to watch striptease with him.

The temptations of sex were not limited to striptease.

In Ann Arbor, a college town, pornographic magazines were available in stores, but within the city there were no adult theaters or striptease bars. In the surrounding area, though, sex-service establishments operated more or less openly.

A twenty-four-year-old student from Fujian studying software design at the university told me of his experience in a sauna bath house operated by a Korean. After the bath, the manager sent in a Korean girl to give him a massage. The girl asked him where he was from. He lied, out of an acute political awareness, saying that he was from Taiwan.[11] *After some rubbing and kneading, she asked him if he desired any special service. Of course he understood what she meant, and he could not resist the temptation. "And then?" I asked. He looked at me and said with a laugh, "Then, I gave her a massage instead."*

Since most Chinese students were single, occasional patronage of the sex trade was understandable. Some educators in China also adopt a more understanding attitude. A student who participated in an orientation program held at the Beijing Language School before leaving China said that the director of the program warned students not to set foot in red-light districts. But the director immediately added, "If you really cannot hold it any longer, it's all right to go. Just don't go there again."

Not every Chinese student escaped becoming trapped in wanton licentiousness, but very few become corrupted by America's pornographic culture.

The sex business was only a part of America's sex culture. The somewhat unrestrained attitude and openness of Americans toward sex gave the Chinese students a much greater cultural lashing.

An American friend of mine, twenty-nine-years old, was a free-"lance writer. Once we drove to New York together, and on the way we passed some cities. She told me that she had a boyfriend living in this city, another living in that city, and so forth. I carelessly blurted out in surprise, "Wow! How can you have so many boyfriends?" She was obviously surprised by my surprise and said, "You know, I'm a mature woman!"

Although some Chinese students learned to adopt a more open attitude toward sex, it was difficult to know how to react in certain situations.

A twenty-two-year-old student, studying in a business college in Miami, lived in the college dormitory during his first year there. His roommate was a handsome and energetic young American named Mike. This young man, who said "Hi!" to whomever he chanced to meet, was easy to get along with and had many girlfriends. Mike and his girlfriends would consummate their dates in the dormitory until late at night, making it impossible for his roommate to study or sleep. One night the commotion in the other bed became so noisy that he decided to leave the room. But Mike said graciously from his bed, "There's no problem—you can stay. I don't mind."

A twenty-eight-year-old graduate student talked about her first-year experience in a rooming house near the campus. On the first day, the landlord, about forty years old, gathered all of his tenants—three men and four women—for a house meeting. He first listed some general house rules, then changed the subject and declared that he had just had an AIDS test and the result was negative. Soon afterward, he started a love affair with a twenty-year-old, one of the four girls. The house was poorly insulated, so the noise they made at night could be heard in every room. A year later, when the lease expired, everybody moved out, and the affair between the landlord and the girl also ended. Such situations were said to occur frequently in rooming houses near the campus.

In America, a sexual relationship can be one between male and female or between individuals of the same sex. In the "Personals" section of classified ads in newspapers, there are "male looking for male companionship" and "female looking for female companionship" listings.

Most Chinese students were naive about homosexuality.

On a winter evening in 1991, I was walking home after studying in the library. An African American youth pushing a bicycle struck up a conversation. At first he was just walking beside me, but then he asked abruptly, "Do you like to do that? I have lots of girls. They're really sexy."

I understood that he was a pimp, so I said, "No, I don't like it."

"Oh, you don't like it." He would not let it go. "Don't worry. I have lots of boys, too." Then he described to me the various modes of homosexual lovemaking.

I was dumbfounded. Only after some time did I begin to realize that he had taken me as gay and was trying to make a sale. Finally I told him I had no interest in his male merchandise. He left swiftly on his bicycle.

Homosexuality had become a hot topic in America in recent years. In early 1993 Bill Clinton's first policy statement as president was not on the basic philosophy of his administration or on the economy, nor on global peace and war, but on lifting the ban of homosexuals in the military. In recent years, the demand for equal rights and privileges by homosexual groups had been rising steadily. Public understanding and acceptance of homosexuality had also risen.

The Journalism Fellowship Program permitted a student's spouse, boyfriend, or girlfriend to participate in school activities. During the year I was there, a reporter from the Associated Press brought along her lesbian friend, a reporter from a newspaper in New York. The director of the institute did not object, and the whole class welcomed her. But it took me some time to figure out the relationship between the two women.

Like heterosexual relationships, same-sex relationships could also cause headaches.

A twenty-five-year-old Tsinghua University graduate told me about his experience. He had come to America in 1986 to study pharmacology at a college in Colorado. During his first summer in America, he worked on a rotating basis in several laboratories. A professor in one of the laboratories was particularly friendly to him and would stop by for a chat or have lunch with him. The professor was tall, about forty, and had some gray hair, a good sense of humor, and a scholarly appearance. Toward the end of the summer, the professor warmly invited him to spend a weekend at his country home. Believing it to be a friendly gesture from an American to a Chinese, the student happily accepted. That night at the country home, the professor built a fire in the fireplace. They lay on the carpet and talked about China, music, art, and American culture. In the midst of the conversation, the professor suddenly said, "Would you like us to touch each other? I mean to masturbate together." Upon hearing this, the Chinese student was shaken up and quickly replied, "No, I'm not a homosexual." The American professor remained calm and said gently, "Sorry." He never mentioned it again.

Of course these stories did not always have a gentle ending. Sometimes they became quite ugly.

In 1993 a Chinese man studying music at a college in Ohio sued the chairman of the department for "male sexual harassment." The story evolved in the following way. One day, the Chinese student visited the professor and noticed that the professor was feeling pain in his neck and back. Out of kindness, the student, who had some training in massage in China, offered to knead the painful spots. After a few massages, the pains and aches were gone, but the professor would not let this free massage service end. Every several days he would call and ask the student to come over and give him a massage. Though unwilling, the student forced himself to go. But when the professor proposed that the massage become more sexual, he refused and stopped going. Their relationship turned sour. Using his authority, the chairman began punishing the student. He denied him graduation, citing insufficient course credits and below-par performance as the reason. This dragged on for two years. Finally the Chinese student, unable to bear any more, sued the professor. I have heard that the suit was dismissed due to insufficient evidence, and the student was allowed to graduate immediately.

Although America is a sexually liberated society, and Americans like to fashion its sex culture with new guises, Chinese students found that in reality Americans were not as they were depicted in popular fiction and Hollywood movies. These representations implied that men had only one thing in mind when they saw a woman, and a woman could go to bed with any man at any time. A professional basketball player wrote in his autobiography that he had slept with more than 20,000 women in a span of a few years. Someone did the arithmetic: at that rate he would have had to sleep with 2.5 women per day, every day. That would have been impossible.

A female American graduate student told me that there were frequent surveys reported in newspapers and on television about Americans' sexual behavior. These surveys cited percentages of men or women who had had many sexual partners. But she had never known anybody who lived like that.

This woman's impression was verified by the latest survey. In 1992 researchers at the University of Chicago and the State University of New York at Stony Brook conducted a survey of the sexual behavior of Americans. They randomly surveyed 3,432 people whose ages ranged from eighteen to fifty-nine. The polling method was much more scientific than that used for the "Kinsey Reports" in 1948. The result, announced in October 1992, showed that Americans' sex lives were far more traditional than people had imagined. More than 80 percent had had only one sexual partner in the previous year, and only 3 percent of men and women had five or more sexual partners; the adults had sex, on the average, once per week, and more than 33 percent had sex only a few times in the previous year or not at all; married couples were most satisfied with their sex life, and 75 percent of men and 85 percent of women said that they were faithful to their spouses.

Some Chinese confused the America in the movies with the real America. They thus mistakenly believed that all Americans, in particular American women, treated sex casually. An American scholar who studied Chinese language and culture for two years in Beijing said that her teacher, a grandfather and a family man, was bold enough to propose a love affair. She believed that the brash proposition was made primarily because she was American. Another American student told me that once while she was working as an interpreter for a young male visiting Chinese artist, he tried to embrace her. She was stunned and very upset.

Another misapprehension is that there is only sex and no love in American society. This is false. I remember the parting scene of a young couple when I was waiting for a Greyhound bus in the bus depot in Cleveland. The young man was carrying his backpack and luggage, apparently leaving for college in another city. The young woman was there to say goodbye. While standing there waiting for the bus, they embraced gently and were immersed in the poignant emotions of parting. She placed her hands on his shoulders, lifted her head, and gazed at him, tears streaking down her cheeks. They stayed for more than an hour, until the boy boarded the bus.

THE SEEPING IN OF DOUBTS

We grew up in a society in which we naturally believed everything to be unassailably right. Even when we disliked some events, we rarely questioned the rationality of their existence; everything was perfectly justified.

One day we walked into another society that had a different social system, political tradition, religious beliefs, values, lifestyles, and social customs, and found that people in that strange society also led a seemingly normal life. We were perplexed and astonished. We began to question our long-held beliefs about our own society.

This perhaps was one of the most profound and complicated feelings experienced by many Chinese students.

A twenty-nine-year-old graduate student studying electrical engineering told me about one of his revelations. In China, like many others, he had made frequent progress reports to the leadership of the Chinese Communist Party on ideology and had always felt this was normal. After being in America for about six months, he suddenly felt that the practice was absurd: "Why should I tell them what I think?"

A thirty-three-year-old Ph.D. candidate studying at the University of California at Berkeley told me the following story. The professor who taught American politics explained that the ideal of the framers of the U.S. Constitution was to create a weak government so that it could not control the citizens. The Chinese student was greatly puzzled. In China he had been used to hearing the argument of "greatly strengthening the proletarian dictatorship," and he had always thought that the government should be powerful. How else could it govern?

Our thoughts are unconsciously confined by the values of our society and further limited by our cultural traditions. Just as human thoughts cannot go beyond the limits of human existence, it is difficult for our thoughts to transcend our social and cultural confines. We naturally think that everything our society represents, whether good or bad, is quite normal. We accept it without questioning. Only when we step into a different society do we begin to appreciate the limits of our consciousness.

But to an individual or a nation, the most frightening thing is not the limits of our consciousness but an absolute mode of thinking resulting from that limited consciousness. We unwittingly use events in our own society as the yardstick to measure and then judge other societies. Sometimes, even after we walk out of our country, we cannot walk out of that absolute mode of thinking.

Many Chinese saw only "foreign scenes" when they went abroad. Those scenes could be new and entertaining, but anything that did not fit the Chinese cultural tradition would be classified as strange and abnormal. This mentality had deep historical roots. Since antiquity, the Chinese had regarded people in surrounding nations as barbarians, or "people on the periphery." They labeled foreigners "ghosts," while regarding themselves as the people of the "Great Central Kingdom."

Of course, this absolute mode of thinking could appear in its opposing extreme. After 1978, when China opened its door to the outside world after several decades of isolation, the Chinese were stunned by what they saw. Quite a few people adopted the opposite view: everything in the West was logical and scientific, and everything in China was ugly and morbid.

For more than a hundred years, the Chinese attitude toward the encroaching foreign culture had remained the same. It consisted of the traditional middle-of-the-road approach—"Chinese learning is the essence, and Western learning is for practical development"[12]—and the modern dialectical method of "discarding the dross while retaining the essence." These were simply two different selection criteria based on the same mode of thinking: Chinese culture forms core values. As a result, that core value became not only the criterion used to judge the usefulness of any aspect of Western culture, but also the means by which we differentiated the grain from the chaff.

Americans have nearly the same problem. The peaceful development of the country for more than a century has led to its strong economic power, advanced science and technology, gradually perfected democratic system, and increasingly popular mass culture. Americans have thus become overly self-righteous, believing that the American form of society is the model that all other countries should emulate and that American values are the absolute standard with which to measure all events in the world. They rarely realize that America is only one example in the history of human social development, and perhaps a special example at that.[13] This insular view is evident in the work of "liberal" writers and in reports by "objective" journalists. Americans need to engage in thoughtful introspection, similar to what the Chinese went through after the Cultural Revolution. A small window of opportunity for Americans to do that was available after their defeat in the Vietnam War. Deplorably, the introspection apparently did not go deep enough.

Based on this absolute mode of thinking, people often form a rigid right-wrong consciousness. They seem to acquire, a priori, the concept of what is "normal" from their own form of social living, and unconsciously use that normality as a criterion for differentiating right and wrong. In regarding ourselves as normal, we regard those who have a different form of social living as abnormal; our unalterable principle becomes universally valid.

I once discussed this problem with an American professor of anthropology at a picnic. I asked him if there was a time in American history when people had acquired a consciousness of absolute right and wrong. His immediate answer was, "No." After some thinking he said, "Yes, during the Puritan era." Still a while later, he added, "At the present, too." In fact, anthropology makes us recognize the diversity of forms of social living and helps free us from narrow right-wrong notions of the past.

Among the legacies of human thought, right-wrong consciousness is the most deeply rooted. It makes us fanatical in defending our moral dogmas and cruel in persecuting heretics. No matter what the guise—whether it be freedom, equality, revolution, or democracy—ultimately it leads to the shackling of the mind, to the closing off of culture, and to autocracy in politics.

In Chinese society this right-wrong consciousness is embodied primarily in the society's nearly subconscious belief in unified thinking, a premise for agreeing on the absolute correctness of an idea.[14] An American professor of political science did a survey in China and found that most Chinese believed in democracy but simultaneously endorsed unified thinking. Almost nobody recognized the inconsistency between the two notions.

Whenever unified thoughts, obtained through criteria based on right-wrong consciousness, become a dogma, a principle, tomorrow's ideal, or an abstract principle that demands great sacrifice today from the people for its realization tomorrow, human society begins a time of tragedy. Historically, when human beings were pushed toward the precipice of disaster, it was not so much that some were intentionally pushing everybody to hell, but that they firmly believed that only they knew the road to heaven.

What I felt during my studies in America was similar to my feeling when I was first exposed to the poetry of the Misty school in 1979.[15] I thought, "Ah, poetry can be written even in this form!" When I arrived in America, my feeling was, "Ah, life can also be lived in this way!"

I am neither discussing the ideological battle between socialism and capitalism nor comparing the virtues and defects of Eastern and Western civilization. To argue which side has a rounder moon[16] is like children arguing about how far the sun is from the Earth, a difficult subject to explain even for an intelligent adult. I am talking about something that is more basic: the mode of human existence and human thought.

As explained by the British philosopher John Stuart Mill in his book *On Liberty*,

> There is no reason that all human existences should be constructed on some one, or some small number of patterns. If a person possesses any tolerable amount of common sense and experience, his own mode of

> laying out his existence is the best, not because it is the best in itself, but because it is his own mode.

I do not know how many of the Chinese students who went abroad share my feelings. I believe that because of what they have learned and brought back, they are more tolerant of human diversity and the endlessly variable possibilities of human society.

CHAPTER 4

Different Generations, Different Talents

THE VISITING SCHOLARS, THE RED-GUARD GENERATION, AND THE VENTURING NEW GENERATION[1]

On December 27, 1978, after nearly thirty years of isolation from the Western world, China sent its first fifty students to America. They flew to Washington, D.C., by way of Paris and New York. At the airport they were welcomed by Han Xu, deputy director of the Chinese liaison office in the United States, and by Mr. John Reinhardt, director of the U.S. office of the International Communication Agency.

The next day the *New York Times* carried the following news:

> *52 Chinese Scholars Arrive in U.S., to Study for Two Years*
>
> Washington, D.C., December 27—Fifty-two Chinese scholars arrived here today, the first such group since the American decision to normalize relations with Peking. The group of six women and 46 men were met by Han Hsu [Xu], deputy chief of the Chinese liaison office, and John E. Reinhardt, director of the International Communication Agency. Mr. Han ... said the visit of the scholars would "enhance mutual understanding and friendship between our two peoples."
>
> "They came to learn advanced technology and sciences from the American people, and to contribute to China in the future," he added.
>
> Though there have been small contingents of scholars from China before this group, Mr. Reinhardt said, this is the "first large group, the first of a series of groups." He said 500 to 600 more Chinese were

> expected this year. The United States will send its first group of 12 scholars, mostly social scientists, to China in February.[2]

Most people in this group were key members of China's major universities and research institutes. According to *People's Daily*, many people had attained the rank of associate research scientist, lecturer, engineer, or physician-in-charge. The youngest was thirty-two, the oldest forty-nine. The mean age was forty-one. As visiting scholars, they would study for two years in American colleges and research institutes.[3]

The *New York Times* also reported that their English proficiency ranged from fluent to spotty. First they would study English at Georgetown University and American University. Then they would go to different universities and research institutions to pursue their studies.[4]

Earlier, a smaller group had been sent to other countries. A nationwide recruiting examination, open to high-school students recommended by their schools, took place in the spring of 1978. Three thousand students took the examination, and twenty-three were selected. One question in the oral examination was "What would you do if you were robbed in a foreign country?" Before they left the country, they received orientation instruction at the Beijing Language School and visited Daqing and Dazhai.[5] Each had an overcoat and two suits tailor-made in the Red Capital.[6] In May and June they left for Canada, Britain, France, Japan, Australia, and New Zealand. The students were required to turn their scholarship money over to the Chinese government, which then paid their tuition and room and board, and gave them six U.S. dollars per month for pocket money.

In those days, since there was only a handful of Chinese students in Western countries, they were frequently received with special courtesy. A student who was studying at the University of Toronto recalled his visit to Washington, D.C., in 1979, the year that China and the United States established diplomatic relations. When he and several other Chinese students went to a Chinese restaurant for dinner, the owner welcomed them with a free dinner; when they visited the Metropolitan Museum of Art in New York City, the museum administration, after learning that they were from "Red China," extended the closing time for their visit.

In the early eighties, except for this young group, most of the Chinese students were middle-aged visiting scholars. According to the visa data of the U.S. government, there were 5,593 visiting scholars from 1979 to 1982; of these, 60 to 66 percent were between forty and forty-nine; and other than those who came in 1979, about 20 percent were fifty or older.[7] There were far fewer students holding J-1 visas indicating that they were studying for a degree. Among these visiting scholars were some of China's best middle-aged talents.

Having endured the Chinese Communist Party's political indoctrination and weathered the political storms for many years, this group tended to be cautious and staid. A visiting scholar, over fifty, who went to study at the University of California at San Diego, recalled that he was the only Chinese student on the whole campus, and he could find hardly anyone to talk to. One day a delegation from mainland China visiting the university chanced to meet him on the campus. One delegate cried out to him, "Comrade!" That single word brought tears to his eyes.

Although many visiting scholars were reputable experts in their own fields, their study broadened their horizons and affected them deeply. An economist who took part in the planning of China's economic reform of rural areas wanted to master all new Western economic theories in his six-month stay in America. After arrival, he checked out many books. But he soon discovered that he simply could not follow these writings because he lacked basic training in the subject. He became humbler.

Although visiting scholars enjoyed some advantages, they had difficulties that were hard to overcome. Since most were middle-aged, it was hard for them to improve their language skills. Because of the short duration of study, it was difficult to adjust to the new academic and social environment. This was especially true for humanities students. A student who studied history at a college on the East Coast told me that he once received a visiting scholar who was the director of a research institute in China.[8] Since the student's American adviser needed data from that research institute, the adviser had invited the director to come to America for three months to lecture. But the director knew no English, and hence could neither lecture nor communicate with his American colleagues. Furthermore, since his financial support was limited, he could afford only to sleep in the living room of an apartment shared by several Chinese students. Since their place was far from the campus and he did not know how to drive, he came to the campus only occasionally and spent most of his three months sitting idly in the living room. The student host, feeling sorry for him, took him out from time to time for a ride, to visit the campus, or shopping. Three months later the "lecturing" came to an end and the visiting scholar was happy that he could finally return to China. Surprisingly, before he left, he repeatedly asked the student to help his daughter come to America.

Unlike the students studying for a degree, the visiting scholars had no academic pressures and hence had more leisure time. A female student studying at a Canadian university talked about a visiting scholar in her school, a man who was over forty and frequently could be seen strolling on the campus. He would often leave her a telephone message, saying, "Hi, this is Old Zhang. Nothing important. We haven't seen each other for a while. Let's get together sometime."

Between approximately 1982 and 1985, a group of much younger students was sent to America and other Western countries after passing a selection examination. According to American visa data for 1982, the number of Chinese students holding J-1 visas who were between twenty and twenty-nine reached 54 percent and exceeded, for the first time, the number of those over thirty. Together, they accounted for 85 percent of all students.[9]

In this group, those students who were about thirty were undergraduate and graduate students who had entered college in 1977 and 1978, after the college entrance examination was restored in 1977. During the Cultural Revolution, these students had been Red Guards. Later they also worked in communes, work corps, or factories.

History can mock us. During the Cultural Revolution, Chairman Mao, in his call for school graduates to work on the communes, said that the rural area is a "vast world where much can be accomplished." Millions of youth answered the call, marched to the communes and border provinces, and were determined to take root there. But soon afterward, they started returning to the cities. After spending some time composing Misty poetry and writing about democracy on Xidan Wall, they finally found the vast world advocated by the chairman.[10] It turned out to be in another country.

When compared to the generation of the middle-aged students, these younger students showed plenty of drive to learn and work, a spirit they had acquired during the Cultural Revolution.

Between 1983 and 1985, the University of Michigan had 185 government-sponsored Chinese students, more than any other campus in America.[11]

A student studying electronics at the University of Michigan, who had graduated from Tsinghua High School years ago and was now in his forties, told me his story. When he left China in 1982, he was supported by the National Education Commission on a monthly stipend of a little more than $400. It was hard to live on that sum. Shortly after arrival, he learned that the monthly pay for a teaching or research assistant was $1,000. Immediately, he maneuvered to win support from the professors. He called on them one by one, stressing his difficulties, and judiciously presented them with some small presents from China. Soon he was given a research assistantship. He said that many other students found financial support from their departments in their first year. In the second year, when the Chinese Consulate mailed them scholarship-renewal forms, many people did not even bother to reply.

These students also were not as placid as the earlier, older generation or as shy in dealing with Americans. A thirty-seven-year-old student from Shanghai who was studying comparative literature at the University of Michigan said that when he and three others lived in a one-bedroom apartment to conserve funds, the landlord objected. They argued back, really without justification. They even used human rights as an argument.

Because of the particular experiences they had gone through, it was not easy for these students to shed their memories of domestic politics. Whenever there was a political storm brewing in China, they would write petitions or organize demonstrations. Shortly after the 1987 Anti–Bourgeois Liberalization Campaign, one of China's leading writers on Marxism-Leninism visited the University of Michigan. During a panel discussion, he was verbally attacked, rather ferociously, by many Chinese students. This elderly gentleman, who had been so used to writing attacks on others, was in a sorry plight. Finally, he resorted to reading the newspaper for more than an hour, nonstop, so as to avoid the students' interrogation.

In the early eighties, privately financed students also began to go abroad through various channels. Because of the need to earn a living, they were not as easily upset by domestic politics as the government-financed students. This was especially true for older students whose only desire, having endured much suffering in the past, was to live quietly. Nevertheless, the suffering left a deep brand in their memories.

He was from Shanxi and was already thirty-six when he left China. During the Cultural Revolution he had worked on a farm. There, for eight years, he ate sorghum and slept on a brick bed. In 1981, helped by their relatives, he and his wife went to America, and they were determined to stay. After finishing his master's degree in two years, he easily found a job at a pharmaceutical company and gradually began to lead a more stable life. But the good days came to an end when he was laid off during a recession. At that time his wife was pregnant, and, because of the circumstances, she aborted the pregnancy. Unable to find work in his field, he decided to return to school to study and work at odd jobs. Although life was hard, it never weakened his determination to stay in America. But one evening he happened to find an old issue of a Chinese magazine that contained a fictional story titled "The Dream We Had When We Were Young." He finished reading the long article. But that night, he said, he could not sleep.

Beginning in 1986 a wave of even younger Chinese students, just over twenty years old, went to America. The decade-long Cultural Revolution did not leave any deep mark in their memories; to them, "to work on the hillside and in the countryside" was only some soppy historical saga of the older generation. After graduating from China's key high schools, they went to China's key colleges. In college, they not only prepared for the TOEFL but also listened to Voice of America broadcasts; they were familiar with democracy and human rights, and the latest rock stars as well. They seemed to be the generation that was born to study in America.

Compared to the two older generations, they led an even less restrained life. They were not burdened with the desire to pay back or to serve their motherland, nor were they planning to start families. They thirsted only for life's adventures and seeing the world. "To study abroad, like life, is a journey," said a male student in Chicago. "I just want to enjoy the journey."

A twenty-four-year-old student, a graduate of Beijing Institute of Metallurgy, went to America in 1988 to study metal cutting at a college in Minnesota. Six months later, he wrote the following letter to his classmates back home:

> *Hi, everybody! After enduring some tough studying, I got by with two* B*'s. I then started my eastward march in my newly purchased car, a used Toyota Crown.*[12] *First stop was* Chicago. *Had a buffet at a* Big Boy. *Since the* service *was lousy, I did not leave a* tip, *to show the determination of the proletariat. At first I wanted to attend a concert, but turned into*

> *Chicago's "42nd Street." It was nothing more than* topless *and* bottomless. *The second stop was* Pittsburgh. *I parked the car on a busy street and did not take out the luggage. When I returned I noticed the window was broken and the luggage was stolen.* Shit! *Initial estimate of the loss was $500. But that did not stop me. I drove straight to* New York. *In* New York, *I stayed in the home of an American classmate. It is a big* mansion *in an affluent section of Brooklyn. It has a sauna and a* greenhouse. *The father is a stockbroker in a big corporation, but well versed in art. With his guidance, I visited several* museums *and* galleries. *It was an eye-opening experience. Later I attended a musical on* Broadway. *After rambling in New York for a few days, I decided to go to* Florida.

Because they were young, these students quickly adapted to American society and the American lifestyle. Someone wrote a ballad describing them:

> In the first year I drive a fast car,
> In the second year I find a lover,
> In the third year I start to argue,
> And in the fourth year I disown my Mom.

Unlike members of the preceding generations, who lived frugally for years to save money for a used car, they wanted to buy a car as soon as they arrived. Not just a used car, but a fancy car, a sports car, a new car. But where did they get the money? They borrowed it. In the second year they began to date, not just Chinese girls, but also the blue-eyed and blonde-haired ones. In the third year their English became fluent and they loved to start arguments, with or without good cause. In the fourth year everything in America had become so natural that it was taken for granted. Meanwhile, China had become distant and vague. A student who went to America to study before he was twenty returned for a visit to China after a few years. After returning to America, he commented about China, "The pitiful sight was almost unbearable." He added, expressing a deep bafflement, "How could it be like that?!"

But no one would disagree that these students had talent.

A forty-year-old Ph.D. candidate at Harvard said that each year the top-scoring students in the physics department were all Chinese, and were often named Hong.[13]

Obviously they were born in the sixties. This was also true in other departments, such as chemistry, biology, and mathematics. He said that among his classmate there was a child prodigy from the University of Science and Technology. In China this student had completed the four-year curriculum in two years and at nineteen had received a master's degree. He was then sent to Harvard for doctoral studies. In his first semester, he took courses that were usually reserved for more advanced students. In his second year he was already pondering how to design the fifth and sixth generations of computers. The Ph.D. candidate said with a sigh, "When you see these kids, you really feel proud for China. It's just a matter of time until the new Chen Ning Yang or T. D. Lee will emerge from them."[14]

American colleges were like a giant smelter. Waves and waves of Chinese students—each with memories of their own time in China, their experiences, and their aspirations—were the raw ore. They were thrown into the furnace to be refined. Perhaps that is how steel is made.

THE FAIRY TALES AND THE REALITY

Since the eighties, numerous success stories of Chinese students in other countries had appeared in China's newspapers and magazines. In these stories, the plot, the scene, and the characters may vary, but there are two basic supporting themes. The first is that Chinese have made their way to the international lecterns; their reports cause a sensation in the audience; the foreigners, thumbs up, say, "The Chinese are great!" The second is that the hero or heroine is determined not to accept a high-salary job overseas but to return to China instead.

This kind of story was useful in boosting the confidence of the Chinese people in themselves, but it often bordered on being a fairy tale. The cause of the misinformation was the great distance and poor communication separating China and America.

In foreign countries, there was nothing special about attending a conference. By the eighties, one could meet Chinese students at all kinds of workshops or annual meetings of scholarly associations in America. At the lectern, they read their papers and answered questions. Off the lectern they had to work hard to find leads on research support or job openings. Furthermore, they had to pay in order to talk; they were not paid for it. In November 1992 I attended the annual meeting of the

American Association of Foreign-Language Teachers in Chicago. I paid $100 for the opportunity to make a fifteen-minute presentation; of that sum, $30 was for dues and $70 for the registration fee.

American's use of the word "great" is misunderstood by the Chinese. A Chinese student studying on the West Coast said that Americans would habitually use the expression "That's great!" as a polite but noncommittal comment. They really meant "That's good!" But when translated literally into Chinese, the phrase meant "That was *really grand*!" He said that he understood this distinction only after coming to America.

The "high-salary" offer also was rather comical. It was frequently $10,000 or $20,000 per year. The sum would be sufficient for subsistence, but nothing more.

Then there were even more ludicrous stories.

A visiting scholar from an interior province told the following story. A teacher from his school stayed in America for a year. After returning to China, he went around boasting that he was so successful in America that the president of the university had tried to retain him with a high salary, a house, and a beautiful lady. The visiting scholar said that the story could not possibly be true; the president of a university was responsible for the school's budget and hence would have some money at his disposal for hiring, but he would have no influence over housing.[15] *But the most absurd part was the "beautiful lady"—where was the president going to find that lady? The visiting scholar said that the teacher, in fact, spent most of his time playing card games or combing through ads for bargains. The teacher, relying on his bragging, was promoted to a full professorship soon after returning to China. His fictional success in America even made its way into a newspaper.*

In the early eighties foreign things still filled people in China with respect and fear because they had lived for a long time in an isolated and sealed-off environment.

A thirty-eight-year-old Chinese talked about his changing fears and aspirations. In 1983, when he first received the admission notice from Harvard, he could hardly bear the emotional impact of the news. To him, Harvard, the most revered academic citadel in America, perhaps even in the world, was mysterious and beyond his comprehension. "Can I do it?" he asked himself. He simply could not believe that such a poor Chinese student could study at that academic shrine. "My parents were just old peasants. When the New Fourth Army came, they just tagged along."[16] *At the time he told me this story, he had already received his Ph.D. from Harvard. His aspiration was to write several books on the history of Western thought; he wanted to have them compared to those written by his colleagues at Harvard. He felt deficient neither in intelligence nor training.*

A thirty-one-year-old student, a graduate of Shanghai Science and Technology University, told me her experiences: Years back, her school engaged a "foreign teacher" to teach English conversation. He was an American, about forty, of average height and slightly plump. That was her first contact with a "foreign scholar." She was so charmed by his courteous manner and humorous conversation that she had retained the memory of him ever since. Later she went to America and, within five years, received two master's degrees, passed her Ph.D. qualifying examination, and started working. One day, during a chat with a professor from her Shanghai school who was visiting America, she learned that the foreign teacher was actually living in the same city. She was excited and, under the pretext of honoring her visiting professor, quickly hosted a party and invited the American teacher. But what she saw that evening was not the cultured and well-mannered American expert that she remembered, but an American who was petty and listless, even a bit tainted with commercial vulgarity. During the party, the foreign teacher carried out a deferential conversation with the visiting professor. Later, the professor told her that the American had not been able to find work after returning to America and was thinking of going back to China to teach English. Could the professor help? She said she felt disappointed and sad, without really knowing why. But she knew that the one who had really changed was not the American teacher, but she.

Within a span of ten years or so, generations and generations of Chinese students had matured.

In the nineties many newly arrived Chinese students were surprised to find that some of their "American professors" were Chinese students who had come to America a few years earlier.

Beginning in 1990, each year three or four Chinese students who had graduated from other universities were hired as assistant professors at the University of Michigan. Their fields of study included political science, economics, languages, mathematics, psychology, computer science, electrical engineering, and business administration. After several years, these former members of branches of the Chinese Students Association at various colleges became members of the Association of Chinese Professors.

At the same time, Chinese students who graduated from the University of Michigan were hired to teach at other universities. Among the people I knew, some went to the East Coast, some to California, and some to Canada.

Today, to Chinese students who have survived tough times, American colleges are no longer the sacred academic shrines they once thought them to be, but a contest arena in life. Like other gathering places, American colleges, where knowledge and scholarship are pursued, have their share of people who plot to help their friends and beat their foes and to engage in intrigues to gain the upper hand.

It is not easy to get a teaching position at an American college. In addition to a degree from a prestigious college and strong recommendation letters from eminent professors, one must possess an intense awareness of the competition and a determination to pursue one's goals.

A thirty-three-year-old Chinese who taught at a college in Missouri said he had sent out more than a hundred letters of inquiry and received three interview appointments. For one of the interviews, he equipped himself with a $300 suit and a briefcase. Before the interview, he did an internet search on each member of the search committee, learning their alma maters, their specialties, their publications, and their hobbies. He also memorized their names. The two-day interview was a torment. The formal discussion lasted only half an hour, but the interview really began as soon as he got off the plane. In addition to giving a seminar about his work, he also had to meet student representatives and to have lunch or coffee separately with each member of the search committee. He was tense all the time and fearful of making some stupid mistake. He had to win the approval of every professor, since each had one vote in the final selection. During the interviews he tried to steer the conversation, as smoothly as possible, to topics that were of interest to the interviewing professor, or to mention casually that he had read a certain article the professor published some years back. He said that during the two days he made only one mistake: he mixed up the names of two professors. But that was a small mistake and was quickly corrected. Upon returning home and facing his wife, who eagerly asked about the interview, he was too exhausted to talk.

However, to receive a professorial appointment is not the end of competition, but only the beginning of a tougher one. All new hires must strive to earn tenure within five or six years, or they will be sent packing. A tenured appointment depends not only on scholarship, research results, and publications, but also on personal relationships.

A thirty-six-year-old assistant professor in the Department of Sociology at a college in Boston said that, in the last year of his eligibility for tenure, he would often wake up in the middle of the night for no particular reason. Actually, he was worried about whether he would be given tenure. A reason for his worry was that he felt the department chair had not been friendly to him recently. If he failed in this competition, he would have a crisis to deal with.

LIFE NO LONGER AN ILLUSION

A college is only a small contest arena. The bigger one is outside the campus.

I met her at a supermarket outside the city shortly after I arrived in America. Being new arrivals, neither of us had a car. I had gotten a ride that day and asked her how she got there. She said, "I walked." But the supermarket was nearly ten miles from the city.

She explained, "I looked at the map and it didn't seem too far. The weather was good. So I walked along that narrow path next to the highway. It was fine in the beginning. But then the footpath ended. The cars zoomed by as I was standing at the expressway. Then I thought, I had already walked halfway and there would be no turning back. So I kept walking and got here."

She was from Beijing, a graduate of a well-known medical college and now in a doctoral program in physiology.

"I don't want to study anymore," she said. "I don't want to work in a lab. I want to be a doctor, a doctor in America."

I was surprised. Many students who studied medicine in China changed their field of study after arriving in America. After graduation, they usually found work in a medical laboratory. Laboratory jobs usually were busy but routine; they paid poorly but were easy to find. To become a physician in America was much harder. After graduating from medical school, one had to pass two examinations that had high failure rates before one could become a resident physician. After another three to five years and a passing grade on a third exam, one could be certified as a practicing physician.

A year later I happened to meet her in a reading room. She had been studying day and night to prepare for her first exam. She said the exam was known to be hard and expensive. The registration fee was more than $500. "I took this path anyway, and I just kept on going," she said.

Soon she passed both examinations and began her residence at a hospital in Miami.

I met another woman who yearned to succeed in the nonacademic world. She was a Ph.D. candidate in sociology and was writing her thesis while working as a teaching assistant. But sociology did not seem to excite her passion. One day I met her in the library busily scanning the financial pages of the New York Times. "I want to be a stockbroker," she said cheerfully. I thought she was joking. A year later, she left school and became a stockbroker.

As waves of Chinese students left their schools after graduation, their appearance in America's workforce became increasingly pronounced. Years ago Chinese students could be seen at the most remote colleges. Today these former students can be found in every profession in American society, and in New York City, Boston, Houston, and San Francisco. In some cases the depth of their infusion into American society is simply astonishing.

In May 1990 I took part in the Understanding America tour sponsored by the National Committee on U.S.-China Relations, designed especially for journalists from mainland China. Being a media group, we visited the sites of early immigrants in Virginia, the Gettysburg battlefield in Pennsylvania, Capitol Hill in Washington, D.C., and the stock exchange in New York City. We also visited many news media—including *USA Today*, the NBC television studio, and the Committee to Protect Journalists—and we attended a news conference at the State Department. Among all of the experiences, the one at Voice of America left me with the deepest impression.

This worldwide broadcasting network, a part of the U.S. Information Agency and scarcely known in America, was well known in China. In mainland China some people used Voice of America as an alternative to the Chinese government as a source of information.

Mr. Hess, director of the VOA Chinese program, received us. He had a big beard and spoke Chinese fluently. He first introduced the Chinese program, saying that it had a staff of about sixty. Then he said they had always insisted on the guidelines of "accuracy, objectivity, and impartiality." Of course, that was how they viewed themselves.

Questions follow the speech.

"Are there Chinese students working here?" I asked.

"Of course," Mr. Hess replied with a pleased air.

"How many?" I continued.

"More than twenty." He paused for a moment and then added, "Twenty-five full-time staff and several temporaries."

More than twenty! This number was astonishing. It meant that mainland Chinese students were a nonnegligible percentage of the staff at Voice of America.

We had to admit that Chinese students' influence on American society had increased. This influence was clearly shown later in their lobbying for the Chinese Student Protection Act.

Why those students could find a place for themselves in the intensely competitive American environment was due almost entirely to their intelligence and diligence.

Most of the Chinese students employed by the big American financial corporations were graduates of prestigious colleges. They worked as lawyers, accountants, brokers, real estate agents. The economic takeoff in China and all of Asia also provided a historical opportunity for them. Between 1993 and 1994, the Hong Kong headquarters of Morgan Bank alone hired more than twenty Chinese students.

Specialists in science and engineering had also become a nonnegligible force in that sector of America. At the Big Three automobile manufacturers, the Boeing Company (airplane manufacturers), or the DuPont Chemical Company you could meet Chinese students who had graduated in recent years. According to a joke, an American who wished to work at IBM first had to learn Chinese, since a sizable percentage of the staff there came either from mainland China or Taiwan.

At the same time, stories of different legendary personalities who had made it big overseas appeared: the ever-rising auction prices in New York and Hong Kong of oil paintings by Shanghai painter Chen Yifei; the winning of the Oscar award by the movie *The Last Emperor,* in which Chen Chong acted and for which Soo Cong, who had studied in Germany, wrote the music; and the publication of books in English by Chinese authors about the hardships they had endured.

Some students were very ambitious. Those studying science had their eyes on the Nobel Prize; those in business aimed at amassing a fortune; those in literature aimed at entering mainstream American culture; even in the arts, many of them aimed at Hollywood or Broadway.

Behind all this ruckus was a progressive spirit that traditional Chinese culture could not cultivate. Because of the influence of the social conditions and the culture of the West, one could hardly see in these students any trace of the Oriental transcendental attitude that "life is an illusion," which had been a trademark of Chinese intellectuals. Instead, they were willing to take risks and try new things. I could not help recalling the advice given by Lu Xun to the Chinese youth of his day. He said that after reading books by foreign authors, you always wished to do something, but books by Chinese authors made you wish to remain placid and do nothing.

Was this transformation of ethos a basic reason for studying abroad?

A PLAYER ON WALL STREET

I first met him at the university's reception for new hires before the start of the semester. He had just gotten his Ph.D. from a midwestern university and had begun to teach mathematics at the University of Michigan. He was just over thirty, short in stature and alert. While busily sampling the refreshments, he told me that he was from Jiangxi and a graduate of Hunan University.

After the semester began each of us became preoccupied with our own business. On Thanksgiving Day I called and asked him to come over for dinner. He came and talked about stocks. "Stocks are interesting," he said. "Every Chinese student should open an account with a stockbroker. Even if you don't buy stocks, your money receives higher interest rates from a brokerage house than from a bank."

I was totally ignorant about stocks. Every day I read the news and cultural sections, not the business section, of the New York Times. *The densely packed fine print of prices was incomprehensible to me. I often doubted that anybody was genuinely interested in reading those utterly dull printouts.*

So he began to educate me. America had three major security exchanges: the New York Stock Exchange, the American Stock Exchange, and the National Association of Securities Dealers Automated Quotations System (NASDAQ), formed through a computer network for securities of companies of smaller capitalization.

"How do you buy stocks?" I asked.

"It's easy. You open an account with a stockbroker. When you've decided what you want to buy or sell, just call the broker. It's all done within a minute."

"Really?" I only half believed him. "When are you going to open an account?"

"Soon. Very soon."

A month later he called me and said he had opened an account and bought some shares of a cosmetic company that produced a shampoo capable of straightening the curly hair of African Americans.

"Has the price gone up yet?" I asked.

"It will go up," he said.

When I saw him again sometime later, he talked like a stock-trading expert. He could not remember clearly what he had bought and sold, but on balance he had had a gain, and his record looked good even when compared to those of professionals. That pleased him.

But he was not satisfied.

"My hardware is not good enough," he complained. "What you read in the newspaper is yesterday's information. It's too slow and you can't compete during rapid trading. It's not working out. I have to become better equipped."

Thus he began to modernize his trading facilities. First, he ordered a $500 price quoter that reported the latest stock prices. But that was not satisfactory. He changed to an electronic system that got price quotations through television. But that too was not good enough. Finally he chose a newly marketed computer network on securities. He could sit at home, like the professionals, and watch the stock market.

He also researched the stock market. He read articles about the market in the Wall Street Journal *and, with his skill in mathematics, used theory and graphs to analyze the market.*

The American stock market was bullish that year. He became more and more confident as time went on, and the magnitude of his trading increased. He caused a mild stock fever in some of the Chinese students. Following his advice, many people opened accounts. His telephone rang constantly, as people called for tips.

But like weather, which can have unpredictable storms, stocks fell sharply one Friday in October 1992. The Dow Jones Industrial Index lost more than a hundred points in two hours. The market was gloomy.

I saw him on the street about five o'clock that afternoon. The oversized shirt he wore made him look rather diminutive. Like the overcast sky of that day, his face looked cloudy.

"I wasn't fast enough. I got caught," he said, referring to his stocks. Although he was sad, he did not lose his lofty aspirations. "It will slowly come back."

I saw him in the library a few days later. He seemed more worried. He said he had gotten a really bad deal. Not long before, he had bought some shares of a pharmaceutical company. The company had reported rising profits in recent years; its stocks were hot, and he joined the scrambling. But a scandal was exposed. Newspapers disclosed that the operation was a fraud and the publicized business figures were fictitious. The general manager went into hiding and was nowhere to be found. The company declared bankruptcy, and the trading of its shares, which had suffered a tumultuous drop, was halted.

"I lost four thousand dollars," he said hopelessly.

After the New Year, the stock market became bullish again, and the Dow Jones

Index repeatedly set new highs. I called him and asked how his stocks were doing. He sounded excited over the phone. "Not bad, not bad. Every day you can bring home a golden doll."[17]

The stock market began to slip again in the spring, and this time he knew to get out early. But those who looked to him for leadership were one step too slow. Many were caught.

We did not see each other for quite a while. One day he came over to see me and said he was still busy trading stocks but thought it would be more exciting to trade currencies. In currency trading, he said, one could borrow a large sum, even hundreds of thousands of dollars, and could trade around the clock, whereas stocks could be traded only between 9:30 A.M. and 4:00 P.M. He said he would try currency trading.

I called him up after a while and asked if he had gotten into the currency-trading business. I was surprised to hear him say that he had some new ideas and was forming a company. A few days later, he gave me his business card, on which the title "President" was printed after his name. In his home there were all kinds of made-in-China toys and samples of children's shoes.

Three years went by. His teaching contract with the university expired, and it was time for him to leave. So we had dinner together again. During dinner he said that since childhood he had been a restless person; he wanted to try everything. When he had first arrived in America, the stipend that he received from the government was pitifully small. Others simply lived frugally, but he delivered pizza. His argument was that money must be made; it did not grow on trees. Making money was one of the many freedoms in America; having money meant that you could enjoy spending it. Many people took up teaching and wanted tenure, but he wanted something else. He said that if you didn't try something, you'd never know whether you were good at it. He had never been jealous of others; it would be all right to discover that he wasn't good at something after trying it out. He said he still would like to try to make his fortune on Wall Street. It would be all right if he did not succeed; he could always go back to delivering pizza.

Wall Street—that was his true dream.

GETTING RICH AND BEING PATRIOTIC

After the June Fourth Incident, the return of the Chinese students to China became a hotly debated political issue in America. Legislation was proposed in Congress to "protect" the Chinese students.[18] President George Bush vetoed that legislation but signed an administrative decree permitting Chinese students to stay in America until January 1, 1994. At that time, a well-known American China scholar expressed privately that, in consideration of America's long-range interests, the U.S. government should encourage, or even force, the Chinese students to return to China. "If they stay," he said, derogatorily, "they can only open restaurants or something like that."

Later events proved that this China scholar was not completely off the mark. One of his Chinese students opened a Chinese restaurant near the campus while he was writing his dissertation. And the business was rather good.

But this China scholar had underestimated the aspirations and abilities of Chinese students. Historically, early Chinese immigrants earned their living almost exclusively in laundry and restaurant businesses, but here history did not repeat itself.

A thirty-five-year-old man came from Beijing in 1986 and eventually received a master's degree from a college in Maine. After graduation he changed jobs several times and finally went to Houston to start his own business. Several years later, he owned five companies and had a six-digit annual income. He bought a big house in the city and a vacation home in the suburbs.

He already had a Green Card, but he kept emphasizing that he still loved China. "To be patriotic, you have to donate money to good causes in China" was his favorite saying. "Look at Li Jiacheng or Bao Yugang in Hong Kong: when they said they were patriotic, they donated money, millions and millions of dollars. If you don't show money, it's just empty talk!"

I had known him for a long time. Toward the end of the Cultural Revolution, we were students in the same high school in the eastern district of Beijing. I was one of the "good students" while he, though not a model student, was not a "bad student." After school I would stay home, feeling bored, but he would run from one classmate's house to another. He was full of energy and interested in many things. Besides doing homework, he wrote poetry, painted, and composed music. He missed nothing.

Years passed. We both graduated from college. He was assigned to work in a foreign-trade company in Beijing, a much-coveted position. Every day he represented the government in trade discussions with foreign business people, and often he was entertained with banquets. But after two years of this leisurely life he felt bored and stifled. So finally he made some contacts and became a privately financed student trying it out in America.

He got a master's degree after two years of hard times. After graduation there was no time for celebration, since the more pressing problem was avoiding starvation.

Even if he had to starve, he said, he would not work in a Chinese restaurant. His reasoning was that once you began to rely on this cheapest mode of earning a living, you would become trapped in a low social stratum and never see daylight again. It sounded rather snobbish but had some validity.

When he arrived in New York, he found work at a company financed by the Chinese government. Being a Chinese student with an American diploma, he thought his skill and talent would be appreciated. Also, like many other Chinese students starting off in business, he had a naive belief that his connections from his old work unit in China would bring some "mainland business" to the company. He was totally wrong.

In this Chinese-run company, in spite of his enthusiasm and accomplishments, he was always treated as a second-class citizen and had to endure all kinds of prejudices. Slowly he understood that in the eyes of his Chinese colleagues, he was just another one of those people who had come there to get paid because he could not make it on his own. His old unit in China was even more chilly toward him. Perhaps he had unintentionally offended someone in that organization in the past; it seemed as if there had been an explicit directive forbidding anyone to do business with him.

He admitted later that those were his most difficult days in America, but he was able to persevere because he was confident that one day he could prove his worth. He quickly left New York and went to Houston, where he became a salesman for an American company. He was forced to take this step, but it decidedly made the difference in his career growth.

He sold shipping routes and container space in ocean-going cargo ships. Within a few years, he quickly learned the American style of salesmanship: finding potential customers from telephone books, getting appointments for sales talks, making people listen to his sales pitches even though they should be attending to more pressing problems, finishing a two-hour conversation in half an hour, and, in the end, making the other party sign the contract because they felt they had gotten a really good deal.

In those few years he learned not only to talk fast and never get discouraged, but also how to deal with Japanese, Korean, Vietnamese, and South American business people. He also acquired an acute market consciousness.

He quickly established himself in that American company. The pay was good. But he knew that there was no future in being a salesman. In 1988 during a visit to Beijing, he enjoyed the play Death of a Salesman *performed by the People's Art Troupe, but he did not wish to die a salesman.*

He patiently waited for an opportunity, and the opportunity finally came—or, rather, he found it.

At that time the South African government practiced apartheid. There was an international embargo on South Africa, with whom many countries had severed diplomatic relationships. In actual fact, these countries had a great deal of indirect trade with South Africa. He knew that there existed a big market in the shipping business.

In 1990 he resigned from his sales job and formed his own company, Ocean Shipping Agency, Inc. Soon afterward the company got its first commission. His business expanded rapidly, from shipping to the related business of insurance and trading. Then he set his eyes, in addition to South Africa, on Eastern Europe and Vietnam. And being Chinese, he could not forget the huge market in China.

In the early nineties he tried repeatedly to negotiate business with representatives of a variety of Chinese-run companies and with trade delegates from China. But he found that his American style of salesmanship was useless. What was useful was a revelation pointed out to him by an old colleague: "You want to do business in China? First, you can't act like the boss calling the shots; you have to learn to beg." To beg meant to wine, dine, and flatter the delegates. But even that was not enough. Some delegates, after eating and drinking, would propose, "How about helping us to open up our sights—show us some things we can't see in China."[19]

To open the China market, he went to China many times. After each trip he sadly commented that China had no market based on fair competition on quality and price. In China everybody was complaining that "the whole country is engaged in business." In fact, what they really should have complained about was the method of doing business, not the number of business people.

He still waited patiently, believing his opportunity would come. He was only one of many Chinese students doing business.

As the number of Chinese students graduating from colleges and becoming American residents increased, they turned to business in a spectacular tide.

Many Chinese students entered America with an enthusiasm for scholarship and a dedication to academic studies. But they soon discovered that the center of gravity in American society was not in politics, not in culture, not even in science, but in business. An American president once said, "The chief business of the American people is business."[20] The value in everything could be measured in terms of commercial value, and business success was one of the critical building blocks of any kind of enterprise. In this fully developed business society, it was far easier to form a corporation than it was to get a passport in China. The business world, full of opportunities and challenges, would inevitably attract Chinese students who had talent and adventurous spirits, because that was the arena in which they could strive for supremacy.

In World War II, men fought and killed one another. After the war, the East and West engaged in the cold war of an intense arms race. Now, with the Cold War over, a new contest based on economic strength in the form of trade and business had quickly begun among nations. In the next century, whether China could rise among the nations would depend to a large extent on its success or failure in this contest.

CHAPTER 5

The Other Side of the Bright Moon

THE MANUAL-LABOR EXPERIENCE

A college friend wrote to me from Japan, "In college we laughed because we were carefree; in the work unit we grumbled because we were discontented; in a foreign country we groaned because we did manual labor."

There have been numerous articles describing this work experience as fun and free and easy—it is an embodiment of the spirit of independence of Western youth. But to most Chinese students, it was unpleasant.

"Don't ever think of having a moment of free time," said a thirty-year-old Ph.D. candidate studying artificial intelligence. He washed dishes two hours a day in a Chinese restaurant. Each day the dishes were already piled high when he started, and he never was able to finish washing them. After two days, the skin on his hands began to peel. He also said that the owner was the first truly wicked person he had ever known. The owner scolded the students and once dismissed a girl on the grounds that her hair was smelly. There was never a day off, since, the owner said, holidays were American ones and there was no need for Chinese to celebrate them; when Chinese New Year came, he would say, "This is America—just forget about it." If you insisted on having a day off, he would dismiss you. He habitually patronized prostitutes, saying that that was how he spent his money.

In New York City I met a young couple who depended on manual labor for a living. They were from Guangzhou, and both had worked for an export company in

China. In 1983, with the help of their relatives, they had come to America under the pretext of studying. On the third day after their arrival, they began looking for work in a rainstorm. They first rented a basement apartment, and that night, in the midst of the squeaking of mice, they slept on old newspapers. The husband then started delivering pizzas on a bicycle. One night, during a driving rain, he was riding uphill and ran into a ditch. He got up and walked up the slope. He returned to his basement home at two o'clock in the morning, soaking wet. The tip for the entire evening was twenty-five cents.

To this generation of Chinese students, manual labor was equivalent to another "reeducation" program, but with a difference.[1] Enduring hardships in China during reeducation had been an implicit act of courage in response to the call of a political movement. Hardship in America, however, was simply the pressure of earning a living, and there was no escape. Regardless of how talented, famous, or ambitious you were in China, in America you had to take on manual labor if you had no money or marketable skills.

So Chinese intellectuals became America's laborers. This role reversal had tremendous impact on those intellectuals; in spite of their experience of "reform through labor" in China, they had never shed their subconscious attitude of class superiority in Chinese society.

Once, during a Chinese students' party, a woman said to me ruefully that she smelled of hot cooking oil because she had just finished work in a restaurant. She was studying art, but the restaurant work kept her busy. She said, "I have no time to think of anything during the day, but all those suppressed feelings surface in my nightmares."

A journalist, just over forty and well known in China for his documentary writings, told me about his feelings when he was growing bean sprouts, in his raincoat and boots, in the damp basement of a Chinese restaurant.[2] *He accepted the work, with resignation, as a learning experience in life. To sustain his spirits, he silently recited the teachings of Mencius: "Before Heaven lays her trust on a man, she will first steel his will with suffering, tire his body with toil, and starve him with hunger."*[3]

Many of the Chinese students had been accustomed to having their livelihood taken care of by the "iron rice bowl" of the socialist system. This American style of reeducation hence forced them to take a second look at their ability to survive and their worth to society. In

America, a Chinese student who could not earn a living would find it difficult to keep the traditional traits of Chinese intellectuals: conceit and aloofness.

A twenty-eight-year-old friend who used to study literature went to America in 1990 to find a new way of living. But things were different from what he had imagined, so he gave up his plan to study and began washing dishes instead. Sometime later he wrote in a letter to a friend, "I have been washing dishes for several days now in a Chinese restaurant. The number of dishes I have washed is probably equal to what I should have washed in China but did not because I was too lazy. When you become a blue-collar worker, you shed fanciful notions of yourself."

A thirty-something economics student said that in his first year in America he had a scholarship and felt that he belonged to the elite. He would attend all the meetings on China's economy and, often to the astonishment of the audience, would argue with anybody. A year later the scholarship stopped. He suddenly discovered that he was so pitifully insignificant in that mammoth society that he could not even feed himself. With no other way out, he started working as a "chicken separator" in a Chinese restaurant—he cut up chickens. He also dispelled the notion of being elite.

It was true. There was a real difference between those who had tasted the manual-labor experience and those who had not. After the June Fourth Incident, a group of leadership stars appeared on the stage in the overseas democracy movement. Their speech and conduct quickly became the target of criticism from the students of an earlier day. One of the most biting remarks was "They've never worked a single day."

What the Chinese students called work included nearly everything: domestic help, babysitting, trash hauling, or taking care of the dead in funeral homes. But working in a Chinese restaurant was the most frequent.

There are countless Chinese restaurants in America. One can find several in every city, along every expressway. A joke went, "If every Chinese restaurant put out a Chinese flag, China could have said long ago that the sun never sets on the Chinese empire."

Most of these restaurants were owned by people from Taiwan, and some by Chinese from Hong Kong, Singapore, or even Vietnam. In recent years, some mainland Chinese students had also entered the restaurant business. I heard of a visiting scholar who, in his first year at a college in Miami, carried his briefcase to school every day to do his scholarly work. In his second year he opened a restaurant with a partner and thereafter reported to work every day with the same briefcase.

Many Chinese restaurants looked like castles. There were no windows, as if to minimize any distraction from eating. Inside, bright red often dominated the splendid decor, showing a heavy Oriental atmosphere unaffected by mainstream American culture.

When you walked into a Chinese restaurant, you would almost always meet waiters or waitresses from mainland China. An inquiry would show that they came from Beijing, Shanghai, or Guangzhou. Most of the Chinese students in America originated from these three cities.

Although they were all Chinese, sometimes conflicts arose that were rooted in their differences in place of origin. A woman from Beijing complained that the people from Shanghai were ganging up on her. They ignored her and would not help her in any way. The Shanghai hostess would lead what looked like a good customer to a table waited on by a Shanghai waiter. Once there was a job vacancy, and the Shanghai workers collectively lobbied for another person from Shanghai, fearful that the owner would hire someone from another city.

If the restaurant was an American fast-food one, then an international conflict could arise.

A Chinese student delivered pizza in Houston. There were three delivery people at the restaurant: a Mexican, a Vietnamese, and he. The Mexican had started the job two months earlier and hence knew which neighborhoods tipped generously and which meagerly. The rules were that the three people delivered the orders in rotation. But unknown to the other two deliverers, the Mexican would often covertly change the sequence of orders so that he got the good ones, leaving orders from low-tipping neighborhoods to the other two. But sometimes things did not turn out the way he had expected. One day a church ordered a hundred pizzas, and the Mexican grabbed the order. It took him a long time to load the pizzas and, of course, to unload them later. When he returned, he was cursing with fury: the church had given no tip. Later, when the other two discovered this sneaky way of doing business, a fight nearly broke out.

The usual wage for waiting on tables was just a couple of dollars per hour, so the principal income for waiters was tips. Customers who walked away after a meal without leaving a tip infuriated the service people.

A twenty-eight-year-old student in Seattle said he had encountered such customers. Once several South Americans came and ate lavishly. After dinner, they departed without leaving a cent. Two days later, they did the same thing. When they came for the third time, the waiter declared, "No tip, no service." Then there were customers who were extraordinarily generous. Once a black brother ordered a dish priced at $8. After the meal, he left a $10 tip. When the waiter thanked him for the generous tip, the black brother replied, "I just got a job."

There were also customers who were even harder to deal with than those who did not tip.

A thirty-three-year-old graduate student said she was once waiting on an American woman. Toward the end of her meal, the woman suddenly screamed, "There's a hair in the soup!" The manager, trying to keep the peace, apologized profusely. But the waitress noticed that the hair in the soup was blonde, whereas every person working in the restaurant had black hair. So she spoke to the woman, and the woman calmed down.

But there were also warm moments in the restaurant business, and among the waiters and waitresses in Chinese restaurants were people of different talents.

A twenty-five-year-old woman working in a Chinese restaurant in Lansing, Michigan, said that one waiter there used to be a singer in an art troupe. He had a beautiful voice and often, overtaken by an impulse, would start singing "Crossing the Ocean of Trees" by Yang Zirong or "I Remember" by Hu Chuankui. His rhythm was precise, the phrasing smooth. He was at his best when he sang,

The stars sprinkle the sky;
The sliver of moon is bright.
In the meeting of the production brigade,
The wrongs will be made right.[4]

A twenty-four-year-old student in St. Louis who worked as a waiter in a Chinese restaurant said he met an elderly American couple there. Every Wednesday they would come for dinner precisely at seven o'clock in the evening, sit at the same table, order the same dishes, and leave the same tip. They had been doing this for several years. Sometimes when they were planning a trip, they would notify the students of their destination and their date of return. This elderly couple were the most welcomed customers of the restaurant and also dear friends of the student waiters.

The most exciting moment of an exhausting day was counting the day's tips. On good days, a waiter could earn $100, wages included. A mediocre day would still bring $60 or $70. A woman recalled her experience as a waitress: "Those were all *American* dollars!" Only in those moments did she feel that all the hard work was worth it.

Many Chinese students studied at colleges in small cities where the opportunity for finding work was limited. Hence during the summer they went to big cities such as New York to pan for gold.

A twenty-eight-year-old studying media broadcasting at Oklahoma City College described her summer making dumplings in New York City. The workplace was in the new Chinese district in Flushing and had very little sunlight during the day. The owner, from Taiwan, said he had been a lieutenant general in the Nationalist Army, a claim hard to verify. He had a wife, but she never returned after a trip to Taiwan. Now he lived with a woman from Thailand who used to work in the dumpling house. The dumpling makers were all from mainland China. Among them was an elderly woman who had come to America to visit her student son, a younger woman who had immigrated to America years ago and lost her fortune in a restaurant venture in another state, and a third woman who had come with her student husband. A young man who could not find a job after finishing his master's degree also worked there. Besides making dumplings, he helped the owner deliver them. The favorite conversational topic was the owner's relationship with the Thai girl—how they brewed tonic and so forth. Other favorite activities were presenting dumplings to one another as gifts. Since they were paid at the rate of three cents per dumpling, friendship could be measured by the number of dumplings in the gift. The best way to express one's affection was to say, "May I present you with this plate of dumplings?"

There were risks to working in New York City. There I met a twenty-five-year-old student from Mississippi who had come to find summer work.

It was raining heavily on the day of his arrival. Carrying a small umbrella that swayed in the raging storm, he walked block after block to find work. After several days he found a job delivering pizza. On the first day, the owner showed him the route by accompanying him on a delivery. On the top floor of an apartment building, they were robbed by two African Americans, and the student was robbed of his three-dollar tip. The owner, not so fortunate, was stabbed in the buttock because he could not remove the gold ring from his finger. But the experience did not scare off the student. After working in several restaurants, he returned to Mississippi fully equipped to pay for the next year's expenses.

A WANDERER'S LIFE

On the day before Thanksgiving in 1989, a visiting scholar who lived in my rooming house bade me farewell. He was about fifty, a historian specializing in China's ethnic groups. At the breakout of the June Fourth Incident he had been in Japan, and with the help of several American professors, he came to America. He had a three-month research appointment at the University of Michigan and was on his way to the University of Arizona, where he would have another temporary appointment. A month before, he had bought a bright red Ford to drive across America's badlands in the West. He needed to get to Arizona before Christmas, and the journey would take about a week.

On the day he left, the sky was dark and gloomy, and a snowstorm threatened. He loaded all his earthly possessions in the car. They consisted of a suitcase, some clothing, chopsticks and bowls, and two boxes of books. He looked westward at the sky and said wryly, "If my colleagues in the work unit knew I was driving across the American continent, they would say, 'What a romantic adventure!' But, in fact, well . . ." I knew that at that moment his family of four was scattered around the globe. He was heading toward the West, his daughter was studying in New York, his wife was working in Hunan, and his son was studying at a college in Beijing. The family did not know when or if ever they would be reunited. His own future, in particular, was so unsettled. After three months in Arizona, he would leave for Seattle. In another three months, he had to go to St. Louis. After that, he really did not know. Upon arriving at a new place, his first order of business was always to make contacts for his next stop. A few days earlier, he had called his daughter in New York and told her, "Study hard. I'm getting old and don't know how much longer I can run around like this."

This was the seventh time he had left China, and the third time he had come to America. He told me that his father had graduated from Yale in the twenties. In 1949, on the eve of the Communist sweep of China, his father decided that the family would remain in China even though he had already purchased plane tickets for the family. One day during Land Reform, his father gathered his five children around him and told them of his sincere regret for the family's landlord background.[5] *His father specialized in electrical engineering but was not allowed to work in that field; he was assigned to teach in a high school. His father learned of the reason for his banishment only during a denunciation rally during the Cultural Revolution.*[6] *During Land Reform, a colleague of his, a professor, before he was executed for being the local tyrant gangster, confessed under torture to a false charge that his father was a member of the Anti-Communist and Save-the-Country Militia. That testimony found its way into his father's dossier. After 1979 the scholar's four siblings left China one after another, while he stayed to keep his father company. The father became ill during a trip to Hong Kong in 1984 but insisted on returning to China. He later died in his hometown. On his deathbed, he said with a sigh, "I have kept faith with the Communist Party, but the Communist Party has let me down." The scholar understood the tragedy that had befallen his father, a tragedy from which nobody of that time could escape. But he was unwilling to let the same tragedy happen to him, much less to his children.*

So he left Michigan. The blizzard came soon afterward and lasted two full days. The whole world seemed to have become so blurred. More than a week later, he called from Arizona. He had arrived there safely. I have not heard from him since.

A few years later, someone saw him in California; another person had met him in New York; still another said he had gone to Boston.

In America there were many Chinese students who drifted from place to place. If you were a student, you followed the sources of financial support; if you were a visiting scholar and wished to stay, you had to change schools from time to time. This drifting, voluntary or otherwise, made more acute the feeling of rootlessness so common to life in an alien country. In my years of study in America, I met quite a few such wandering Chinese students.

They were a wandering couple. Both were about thirty and had worked as editors of an English magazine in Beijing. In 1987 they had come to America together to study broadcasting at a university in West Virginia. Everything went smoothly in the beginning: they lived in an inexpensive student apartment, the local church organization gave them furniture, and each had a scholarship. Two years later they received their master's degrees, but neither could find work. Finally they went to work at a gas station; she worked during the day and he at night. But now they hardly had any time together. They concluded that this was no life at all and decided to either return to school for doctoral study or find real jobs. Thus they began to wander. They drove from place to place, staying with their friends or friends of friends, inquiring about schools and job opportunities. When they came through Michigan, there still had been no clear leads, and they looked dejected. In addition, the husband's face and body had become swollen from an allergic reaction to the Mexican fast food made with beans and corn that they had been eating so often.

He was thirty-eight years old, a wandering Chinese student. I met him in a market in a small city. He was selling a variety of small Chinese arts and crafts merchandise displayed on a blanket spread on the ground. He was from Beijing and had worked for an export company specializing in arts and crafts products. In 1988 he came to America to study. After a while he did not wish to continue, but he could not find work. That was how he decided to become a mobile vendor. He began by importing some Chinese products and selling them in markets in nearby small cities. Then he started going to wherever there was an arts and crafts market. Finally he bought a van and loaded it with all his belongings. Then he followed the calendar of markets, planned his routes, and traveled from place to place throughout the year. He slept in his van and never spent more than $3 on a meal. I asked him how his business was. He said not bad; he earned enough to survive. He then added that once he was very lucky and made more than $1,000 in a week.

An elderly man in China said, "Now there are not only students studying overseas, but also students in exile overseas."

THE SURVIVAL PRESSURE

The Christmas of 1991 was an ordinary one. A heavy snow fell in Ann Arbor. The white campus and the streets were deserted. Families were spending the holiday together. Christmas trees, colorful lights, and beautifully wrapped gift packages filled every home with warmth and happiness.

Being separated from their families, most Chinese students could not count on having a family reunion. But taking advantage of the holiday, they shopped or invited friends over for dinner, conversation, or watching videos. Still, I know that it was a rather gloomy Christmas in the home of some Chinese students.

The couple had a fight on Christmas Day, and in a fit of pique she drove away. Her forty-three-year-old husband was studying manufacturing. He had finished his doctoral dissertation two years earlier but had yet to take his thesis-defense examination. In the previous two years he had mailed several hundred letters to prospective employers, but every reply began with "We regret . . ." Now he had become totally discouraged; he would still go through the motion of writing, but he did not feel like even opening the replies. That Christmas Day I met his wife in a supermarket, and she immediately started to complain about her husband: "He doesn't want to do anything—so listless, all day. I asked him to try again, perhaps try Singapore, or Hong Kong, but he won't listen."

On Christmas he went to his laboratory and left his wife and children at home. He was thirty-five and had just completed his Ph.D. He stayed on as a postdoctorate scholar since he could not find another job. Six months earlier his wife had given birth to twin girls. It was not that he did not like girls, but the two extra mouths in the house had changed their lives from little-to-spare to extremely tight. "I hate Christmas," he said. "There is absolutely no meaning in it. I just don't want to stay home—it's so irritating." But I know that it was not Christmas that irritated him. A week before Christmas, his boss apologetically told him that he could not retain him the following year because of a shortage of research funds. The boss said he would be very willing to write letters of recommendation, and he could work until the following summer.

During the Christmas holidays the couple worried about how they were going to survive the next year. The husband, close to forty and studying political science, had been a teaching assistant for five years, and that was the maximum duration allowed by school rules. But another crisis struck: his wife, who washed vegetables in the student cafeteria, had lost her job a few days earlier because of arm pain. Following the custom in China, she asked her boss to help her. The boss, however, dismissed her, saying that she needed rest.

America is a country of survival pressure. The instant you set foot there, you become deeply affected by this pressure, which arises from the threat of joblessness, poverty, even starvation. When you walk off the campus, you sense it even more acutely.

Many students could pass examinations, complete their degrees, and work at temporary jobs but could not find a real job after they graduated. When they could not cross that threshold, their lives in America suddenly became grim and cruel.

For Americans, especially middle-class Americans, work is a matter of great concern. A good job not only provides a comfortable life with cars and home ownership, but also confers social status. Losing a job means loss of status and a sense of failure. American society has never been known for its sympathy for those who have failed.

Quite a few Chinese students found jobs after they completed their studies, but many could not. This was especially true for humanities students, students who had specialized in sciences that had no industrial applications, and older students.

There were many reasons for this difficulty. First, aliens and recent immigrants, even those with a higher education, found it hard to blend into the world outside the campus because of the background factors of race, culture, and language. Second, in the early nineties, America was in a long post–Cold War economic slowdown; thousands and thousands of Americans lost their jobs, and many graduating students could not find employment.

Feeling the survival pressure and the predicament of joblessness, many Chinese students, to different degrees, changed their attitude toward life. In China they had tended to consider themselves talented but complained about having no opportunity to use that talent; very few people seemed happy with their work. In America, after having tasted the difficulty of landing a job, they did their work diligently, conscientiously, reliably, and willingly.

Among the students I knew on campus, he was the one who felt the most satisfied with his work. He was twenty-nine, from Jiangsu. He had come in 1988 as a privately financed student of biochemistry. Because he could not afford the high tuition of a top college, he attended a nearby community college. He said that on his poorest day he had only $10 in his pocket and felt as if he was in a trance while sitting on a street bench. Later, with the help of a Chinese American professor, he found work in the biology laboratory of the college, feeding mice and washing bottles. The pay was $700 a month. Although that was a pitiful sum, he did not mind it at all. He worked day and night and on holidays; he just wanted to keep that job. Seeing that so many Chinese students could not find work, he felt he was lucky.

In order to remain in America, it was common for Chinese students to work for very low wages. It was well known in American colleges that a Chinese student could be hired for very little money for doing laboratory work; sometimes the cost was only half as much as supporting a graduate student.

But sometimes events took an extreme course. In March 1993 a case of modern slavery was exposed at Northwestern University in Evanston, Illinois.

A woman visiting scholar, age forty, worked for more than two years, from March 1990 through August 1992, in a psychology laboratory at the university without receiving pay. On August 13, 1992, after asking about her pay, she was beaten, kicked, and pushed to the ground by one of the researchers who had hired her. She was taken to the hospital because of the injury. A few days later, her American boss dismissed her.

She had been a technician in a college of Chinese medicine in Beijing and had come to America in 1990. According to the agreement, she was to work in the laboratory for three years at an annual stipend of $12,000. Striving to maintain a functional rapport with her boss, she dared not complain during the two years in which she was paid nothing. To earn a living, she moonlighted as a kitchen helper in a student cafeteria, washing and cutting vegetables.

After this case of modern slavery was exposed, the students and faculty at the university were outraged. The university administration agreed to pay her a lump sum of $32,000 to settle the case. But the visiting scholar finally decided she would no longer be pushed around; she engaged a lawyer and sued the university.

ARTISTS: FEW RICH, MOST POOR, SOME WHO DIE

In summer 1992 the English-language *Asia Magazine* wrote about three Chinese painters who had enjoyed success in America. Chen Yifei left Shanghai for New York in 1980. His painting *Night Banquet* had just set an auction record of $250,000 in Hong Kong. The reporter wrote that the forty-six-year-old artist admitted happily that he was already a millionaire. He had a studio in the heart of New York City and owned a luxury apartment in the most expensive part of Manhattan. The second artist was a Mr. Ding. The highest price paid for one of his paintings was $300,000. He now lived in a $6 million mansion outside Hollywood, with movie stars as neighbors. The third was a thirty-three-year-old Mr. Chen. One of his paintings was auctioned for $50,000 in Hong Kong. He had an oceanfront studio in California overlooking the vast Pacific Ocean and a beautiful beach.[7]

But just one year earlier, a young Chinese artist, thirty-four-year-old Lin Ling, was shot and killed while painting sidewalk portraits in New York City.

The shooting occurred at two o'clock in the morning, August 18, 1991. Lin Ling was working near a hotel at the intersection of Forty-fifth Street and Eighth Avenue. Four African American youths walked over, chased away the spectators, and began taunting him. They threw chicken bones at his head. Lin and his wife, who was also present, fought back with a soda bottle. Lin was shot to death by twenty-one-year-old James Skinner.[8]

Lin Ling had graduated from Zhejiang Fine Arts College in 1982, where he specialized in oil painting. After going to America in 1986, he studied and received a master's degree from an art college in New York. According to his friends, life had always been hard for this dedicated and talented artist. New York Times *reporter Seth Faison, Jr., said that Mr. Lin's apartment on 145th Street was cramped, as he shared it with three other families. To survive, Lin Ling had worked as a sidewalk artist, carrying a bench and soliciting patrons for portrait painting. He painted at two o'clock in the morning so as to avoid being chased and arrested by the police, for although the city had a long tradition of tolerating such practices, its ordinances forbade them.*

The tragedy of Lin Ling may be an extreme example, but there were more than a hundred such Chinese sidewalk artists in New York City alone. They had been well trained in China but became illicit street-vendor artists in America. Many had mixed feelings about their plight. In May 1990 several Chinese students and I took a ferry to Ellis Island to visit the Statue of Liberty. On the wharf we met a painter whose appearance, manners, and clothing indicated that he was from the mainland. He was sitting on a long bench in the garden with his easel up, waiting for patrons. One of us went over to him and, trying to strike a conversation, asked where he was from. The painter, seeing that we were Chinese students, made it clear that he did not wish to talk. In a very formal manner, he answered in perfect Beijing dialect, "Germany." He then turned his head away.

A portrait artist earned about $10 to $15 for each portrait. Even on a good day, the income was meager. Hence many artists were in a constant struggle for survival. A student who had some contacts with these artists said that she once went with several of them to their living quarters and discovered, to her dismay, that they lived in a run-down warehouse.

If we piece together these two extremes, we can obtain a somewhat more realistic and complete picture of the struggles of Chinese students in America: some succeeded, some failed; some soared, some crashed.

This was true for the Chinese artists in New York City, and also true for the Chinese students who had tried to break into American society in recent years. One thing was clear: as in all contests, winners were few.

The lyrics to a popular Chinese song said, "The world outside is wonderful; / The world outside gives you no choice." We could add another line: "The world outside is also very cruel."

This cruelty left no room at all for the kind of romanticism in which the Chinese literary artists had indulged. The tragedy of the poet Gu Cheng is a good example.

Gu Cheng was a representative poet of the Misty style of poetry.[9] *In 1986 he went to New Zealand as a visiting scholar at the University of Auckland. Later he and his wife, Xie Ye, moved to a sparsely habited island and began a life of seclusion.*

In August 1993 a Hong Kong magazine reported the idyllic life of Gu Cheng. He admired wildflowers, ate mussels, tilled the vegetable garden, and raised chickens; he seemed to be totally intoxicated by the beauty of nature, had completely forgotten chaotic human society, and had found the Peach Blossom Spring.[10]

On October 11, 1993, while that issue of the magazine was still on the shelves of college libraries, a wire service reported that the well-known fairy-tale poet Gu Cheng had, after killing his wife with an ax, committed suicide by hanging himself from a tree.

There were probably many factors that contributed to this tragedy, such as a love affair outside the marriage and the poet's unstable mental state. But behind the specific reasons, the fatal one was probably the tremendous struggle to survive. Gu Cheng's hermit life was far from romantic, and he was actually backed against a wall. He could not support his wife, his child, or even himself. Frequently he had to go to the arts and crafts market to earn some money by doing sketches, and the whole family relied primarily on his wife's income from selling eggs and eggrolls. It was this survival pressure that caused the collapse of the marriage and led to the homicide and suicide.

Since 1978 tens of thousands of Chinese had rushed out of the country to realize their dreams elsewhere. Among them were people who were well established in China. Some quickly reestablished themselves, while others encountered the harsh life in a foreign land.

What was so interesting was that many intellectuals who had in the past yearned for the idyllic society of the West became disillusioned to various degrees after they went abroad. This change of mind was not really a result of improved perception, but of their feeling that Western society was cold and cruel. Moreover, both the yearning in the past and the disillusionment of the present were of their own making; neither had much to do with the reality of Western society.

"Yes, there are many freedoms here," said a thirty-three-year-old Chinese student in Maine who could not find a job after completing his master's degree, "and one of them is the freedom to starve to death."

He was not simply grumbling but also recognizing a real aspect of American society.

THE JUNGLE IN THE BRONX

The American writer Tom Wolfe wrote a well-known work of fiction, *The Bonfire of the Vanities.* The story begins with a young, vigorous, ambitious Wall Street broker who is on his way to the airport to meet his lover. On his return he takes a wrong turn at an expressway exit. Instead of going to Manhattan, he ends up in the Bronx, a place known for its poverty, chaos, and murder rate. His troubles thus begin.

In the winter of 1990, I stayed in the Bronx for a week. The dilapidation I saw was shocking. Trash was piled up on desolate streets with broken pavement. Abandoned buildings on both sides of the streets, their windows sealed with bricks over which window curtains were painted, created an eerie atmosphere. There were few pedestrians on the street; now and then you could see one or two black youths walking aimlessly or leaning against a wall. I rode through the area on a bus on which most passengers were black or Hispanic, with a few whites. All looked despondent, and their eyes betrayed gloom. Even on the bus you felt that someone was sizing you up from behind.

The Bronx was separated by a river from Manhattan, where the giant corporations congregated in skyscrapers in which the price of real estate was measured in hundreds of dollars per square foot. But the Bronx was frightening, filthy, and forgotten. During the day, huge sums of money flowed in and out of the Wall Street Stock Exchange; at night, plays and musicals were performed in theaters big and small. But in the Bronx were destruction, terror, homeless people, and drug addicts.

The Bronx has been described as a city jungle in which human beings are reduced to jungle animals who attack, injure, and even kill one another. This phenomenon could be seen in other cities as well:

Detroit, Chicago, Los Angeles, even Washington, D.C. Once I was changing buses at Detroit's bus depot, which was only a ten-minute walk from the city center. It was late afternoon. I looked at the towering skyscrapers bathed in light from the setting sun and was ready to walk over to visit the renowned city of automobiles. A nearby elderly man sensed my intentions and said to me, very seriously, "Don't go. You could be killed."

Many Chinese students who lived or studied in the Bronx had been robbed.

A thirty-nine-year-old student said that once he was returning to his living quarters from school after work and was forced into a corner by several Hispanic youths. There he was robbed of more than $60. He felt fortunate that he was not hurt. His roommate, from China's northeast, was tall and big.[11] *One day he returned home with blood streaming down his face. He had been robbed in the street by several black youths who, fearful that they might not be able to subdue him in a fight, first beat him severely.*

These random robberies, beatings, and murders were not confined to New York.

In the summer of 1989 a Ms. Mei in Dallas was killed late at night when she returned home from work.

On the night of November 18, 1993, a twenty-five-year-old Mr. Huang from Shanghai, who was studying for his master's degree at Kansas State University, was struck unconscious from behind and suffered a severe concussion. He had been returning to his dormitory from campus.

On the evening of February 28, 1994, a Mr. Wang from Guangxi, who was studying at a college in New York, was shot to death by two black youths robbing the restaurant where he was working.

In some big cities, the danger existed not only on the streets.

A thirty-three-year-old student in Houston told me of a terrifying experience he went through one evening. He had come to America in 1986 and found work in Houston after completing his master's degree. There he bought a house in a fairly decent neighborhood. One night his wife woke up and noticed someone moving about in the bedroom. At first she thought it was her husband, but then she felt him sleeping soundly next to her. She pushed him and screamed, "Someone's in the room!" and the intruder calmly left the room. The frightened couple lay on the floor, face down, as their waterbed offered no crawlspace. After they were sure that nothing was stirring, they got up, locked the door, and dialed 911. After a few minutes the police came. The police were not as brave as they were depicted in the movies. With their guns drawn, they asked the couple to lead the way. The commotion lasted until dawn. Later it was found that the intruder had come in through an unbarred window and had stolen some cash and credit cards. Fortunately, the robbery did not turn into murder. Several neighbors were also robbed that night. The couple has since kept two watchdogs and three guns—one gun in the study, one in the bedroom, and the third under the pillow. The student said that if it happened again, he would be ready to shoot.

There are many factors contributing to crime in America, such as poverty, unemployment, drugs, and the ready availability of firearms. But the Bronx jungle phenomenon was largely rooted in the racial conflict in American society. The decline and fall of Detroit was directly related to sixties race riots, after which white people moved out of the city. Big corporations followed suit. The once thriving downtown area became dilapidated, and black people were trapped in unemployment and poverty. Black youth, as vividly described in the movie *Boyz N the Hood*, directed by a twenty-three-year-old black man, had no chance of developing themselves other than by becoming sports stars. Thus they began using drugs, selling drugs, robbing, killing, and finally killing each other. The story of Detroit now seems to be replayed in other cities.

Today nobody in America is willing to be tainted with the label "racist." But racial prejudice exists subtly and not so subtly. Some white people are unwilling to have black neighbors, for fear of racial troubles and a drop in the value of their property. Black people frequently complain that white people purposely inflate home prices so as to exclude them from white neighborhoods. In the workplace, the opportunity for promotion is apparently higher for whites than for blacks. Some white people say privately that black people are lazy and unwilling to work hard. But a black youth once told me that whites are afraid of blacks because the whites, like a child holding a candy bar, are fearful that what they have will be snatched away.

The social status of Chinese seemed to be somewhere in between.

A twenty-nine-year-old woman studying at a college in Mississippi said that once she politely said "Hi!" to a black woman whom she met in a public park. The black woman returned the greeting with "Asians, get out!"

But the Chinese were not to be outdone by blacks or whites in their racial consciousness. In New York City, I frequently heard Chinese students referring to a "black ghost" doing this and that. Nowadays they would more or less accept the marriage of a Chinese woman to a white man but would sneer at her if she married a black man. I have heard that in Boston a woman from Shanghai married a black man. Later, after she gave birth to a child, the baby became the butt of a joke among the Chinese: "Look, he's even darker than his father!" Toward white people, Chinese showed more reverence than affection—the characteristic of a weak nation imbued with an inferiority complex and its accompanying arrogance. An autobiographical-style novel that was quite popular for a while described the struggle of Chinese students in Manhattan. The heroine of the story, after her success in starting a small business, felt immensely pleased with herself when she saw several women with "blonde hair and blue eyes" earning a pittance for doing some trivial work.

Just as China's political system was frequently the cause of social unrest in China, racial conflict was the root cause of America's social problems.

I have often thought that, if I had spent my first day in America in the Bronx, or a similar district in Detroit or Los Angeles, I probably would have left the country on the second day. But I was fortunate to have the opportunity to see this other aspect of America at a later date.

A BESIEGED-FORTRESS MENTALITY

Near the end of 1992 the Chinese government sent a large recruiting team to America. After the team arrived, it was divided into smaller groups to recruit on regional campuses on the East and West Coasts and in the Midwest. On November 8 and 9 one group reached the University of Michigan. At eight o'clock in the evening on the first day, the delegation sponsored a movie-viewing as a way to meet with Chinese students already at Michigan. The group leader, who was deputy head of the recruiting team, gave a speech. He made some introductory remarks about the latest political and economical developments in China, recent policy changes concerning studying abroad, and the mission of the recruiting team. Then he raised his voice and spoke with passion: "Dear students, China is now entering an era in which great men and women are needed. I believe that a generation of great men and women has been born in you!"

During his ardent speech, the meeting place was chaotic and noisy. A few students had shown up, but most of the audience was made up of spouses and elderly parents of the students. They were jabbering the whole time, waiting for the movie to begin, and there were many children chasing one another on and off the stage, shouting "Yes" and "No" incessantly. The scene was similar to a community-wide meeting called by an agrarian production brigade in a Chinese village in a past era. It was not apparent that any great man or woman would emerge from the crowd.

Certainly, studying abroad could endow a student with talent. But not every student who studied abroad would become endowed with talent.

In modern Chinese literature, two writers leveled penetrating criticism on Chinese who went abroad to study: Lu Xun and Qian Zhongshu.[12] Although the primary target of Lu Xun's satire was traditional Chinese intellectuals, he sculpted the everlasting image of the "bogus foreign ghost" in "The True Story of Ah Q." There he let the Chinese see how their minds had been distorted by a colonial mentality.

In comparison, *Fortress Besieged* (Weicheng) by Qian Zhongshu mocked modern Chinese intellectuals who returned after studying abroad. Qian used the stories of a group of students, some genuinely studying while abroad and others mere charlatans, to tell us that even the experience of studying abroad would not remove the despicable and trifling character of the Chinese.

Today the "bogus foreign ghost" has become a household word. It has also become a mirror in which Chinese students can see and examine themselves. Few people are aware that, after living abroad for a long time, not only can they become a "bogus foreign ghost," but they can become trapped in the besieged fortress of their minds.

This under-siege mentality was not a rare occurrence among Chinese students. Some students showed a surprising tendency to become increasingly parochial, bored, and passive. This tendency was also mixed with an unrealistic appraisal of their self-worth.

Both husband and wife were over thirty. In 1985 they had come as privately financed students from a southern city in China and had led a hard student life at a Midwestern university for several years. He completed his Ph.D. and she, her master's degree. Afterward they found jobs at two small companies near Detroit. When I met them their lives had apparently settled down. Soon after we began talking, the wife informed me voluntarily that they had already received their Green Cards. Then, as if to console those of us who had not yet gotten one, she added immediately, "You'll get one too." I asked if they had gone back for a visit. The husband said indifferently, "We really have no more ties with China." The wife said that they were planning a European vacation, and then she began to complain about the monotony of food in America: "Every day all you have to eat is chicken, duck, pork, or beef. There isn't really anything good to eat."

I have not seen them since, but I heard that they had bought a house in a town nearby. To find a chandelier for their living room, they shopped at more than fifty stores. After the chandelier was installed, they put in only one lightbulb instead of the full set of eight, so as to be able to pay back the installment loan. Sometimes I received e-mail from the husband through the university's network. Once he gave a detailed comparison of menus and prices from nearby Chinese restaurants. At the end of the message he did not neglect to add "Ph.D." after his name.

Perhaps because life was rather bland, many students liked to argue on the Internet. It usually started with some insignificant problem and then escalated into a heated debate without a focal point but with a political fervor. Reading these arguments, you felt that you were back in the era of the big-character wall posters during the Cultural Revolution.[13]

Once at a Chinese New Year's dinner party, some guests ate and then left without paying the five-dollar charge. This started a heated argument.

A: Eat and run, the deeply rooted bad habit of Chinese!

B: That was the behavior of a few individuals, not of all Chinese. The organizers also should take some blame. Why is it always either a June Fourth memorial ceremony or the New Year's dinner? There should be some academic activities to attract some campus-wide attention.

C: All of you should mind your own business! What right have you to tell others what to do? Did President Bush tell you what to do?

A: B, you claim that we should have more academic activities. But I know you're not the scholarly type yourself, but an opportunist. After June Fourth, you still went to register to form a trading company, hoping to land some business from the mainland. I suspect you're just a businessman.[14]

B: *People put labels on me, just as in China. Frankly, I came to America precisely to avoid these people. You say I'm a businessman, but I want to know what you're doing here. Are you a student, or a Chinese KGB agent? How did you find out about other people's personal business? This is the behavior of a spy!*

D: *B is really a good actor. Tell us what you really are.*

B: *D, may I ask you a personal question? You talk just like A. Why? Are you two from the same father but different mothers? Let me tell you seriously that I've never taken a single cent from the government.*

There were many reasons for this under-siege mentality. First, the students often remained stuck in their image of the China they used to know. All students who left China retained their own memories of the country. Those who left in the early eighties and those who left in the nineties each had their corresponding images. These subconsciously preserved images were difficult to shed and made Chinese students abroad become increasingly estranged from the continuously changing China. A student who had come to America in 1992 said that it was hard to communicate with students who left China a few years earlier, as they seemed to have little understanding of China in the nineties. "I told them that China is different now, but they won't believe it," he said. In recent years, only the students who returned for family visits were stunned and overwhelmed with feelings about the changes in China. A thirty-two-year-old who had gone to America in 1984 for doctoral studies at a medical school returned to China in 1993 for a visit. He was astonished to see the un-Chinese behavior of the returned students: they spoke with American mannerisms, dressed casually at work, and verified their dinner bills to the penny with waiters in restaurants.

The impressions that the students preserved in their minds about China affected their thinking and their lifestyles. When a chasm appeared between China today and the China they remembered, they tended to become more conservative. Some students used the same old language to discuss current events in China, while others would attack recently emerged new phenomena in China with a condescending attitude. Rarely would they have an inkling that maybe they were the ones who had been left behind by time. It was similar to a pattern in the old days, in which only the elderly Chinese overseas showed much reverence for traditional Chinese values. Some students, after living abroad for some time, were less open-minded than the current generation of youth in China.

Another manifestation of the under-siege mentality was that students often confined their lives to a small circle of friends and activities.

Studying abroad could provide an opportunity for radically broadening a person's perspective on life. In fact, however, most students lived very confined lives. Frequently they lived in the same place for several years. On campus they met the same people, said the same things, and even bought the same merchandise from the same stores. During holidays the same families took turns hosting get-togethers. I spent several Christmases with the same people, but in different homes. The topics of conversation were the same as those of the previous year, except that the speakers could no longer remember what they had said the year before and the listeners did not recall that they had heard it before.

The monotony in life generated a void in spirit. For some students the things they were concerned about became increasingly trivial, such as where to get a bargain or who had been paid how much, and the most important issue in life was how to apply for a Green Card. Boredom also bred small talk, especially in the form of gossip between spouses of students. Sometimes even what happened in bedrooms, their own or others', became the subject of conversation.

Not all students were aware of the provincial character of their lives. American high-tech communication gave people a false sense of participation. When they turned on the television, world events, including those in China, would parade in front of them. This false sense of participation often made them overlook the chasm that separated them from the real world.

A third manifestation, and a fatal one, was that some students became intoxicated with feeling good about themselves. Because of the intense competition in securing an opportunity to study abroad, many people felt that realizing this goal in itself was a proud accomplishment. The large gap between East and West in science, technology, and culture was also taken by some students as a gap in worth between themselves and those still in China; they could scarcely hide their feelings of superiority.

This mentality led some students to live a mediocre life abroad while, at the same time, believing they were on a higher ethical ground. Hence, although they were trapped in extreme boredom, they were not aware of it. Some even tried to adopt the vulgarities of foreign culture, thinking these vulgarities were part of a refined and elegant foreign lifestyle. They were pleased to be small-city people in a foreign country.

Whether great men and women would emerge from this generation of Chinese students would be determined by many factors. But anyone who wishes to accomplish something, whether in or out of China, must have a progressive spirit. If the generation of students who had had dreams, embraced great aspirations, and endured enormous hardships in China all became tamed by comfortable housing and the abundance of food and were content with a life of mediocrity, it would be a great tragedy for the individual students as well as for the whole study-abroad program.

CHAPTER 6

Some Marriages Hold Together, Many Fall Apart

CONFUSED MEN

I met him on the first day of registration at the University of Michigan, on the lawn outside the library. It was sunny, and many students, dressed in T-shirts and shorts, were lying on the lawn and enjoying the warm sun. The semester would begin the next day.

He was sitting alone in the shade in a far corner of the lawn, staring blankly at the distant space. He seemed depressed.

He was wearing glasses and looked about thirty. The reserved style of his shirt and pants showed that he was from the mainland.

I walked over and asked him if he was from China. He looked at me with a start, then nodded. I said I had just come from China. Knowing that I was a new arrival, he appeared to relax a bit. He said he had been there for three months.

We chatted. He said he had come to visit his wife, who was studying for her Ph.D. He had graduated from Tsinghua University, class of 1982. His specialty was architecture, and he had been doing city planning for the Chinese Ministry of Construction.

"How is life treating you here?" I asked.

"Not bad," he said with a rather spirited voice. "I just received my work permit."

"Is it easy to find work?"

"You see those stores displaying the sign 'Help Wanted'? That means they are hiring. Just walk in and ask." He was trying to be helpful.

"Have you found work yet?"

"I tried several places. They need people with experience. I'm unseasoned, so I

haven't found work yet." Then he sighed, "But Americans have good manners. They're courteous."

"Perhaps it's easier to find work in a Chinese restaurant," I said.

"Not necessarily. I was going to work in a Chinese restaurant. We had already agreed on the wage. The owner called me, asking me to start working the next day. Then I asked one question too many. I asked if I could have Wednesday and Friday afternoons off so I could attend an English class. That made him angry. He said curtly, 'You're not qualified to discuss hours with me yet!' and slammed down the phone. These owners are really bastards!"

"What do you plan to do now?"

"I'll take time to look for work. I have to continue to sell myself, to see how much I'm worth." He appeared to be at a loss. "If I stay home, I either watch television or we get into a fight."

After a moment of silence, he suddenly blurted out, "In China I was on my way to being promoted to section chief."

We exchanged telephone numbers. I have not seen him since.

Other than revolution, there was nothing like going abroad that changed the social status of a Chinese so abruptly. And in that transformation, no other class of people were more vulnerable to feeling lost than were Chinese men. They had grown up in a traditional patriarchal society, and their dominant status within the family and in society had never been challenged. Many also belonged to an enviable social stratum. But as soon as they left China, their status began a free fall. Not only could they not adapt to the sudden change of social environment, but it was hard to bear the psychological impact of that abrupt change. In comparison, Chinese women, who had long been held back by various social constraints and hence had a less acute consciousness of social class, were more flexible in adapting to the transformation.

A man's loss of social status frequently marked the beginning of a loss of equilibrium in his marriage. Many marriages that had been viewed as perfect matches in China began to show fissures soon after the couple went to America. Some quickly broke up.

While in Beijing they were an enviable couple. He was studying the international Communist movement in the Department of Political Science, and she specialized in English. They entered college in 1979 and began to date in their sophomore year. At that time they studied together in the reading room, ate together in the cafeteria, and held hands publicly while strolling on campus. They were married after graduation. He was retained in the school as a Party secretary, and she went on to graduate school.

A year later she passed the screening examination given by the National Education Commission and won an opportunity to study in America with government funds. In 1988 she went to America to study English literature at a college in the Midwest. At the time of parting they were both feeling more excited than sad, indulging in the dream of a student life abroad. Half a year later, her husband joined her on a visitor visa.

Although they had been separated for only six months, each noticed that the other had changed. The husband felt that his wife, who had not liked social gatherings in China, had become fond of these occasions. She would attend all kinds of gatherings organized by American students and was usually one of the most lively people there. Holding a wine glass, she would chat with this person or hug that person. Her English was good and her appearance attractive, and so she was welcomed everywhere. "At that time, I didn't feel comfortable," her husband said later. At first he would go with her to these parties, but since he had only a limited command of English, he was often left alone, feeling like a fool. Later, he was no longer willing to go. She would not force him, and often on weekends she would be picked up and taken to parties without him.

The wife felt that the husband, who had been quite broad-minded in China, had suddenly become narrow-minded after coming to America. At times his pride was unreasonable. "If English was the problem, all he had to do was to be modest enough to study and practice," she complained later. "To bring him to a party was like you owed him something—he always had this long face," she said. The thing that irked her most was that after a year, not only had his English not improved, but he still did not know how to drive. She had asked several American students to teach him to drive, but because he felt embarrassed, he did not wish to learn.

At first the husband was unwilling to work. But he could neither attend school nor simply stay home and live on his wife's scholarship. So finally he agreed to work in a nearby Chinese restaurant. She believed that there was nothing disgraceful in manual labor in America, but he would not allow her to tell anybody. In letters or phone calls to their parents or schoolmates in China, he would say he was studying for the TOEFL *and would soon start attending school.*

Working in a Chinese restaurant was not always a happy experience. He would return home late at night, sighing. Busy with her schoolwork, she had neither the time nor the inclination to worry about him. They no longer argued as they had in the beginning, but they also had little dialogue on common concerns. Time passed blandly.

One day he came home early, at three o'clock in the afternoon, with one hand wrapped in gauze. He had cut his little finger while working. She immediately cleaned and dressed the wound. When she saw the deep cut and the blood-soaked gauze, she felt a stir inside.

He told her that he had accidentally cut his finger after three hours of slicing meat and that the blood had covered the chopping board. The owner found some gauze, wrapped up the wound, and sent him home. He was told not to return in the near future; in fact, he was dismissed.

As he was relating these events, he began to cry. For some inexplicable reason, the sight of a sobbing husband changed her budding sympathy into contempt. She later admitted that from that time on she despised him.

Soon afterward, in the heat of an argument, he slapped her. She moved out of the house.

"She was so heartless," was all he said afterward. The Chinese students at the university knew that she had an overly intimate relationship with a young American man.

"We were finished after he struck me," she said. "I had an American friend. He was very nice to me—at least he didn't hit me."

These overseas marital tragedies, heartbreaking for the Chinese men, were not rare occurrences. But one could not simply blame the women for being fickle.

Even when both parties preserved the personalities that they had in China, marriages changed in America because of the new social environment. As in a play, when the roles or the stage set changed, the plot had to change, too. In this change of roles and stage set, if the men lost status, the story would more likely end sadly.

Her husband had left China one year ahead of her. He went to Canada in 1988, to study English in a language school. She left China after the June Fourth Incident in 1989 and went to a Midwest college to study chemistry in a Ph.D. program. He was thirty-three, she was thirty-two, and they had been married for four years.

In the next three years, they both focused on getting him to America so they could reunite. But his visa application was turned down repeatedly by the American consulate in Canada. During those three years, she went to Canada several times. They also spent long hours on the telephone maintaining their long-distance love. Many times she cried over the phone because life was hard and she was lonely. Their monthly telephone bills often exceeded $500.

She believed that life would improve as soon as he came to America; the harsh life shared by two people would be far easier than that borne by herself alone.

In the summer of 1992 the American consulate, in a moment of compassion or carelessness, granted him the visa. When she heard the news over the phone, she wept. That was her happiest day since she had come to America. But the reunion was not as stirring as she had imagined. When she cast her first glance at her husband at the airport, she felt suddenly that they were strangers. However, she paid little attention to that feeling, thinking it would soon pass.

But the feeling remained. Her husband loved her and was as considerate of her as always. Also, as in the old days, he was full of optimism and loved to talk about politics and grand, unrealistic plans. However, she sensed now that something had gone wrong. Had he, or she, changed? Or was it simply the environment that was different?

After he settled down, he could not find his place in the new environment. His specialty was philosophy. He had done much work on the theory of construction and deconstruction, but nobody would pay for that knowledge. Nevertheless, he was not discouraged. He would talk one day about becoming a real-estate agent or car salesman and another day about taking the TOEFL *and* GRE.

They lived on her research assistantship. She worked in the laboratory while he stayed home preparing meals.

Her feeling that they were strangers became more acute over time. Sometimes while in the laboratory, she thought, Tonight I should be kind to him. On the way home, she would force herself to recall the care he had lovingly showered on her in the past, hoping to awaken a breath of warmth toward him in her heart. But as soon as she arrived home and saw him so completely occupied with cooking, that wisp of warmth simply vanished.

The familiar husband of the past increasingly became a stranger. Before, she had seen his disheveled hair as a sign of distinction; now it was just an unbearably filthy mess.

She no longer wished to tell him about her problems at work and had no desire to hear his series of grand plans. Sometimes, in bed, she did not even want him to touch her. She blamed herself for that; she knew her husband was a good person and loved her.

But she could no longer fool herself about her own feelings: she no longer loved him. One year later, she proposed a separation. He accepted on the condition that she not tell their friends and relatives in China about the breakup just yet.

Many factors contributed to the breakup of such marriages, but the most serious was the inability of the husband to provide financial support for the family. In a society in which money is the yardstick for measuring value in everything, a person who cannot support the family or even himself is considered worthless by others and begins to doubt his self-worth. When a man encounters setbacks in his career, a crisis often emerges in his marriage. Love alone is not sufficient to maintain a marriage. This was especially true for couples who encountered survival pressure abroad.

She worshiped her husband. For years, both of them had worked for an export company in Shanghai. At the age of thirty-three he suddenly decided to go abroad as a privately financed student. She was eight years younger and had doubts about abandoning their enviable work and fragmenting the cozy family that had taken them considerable effort to put together. But she believed in her husband. In 1987 he went to America and studied business administration at a college in Texas. A year later, she went to America as a visitor.

On the day after her arrival, her husband said she had to find work, as they would need the income for survival. She said nothing and that same day found a waitress job at a nearby Chinese restaurant. In the beginning the owner thought she was too fragile to carry heavy dishes. To convince the owner, she clenched her teeth and carried a heavy load.

The dish-carrying work lasted two-and-a-half years. She worked either from eleven o'clock A.M. to six P.M., or from six P.M. to eleven P.M. every day. She could no longer count the number of plates carried, the number of guests served, or the amount of tips brought home. After two years, he finally finished his MBA study. They both expected a sweet life to follow. She believed that he would soon find a good job.

The husband made job inquiries in some big corporations, but there was no reply. A year later he started mailing job applications to smaller companies, but that too failed to secure an interview. The disappointment led him to consider continuing his studies as a haven from the current financial storm. But all of the universities turned down his applications for financial support.

The husband lost self-confidence and gradually became bad tempered. He would fly into a rage for no obvious reason, and he suffered insomnia, tossing and turning in bed while complaining about the television noise across the hall or the snoring next door.

She still went to work every day, but no longer in the same state of mind. The hope that enabled her to endure the waitressing work had evaporated. One day she told him that she wanted to go back to school. The husband said, "What will we live on?" She said, "You go to work." He looked at her incredulously and said, "I've never thought of that as an option."

"It's your turn now," she said firmly.

Her husband refused to work in a restaurant. He was unwilling to concede that he could not find a job. Soon he became impotent. The marriage could not survive, and she finally proposed divorce.

In my few years in America I had witnessed and heard of many such sad endings of marriages. Sometimes I thought that perhaps the marriages would not have broken up had the couples remained in China. Of course, a marriage that endured was not necessarily happy. An overseas student faced a variety of pressures that did not exist in Chinese society, and each side had to rediscover, recognize, and learn to adapt to the other.

In my interviews with married couples, an interesting pattern caught my attention. In the first three months of their hard-earned reunion in America after a long separation, most couples had frequent domestic arguments. This was true whether it was the husband or the wife who had come to America first. To various extents the recovery of domestic peace depended on how well each side adapted to the changes in social environment. After three months or so, if the husband was the one who had come first, and if he was successful in his career or was otherwise able to support the family, the couple would quickly adapt to the new environment and the marriage could be maintained. On the other hand, if the wife had come first, had a more successful career, and was the principal financial supporter of the family, while the husband was slow to adapt to the new environment, the marriage most likely would break up.

Why was this so? A possible explanation is that Chinese men, consciously or unconsciously, continued to play their traditional male roles in the Chinese family and Chinese society even in America. When they failed in that role, the traditional foundation of marriage would crumble.

LIBERATED WOMEN

In 1988 a middle-aged Chinese scholar visited Europe as a member of a delegation. Being the only woman, though not the head of the delegation, she was treated with "ladies first" courtesy in Europe: people opened doors for her, carried her luggage, and brought chairs for her to sit on. After her return to China, she commented, "Now I know what it's like to be a woman!"

What moved this woman were the traditional Western customs now rejected by contemporary feminists. But her feeling of "what it's like to be a woman" had a ring of the awareness of modern womanhood.

Chinese revolutions had brought about the liberation of women in society: women had equal political, economic, and legal rights. But the revolutions did not bring them liberation in respect to their relationships with men. Women have continued to obey the rules of a male-dominated society and have played the roles demanded of them.

The younger generation of Chinese women became aware, soon after they went abroad to study, that they not only had to be daughter, wife, or mother, but they also had to learn to be a woman.

Among the Chinese students in the university, she was the one who attracted disparaging remarks. She was thirty years old, open-minded, and passionate. She had come to America in 1989 and worked as a laboratory technician at a medical school in the Midwest. The gossip about her first came from the family that shared an apartment with her. She had many male visitors. They were all Americans, mostly white and a few black. On weekends, she would be picked up and would not return until late at night.

She admitted that she had many boyfriends. "It's hard for a woman to live by herself. You always need help, here and there." She said as if to explain herself, "When other people treat you well, you can't just always turn them away."

She soon moved to her own apartment. She still had many boyfriends—some helped her move, some taught her to drive, and still others helped her shop. The gossip continued. She brought in male guests for overnight stays. She changed boyfriends frequently. She no longer bothered to defend herself with explanations. She said she was simply too lonely and had no desire to be a virtuous woman—why should she suffer for the sake of earning a good reputation?

People who knew her thought she was single, but word suddenly came out that she had a husband working as an editor in a publishing house in China. In fact, she had been married for many years and had been trying to get her husband to come over ever since she had arrived in America.

In the summer of 1991, two years after her own arrival, her husband received a visa to visit her. She drove to the airport to meet him. When they got home, her husband tried to embrace and caress her. But she pushed him away and said, "I've become used to living by myself—I'm not accustomed to this kind of thing." She then told him that there was food in the refrigerator and $100 on the table, she was not coming back that night, and she would return the next morning to teach him to drive. The husband, too stunned to say a word, was at a complete loss.

Early the next morning she returned to teach her husband to drive. She also told him that she had found work for him at a Chinese restaurant. During the driving practice, the husband tried again to be affectionate. Once more she pushed him away. "I think it's best that we separate," she said, "and after you settle down to go to school or get a student visa, we can get a divorce."

"What happened to you? I barely get here and you want a divorce!" He was annoyed and angry. "Do you have another man?"

"It's not because of that," she said.

Later she said that she had learned after she came to America what a pitiful woman she had been in the past. Even on her wedding day, she had not felt particularly fortunate. Perhaps she had married because she was already twenty-seven, or perhaps they had already had sex.

The marriage did not bring any great happiness. At first she did not want to have a baby, but her husband did and so did her in-laws. In the first year she had a daughter. She knew this disappointed her husband and in-laws, as he had said to her earlier that he would get down on his knees if she gave birth to a son. She also felt guilty about disappointing them, as her husband was the only child in his family.

Later she had two abortions. Each time she went to the hospital alone after fighting her way to get onto a crowded bus. Her husband said that he was too busy to accompany her.

"I've always lived for others, and now I want to live for myself," she said. "I don't regret being a woman. A woman can live just as happily." She said that her husband was not a bad person and she did not hate him. But it would be impossible for her to resume the old way of life with him. She had helped to get him out so that he could see the world outside. It was her final obligation as a wife.

The essence of the second liberation of Chinese women was a new consciousness about themselves. In fact, to a large extent, the self-consciousness they had held in the past was a result of the indoctrination they had received from the traditional, male-dominated society. They had accepted it without questioning.

"I've always regarded myself as a bad girl," she said. She was twenty-eight and studied at a college in Minnesota. In China she had been a medical student in Beijing but was expelled the year before graduation because the school discovered that she had kept a male student overnight in her dormitory. She said the expulsion humiliated her and gave her an inferiority complex. It seemed that her whole life was finished. "After I came to America, I began to realize that I really had not done anything disgraceful. Why should I believe others who think I'm bad?"

When Chinese women gradually understood that everything they had—including their thoughts, feelings, and bodies—belonged to themselves, and themselves alone, their attitude toward sex became more open.

A thirty-five-year-old student of American culture at a state university in California was near the completion of his Ph.D. program. He found out that it was just as hard to find a wife as to find a job, although finding a girlfriend was easy. "The Chinese girls here have all changed," he said. "Dating is okay. For some, going to bed or even living together is okay, too. But don't mention marriage. If you want to talk about marriage, you must find work or get a Green Card first. But they weren't that way when they were in China," he said. "There, they would guard their virginity during dating. But once they lost that, they wanted to be married to you under any circumstances."

In America it was Chinese men who felt lost. Chinese women lost only the traditional shackles, gaining greater freedom. Just like men, they wanted to taste all the enjoyment that life had to offer, including the one that had always been monopolized by men: sex.

A twenty-nine-year-old Chinese woman, studying in Sydney, Australia, wrote in a local Chinese magazine that as sex partners, Western men were far superior to Chinese because they were more considerate, more sensitive, and more eager to satisfy women's needs. This woman, who was once a journalist in Shanghai, said that eight out of ten Western men performed "outstandingly" in bed, and two were "so-so." As to Chinese men, about two out of ten could be classified as "so-so," and the rest were simply miserable. She said her conclusion was based on her own experience and that of her friends; she first married an Australian, and later, after separating, she had a French boyfriend. The article caused a great uproar in the Chinese community in Sydney. The magazine received numerous letters of protest. Later, angry male readers held a rally that drew a crowd of about five hundred. Among the many criticisms of the author was that she "lacked patriotic spirit."[1]

Those who liked her said she was so natural and always at ease, and those who despised her labeled her a national disgrace. But she paid little attention to what other people said about her. She just wanted to enjoy her life. She was thirty-five, had come to America in 1989, and studied education at a college in Washington, D.C. She had divorced her husband in China after coming to America. She was good-looking and attracted many suitors but was in no hurry to remarry. She wanted to hold on tightly to the freedom of the single life. She did not hide her feelings. She said privately that in the past she did not understand sex; she only understood it after coming to America. Sometimes she would say flauntingly, "American men are really great—the feeling is just not the same with Chinese men." When asked whether she was afraid of contracting AIDS, she answered readily, "Just let them wear condoms!"

Feminine consciousness in Chinese women soared rapidly after they went abroad. This was not simply because of the influence of Western culture and the change in social environment. More important, it was because they had become financially independent. That independence enabled them to be the masters of their own destiny. Women who completed their studies, found work, and lived by themselves often had more difficulty enduring a defective marriage and were more courageous in pursuing love. In contrast, those who relied on their husbands or went as companions to their student husbands and hence were unable to survive independently often had to retreat to the home to play a female role that was even more traditional than in China.

THE MARRIAGE SURVIVAL TEST

Sometimes the life of a student studying abroad was like a survival test for a marriage. The marriage, placed in a new social environment, was subject to the intense hammering of ideology, money, culture, and perspectives on sex. Numerous sad partings and happy unions came out of this survival test. These stories—some sad, some happy, and some ordinary—were filled with the joys and sorrows of life.

At thirty-six she had gone to America from Nanjing in 1986 and received a master's degree in education from a college in Seattle. Her relationship with her husband turned sour a year after they arrived in America. The principal reason, according to her, was that her husband had become overly intimate with a woman from Beijing. One day upon returning home, she heard a telephone message left by that woman for her husband. It began with "We . . ."

Both had been teachers at a high school in Nanjing. She taught literature, and he, physics. In graduate school her father was his adviser, and he courted her for three years. They got married after graduation, and because of the marriage he was retained in the school instead of being assigned to his hometown in Henan. One year after the wedding, she gave birth to a boy.

"He was so considerate then," she commented about her husband at that time. "He would do anything for me."

In 1988 her husband went to a college in California as a government-sponsored visiting scholar. Soon afterward, with the help of an American professor, he changed his status to that of a regular student. A year and a half later she and her two-year-old son went to visit him.

As soon as they arrived she felt that his manners were no longer the same. "Probably he felt that he now had financial resources. He had income, helped me to leave China, and supported me when I went to graduate school. Also, he was a doctoral student and wouldn't have trouble finding a job and getting a Green Card." Not long after, the other woman appeared on the scene.

They got into frequent fights. The wife said she could not take the bullying. A year later, she went back to China with her son. There was no formal divorce proceeding, but both sides understood that it was just a matter of time.

Half a year later, the husband was diagnosed with lymphatic cancer that was spreading rapidly. He could not afford treatment at an American hospital. Because he could not work, the medical coverage in his research assistantship no longer covered him. He asked to be sent back to China. He did not wish to wait in America for the coming of death and to die there. His family made arrangements for him to be treated at a hospital in Shanghai. He was carried to the airplane and could barely breathe when he reached Shanghai.

His wife and son came from Nanjing to see him for the last time. "Seeing him in that state, I no longer hated him. He loved the boy very much. He said the money he had saved could be used for his education. Neither of us mentioned divorce," she said. He died a few days later.

A thirty-four-year-old man from Wuhan went to America in 1987 as a Ph.D. student in computer science at a college in St. Louis.

Four years later, on the evening that he passed his doctoral qualifying examination, his wife told him she wanted a divorce. That evening he had plans to take her out to dinner at a good Chinese restaurant to celebrate. She wanted something different. She said, "I've been wanting to tell you for a long time, but I put it off until today so as not to disturb your preparation for the examination."

"Why?" he asked.

"I love somebody else now," she replied.

At that time they were both Ph.D. students. She was also thirty when she went to America, first as a visitor and then as a student half a year later. She studied Western art history at the same school.

Their marriage never seemed to have problems. Their parents were friends, and they had known each other since childhood. Although they went to different colleges, they "fell in love" with the approval of their parents. In those days they studied together whenever possible. Often they discussed their characters and helped each other to improve. The marriage, which came at a later date, was also natural, although she had jokingly complained that the courtship was bland and lacked passion.

He did not know when she met the other man. The husband worked day and night in the laboratory, writing computer programs and preparing manuscripts. Often he would return home at two or three o'clock in the morning. After eating whatever he could find in the refrigerator, he fell into bed and slept until noon. By that time she had already left for class. When she returned home in the afternoon, he had already left for the laboratory.

He heard later from a friend of hers that she met the man at a dance organized by the Chinese students on campus. The other man was rather well known among the Chinese students at the college. He had come to America in the early eighties. First he studied in Arizona. After two years he dropped out of school for unknown reasons. Later he married an American but got divorced two years later. After that, he came to St. Louis but not as a student. At first he was a street vendor selling Chinese paintings, calligraphy, and Chairman Mao pins. Later he worked as a manager at a Chinese restaurant.

The wife told her girlfriend that she was depressed but felt energized in the presence of the other man. The man told her that he would soon start his own business and it was going to be a smashing success. He made an all-out effort to woo her, and it was indeed a success. She said that the man made her feel for the first time that she was loved as a woman.

The divorce caused a sensation among the local Chinese students.

At first the husband would not agree to the divorce. During one fight he was so upset that he slapped her. When her boyfriend heard of this, he called the police. When the siren of the police patrol car was heard outside their apartment building, the neighbors thought there had been a homicide. Finally the husband gave in. Two years later he graduated, left school, and found work at a computer company in San Francisco. His life became more settled. He bought a new car and then a house. But he did not remarry.

Her passionate love of the other man did not last long. Her boyfriend, though he talked about grand business plans and big money, could not even hold on to his job at the restaurant. In the days that followed, when he could not find work to support her, they began to quarrel. Later he simply walked out, claiming that he was going to start some big business in New York City. No one heard news of him after that, and she was soon liberated from her romantic fervor.

One day three years later, her former husband called her from San Francisco, saying that his parents, her former parents-in-law, were coming to America for a visit and he hoped she would help entertain them. Not wishing to worry their parents or cause friction between the two elderly couples, who had been lifelong friends, they had never told their parents about the divorce. She agreed to come.

In San Francisco she cooked for her "parents-in-law," giving welcoming banquets, and drove them around for sightseeing. The happy old couple ceaselessly praised their virtuous "daughter-in-law." Soon afterward she did become the capable and virtuous daughter-in-law, for after the elderly couple left, her ex-husband called and asked her to come back. They remarried. Of course, there was no need to tell the old folks back home.

She was thirty-three, a graduate of the foreign-language department of a prestigious university in Beijing. In 1988 she and her husband had gone to America as government-sponsored students and studied at a university in the West. She was a visiting scholar studying English, and he, comparative literature. At first she hoped that her husband, who already had a decent reputation in China, would soar to great heights so that they could stay in America. But after two years she became disillusioned. She realized that it was even questionable whether he could find any sort of job after he finished his Ph.D. studies, to say nothing about getting a Green Card. And even with a Green Card, their life would be very tight.

At that time she met the owner of a Chinese restaurant, a man who was also from China. He was thirty-eight, from Zhejiang, short in stature and ordinary in appearance. He had immigrated to America in 1982, and within a few years he had opened two Chinese restaurants and his wife had given birth to four children. He had worked as a disk jockey in China and, after coming to America, acquired a taste for karaoke singing. On weekends his pastime was singing popular songs from Taiwan and Hong Kong with his not-so-great voice.

She and the owner met during one of these karaoke performances. The restaurant owner had never been to Beijing, but he left no stone unturned in wooing this young woman from Beijing. He invited her for dinner, gave her jewelry, and finally bought her a house. It was the house that moved her heart. She divorced her husband, moved into the house, and became a not-so-covert mistress. Then one day the restaurant owner's wife learned of the relationship. She charged into the house with her four children, some big and tall and some quite small . . .

She was a twenty-three-year-old from Hangzhou who had left China in 1989 to study at a language school in Toronto. She went to Canada ostensibly to study, but actually to use Canada as a stepping stone to America. Her husband was a Ph.D. student in electrical engineering at a college in Detroit. She wanted badly to be with him but could not obtain an American visa.

She went to classes during the day and worked as a waitress in a Chinese restaurant in the evening. At night she would often cry in bed. Her whole life was supported by a single hope: to be reunited with her husband in America, but twice the American consul turned down her visa application.

It was at that time that she met him. He was twenty-five, from Shenyang, and also worked in the restaurant. He had come to Toronto six months after her arrival and was also studying English at a language school. His dream was not to go to a university to earn a Ph.D., but to own a Chinese restaurant in Toronto's Chinatown.

He cared for her. He helped her carry heavy plates at work, took her home late at night, and drove her shopping in his car. They began to chat over the phone. At first it was only a brief conversation every few days, but gradually it became several phone calls a day. Sometimes the calls lasted for hours. She felt she was becoming increasingly attached to him. Finally, she seemed to fall incurably in love with him. One night, he stayed at her place.

She felt guilty about having let her husband down, so she tried even harder to get an American visa. Each time she went to the American consulate, her boyfriend accompanied her. In the summer of 1991 the visa finally came. She could finally leave her waitressing job and be reunited with her husband.

Before their parting, they cried together. They vowed never to contact each other again; the parting was forever. She flew to America. A month later, she called him. Several days later, she called again. Three months later, she left her thesis-writing husband and flew back to Canada.

He was twenty-five years old, from Beijing, and had gone with his wife to America in 1990 to study American history at a college in Tennessee.

It was very hard the first year. Since he was on his own, he had to earn money to pay his living expenses in spite of the presidential scholarship that covered his tuition. Every weekend he worked at odd jobs: cleaning, mowing lawns, or cooking. His wife took care of a two-year-old child in an American household. They muddled through their first year.

He set his hopes on the long summer. The school session would finish near the end of April and the next would not begin until early September. He hoped the four-month summer would allow him to earn enough money to cover the next year's expenses. But there were few work opportunities in that small city. It took only five minutes to walk along the main street from end to end. There was only one Chinese restaurant, owned by a Vietnamese. So he decided to go to New York City. There were so many Chinese restaurants in New York's Chinatown; the opportunity for finding work would be far better.

He left his wife in Tennessee. But before his departure he found a domestic-help job for her by means of an ad in the local newspaper. The monthly pay, after food and lodging, was $800. The man of the house was between forty and fifty. He was gentle, polite, and friendly, and worked in an insurance company. At their first meeting, he took the Chinese couple for a ride in his Mercedes Benz. That evening they were his dinner guests in a restaurant. The woman of the house was bedridden, and the Chinese wife's principal duty was caring for her.

After a month in New York and several job changes, the husband found a fairly decent job in a Chinese restaurant. He called his wife once a week. She told him that everything was fine, and there was nothing to worry about. A little more than a month later, he received a call from her. She said that the woman of the house had died and the man of the house asked her to stay a little longer. She estimated that she could work until her husband returned from New York.

In New York, he worked as hard as he could, saving nearly $4,000 in three months, after living expenses. At that rate, in another month he would have saved a total of $5,000. That was his aim. However, about two weeks before his return, he received another call from his wife. She said, "I'm sorry. I want a divorce." He was dumbfounded and asked for an explanation. She told him that the man of the house had asked her to marry him. He bought a plane ticket and flew to Tennessee.

He could hardly recognize his wife when he saw her. Gone were the unattractive clothes she had brought over from China; they were replaced by a stylish, well-tailored, high-quality Western suit. The poor Beijing girl had been suddenly transformed into the woman of the house. The man of the house still welcomed the Chinese husband warmly. He also took him aside for a man-to-man talk. He said he regretted that things had turned out this way, but he was not going to apologize for what had happened. After all, in the battlefield of love, like the battlefield of war, there were losers as well as winners. The husband said nothing. He bought a plane ticket and returned to New York.

MIXED MARRIAGE: TWO DIFFERENT PERSPECTIVES

It was like a modern version of "Cinderella."

Time: summer of 1989. Place: Tokyo. An American man who had come to Japan for business discussions was having lunch in a restaurant. One of the waitresses caught his attention. She had a delicate face and a soft voice, and was the only waitress who could speak English. He sought her out for a talk and learned that she was a professional ballet dancer from Shanghai and had come to Japan in 1989 as a privately financed student. Now she was studying Japanese at a language school and worked in the restaurant for her tuition and living expenses.

After dining several times at the restaurant, the American asked her if she would be willing to go to America with him. From that day on they began their "Tokyo love." A week later the American concluded his business in Japan. At parting he promised he would return in three months to take her to America. Three months later he returned. He brought with him a ring and proposed marriage. He was neither a charlatan nor a drifter; he was the chief executive of an American high-tech corporation. So he took her to America.

And then? Probably like the ending of all fairy tales, "they lived happily ever after."

This children's tale of a wealthy hero of the West who rescued a poverty-stricken beauty of the East is true. An interview with our hero was reported in a well-known business newspaper in America. Hollywood has yet to write a screen version of the story, an East-West version of the box-office success *Pretty Woman.*

More than a decade ago, when China was just opening up to the outside world, the marriage of a Chinese to a foreigner was a fashionable but risky business. An incident that started when a woman painter of the Xinxin school planned to marry a French diplomat evolved into a diplomatic dispute with political overtones. Toward the end of 1983 the issue of mixed marriage was discussed in a memorandum from the Ministry of Education. The proposed solution was to discourage it by letting it slide or to encourage dissolution.

A thirty-six-year-old Chinese student at the University of Hawaii said that there were considerable disquieting comments in the Chinese-student circle when she and her husband-to-be were courting in the community kitchen of the dormitory while preparing meals. At that time, marrying a foreigner, although not regarded as an act of political betrayal, was still regarded as showing a lack of patriotic sentiment. "If I could have found a husband in Beijing, I would have been married long ago—there wouldn't have been any need for me to travel all this distance to find one here," she angrily defended herself. In China she had never met the right person. She was then over thirty and single, falling into the category of "advanced-age female youth" in her work unit.

As more students went abroad, mixed marriages became more common. Today very few people regard it as a political act, and most consider it a personal choice. People have begun to accept mixed marriages that result from mutual attraction.

Distinct from the blind or the calculating lightning-speed "multinational" marriages, mixed marriages are generally based on deeper mutual understanding. But in reality mixed marriages did not play out in the form of "the Western hero rescuing the Eastern beauty" and, also unlike fairy tales, they usually did not have happy endings.

"Sometimes it is lonely to be in a mixed marriage," the thirty-eight-year-old Chinese wife of an American professor said. Even in the nineties she was often reluctant to attend gatherings in the homes of her husband's colleagues. Very rarely was she interested in the subjects they discussed so enthusiastically. And she seldom invited Chinese friends to her home. As for her husband, aside from the Great Wall and the giant panda, he knew next to nothing about China. When she chatted with her Chinese friends, he sat by himself and read the newspaper. She had come from Shanghai and was once a top student of Fudan University. She went to America in 1984 and studied anthropology at a university in New England. Two years later she married a chemistry professor who was divorced and twenty years her senior, and she became the step-mother of two children from his previous marriage. She dropped her Ph.D. studies. What comforted her was that she no longer needed to work in a Chinese restaurant like many others, or to worry about next year's tuition, as she would have had she remained unmarried and in school. Being a professor, he had an excellent, though not extraordinary, income. She opened a little store in the city, selling Chinese arts and crafts. They had a four-bedroom house with a backyard. Every day, when she was not chauffeuring the two children to kindergarten or looking after her small store, she spent time in the backyard. There she planted vegetables. She said, "As long as I'm busy, I'm happy."

"It was I who proposed the divorce," a recently divorced thirty-nine-year-old Ph.D. student said. "He was utterly unreliable." She had come to America in 1984 and studied comparative literature at a university in Virginia. She met her Irish American husband on campus. At that time they both were attending a class on British and American poetry, studying Yeats, Eliot, and Pound. He was warm, friendly, and imaginative. Besides literature, he liked unusual things, such as the cannibalistic fish of Africa and posters of Western movies. One day he told her he would like to learn Chinese and asked if she would be willing to teach him. Thus they began dating, then lived together, and finally got married. The crisis in their marriage

began with his graduation. Since his field was comparative literature, he could not find a job, so they relied on her income as a teaching assistant. Sometimes they could not pay the rent. But the husband was as carefree as usual and spent his days in coffee houses. "He never gave an iota of thought to supporting the family," she said. "All I could do was leave him."

Every mixed marriage with a crisis brewing, like any other marriage, had its own specific problems. Sometimes the problems arose from lack of communication of what the spouses thought and felt, and sometimes from lack of money. But all mixed marriages faced common problems: differences in living habits and cultural concepts.

These differences were often revealed in minor things.

A thirty-six-year-old student who married an American China scholar said she was very much annoyed by the American custom of gift-giving at Christmas. Each Christmas she had to prepare presents for each member of her husband's family. First was the shopping, then the wrapping. It was not only expensive and time consuming but mentally exhausting as well. The most ludicrous aspect of the custom was going around and asking the receivers what they would like or needed so that the gift would be well received. Then when one delivered the gift, the receiver feigned surprise when opening the package. On his part, her husband found it hard to understand why she had to boil milk before drinking it and why she heated cooking oil to a sizzling temperature before stir-frying the vegetables.[2] *He regarded these as acts of barbarism.*

Frequently the marriages stumbled on small differences.

A thirty-eight-year-old student from Tianjin, after finishing her study in Massachusetts, married an American engineer who worked for a local electrical appliance company. Married life was not bad. They bought a new car and a house and were planning to have a baby. But one day her husband abruptly and firmly announced that he wanted a divorce. She was at a loss and only later she understood that he had found out that she had kept some "personal money" (sifangqian).[3] *To her, this was a custom frequently practiced by married women in Asia. But to her American husband it was an unforgivable act of dishonesty. They planned a divorce after a three-month separation.*

The differences in attitudes toward marriage were far more serious than those in living habits and cultural concepts. However, it was often only at the breakup of the marriage that the two sides realized that differences existed.

In the tradition of the East, marriage is a union of a man and a woman in totality. One partner bears a moral responsibility should any change in the marital relation occur. In today's Western concept, marriage simply allows a man and a woman to establish a stable, mutually independent companionship. The termination of a marriage "contract" caused by the change of one party is both natural and reasonable.

Thus in a Western marriage, even though the partners vow to love each other "in sickness and in health, for richer or poorer . . . ," the concept of marriage that an Eastern woman holds—"from now on, I am your woman"—was not appreciated in many of these mixed marriages. The older generation of overseas Chinese often tried to convince the younger generation never to marry a foreigner, because a foreigner was unreliable; a Chinese would be more reliable.

A twenty-eight-year-old Chinese woman who was studying in New York said she had never even dreamed that her American husband would want a divorce after a year of marriage. She asked him why.

He said, "I don't love you any more."

She pressed on: "But you always said you loved me."

He said, "Yes, I loved you before, but I don't love you now."

"How can you be like that?!" she said furiously. "How can you say 'I love you' yesterday and 'I don't love you' today?!"

To her this was simply dishonest. Her American husband had his own philosophy. He loved her then and hence married her; he did not love her now and hence wanted a divorce. He was totally sincere. "Life is short. Why torture yourself when there is no reason to keep the marriage?" he said.

In mixed marriages, conflicting concepts of marriage brought setbacks and dashed hopes to Chinese women. It also made Chinese men bitter.

For a long time he had had a hunch that his American wife would finally leave him. He felt this as soon as he set foot in America, but he never thought that the relationship would become so awkward.

Their love and marriage were quite romantic. They had met on their way to the scenic Jiuzhai Valley (Jiuzhaigou) in Sichuan. At that time he worked as a photographer for a newspaper, and his work had just won a national award. He also published poetry and exhibited his paintings; his friends said he was gifted. She had come to China to study Chinese at Peking University. The bus ride from Chengdu to Jiuzhaigou lasted two and a half days, and they were seated next to each other the whole time. The rickety bus ride was filled with adventure as well as laughter. After visiting Jiuzhaigou, they took a cruise down the Yangzi River, stopping for sightseeing at the Three Gorges, which would eventually be partially submerged under a reservoir behind a dam. They parted in Wuhan. Half a year later they got married. In August 1989 they went to America together.

At that time he was twenty-nine and she was thirty-one.

In America she entered a college in Boston, studying for an MBA while he could get into only a language school to study English. But to him, Chinese politics was more important, or perhaps more interesting, than English. During the first year, every day he hungrily pored through all of the local Chinese newspapers and magazines for bits and pieces of news about China, or engaged in impassioned discussions with other Chinese students about China's future. Sometimes he went to New York City or Washington, D.C., to attend meetings about politics in China.

She advised him not to go to these meetings too often but to spend more time studying English or looking for work.

But he was not interested in a mundane life. He wanted to write a book about politics in China. He claimed that its publication would cause a sensation. But even with her help, he could not find an interested publisher. He said that later he would return to photography for newspapers and magazines, but when he did so, no one was interested in what he had to offer.

He admitted that it was the most difficult period in his life. But he believed that he would succeed, and he hoped his wife would understand and support him. Unexpectedly, it was at this time that she proposed a divorce. After the shock, he refused to move out. She told him calmly that the apartment was rented from the university under her name and, if he did not move out, she would call the police. So he moved out.

During the separation, he hoped that she would change her mind. He called her repeatedly, but she would not answer. One night he sat outside her apartment, waiting for her to return from the library. A few days later, the police knocked on his door. They politely warned him that he should not continue to harass his wife.

He was both angry and worried. He went to see her adviser, hoping the professor would help to mediate. But this Chinese-style maneuver only made his wife more furious. She screamed at him, "I'm so ashamed of you!"

Three months later he received the divorce document mailed by the court. Since they did not have children or property, the procedure was fairly simple: all he had to do was sign it. If he did not agree with the divorce, he could contest the proceedings within sixty days.

He signed it.

"I felt bad for him. But this kind of marriage could lead nowhere," his wife said later. "He didn't understand—he always believed there was another man." She also said that after graduation she would go to law school. In that situation, there was no way that she could be encumbered by such a marriage.

"I don't want to say that we should not have married. I really loved him then," she said. "I hope in the future he'll find a more suitable, Chinese girl."

THE GREEN CARD MARRIAGE

Among the Chinese students, some marriages were undertaken as a means to gain legitimate status for staying in America or for earning a living.

For Chinese who wished to stay abroad for a prolonged period, the most critical need was a permanent-resident permit that would allow them to work and live abroad. In America, this permit is called a Green Card. There were many avenues for getting a Green Card. You could apply for political asylum by declaring that you had advocated democracy and human rights in Tiananmen Square during the June Fourth period; that you were an intimate friend of the Dalai Lama; or that you suffered political persecution by the government because you wished to have a third child. In addition, you could apply as an immigrant through family ties if you had a close relative who was an American citizen, or as an "immigrant investor" if you had $1 million in your pocket. Of course, there was also the arduous but not impossible route of becoming a working immigrant. If you choose this route, you would find a job after graduation, change to an H-1 visa, complete a series of complicated paperwork, pay a lawyer several thousand dollars, and wait patiently for two or three years. You would be able to get a Green Card.

But the fastest route was marriage.

He was forty-four years old, a visiting scholar who had come to study in a university in southern California in the early eighties. In his second year he rather abruptly married a twice-divorced American woman with three children. Because of that, he did not have to return to China.

After the marriage he never permitted his Chinese friends to meet his wife. On the contrary, he purposely distanced himself from them and rarely attended functions organized by the students.

His marriage quickly aroused numerous comments in the small circle of Chinese students: the two just did not look like a good match. At the time of the marriage he was over thirty and skinny, and his wife was over forty, tall, and plump. Furthermore, in the early eighties, most Chinese students were narrow-minded and felt strange about this Green-Card marriage.

The Chinese students learned later that there was a contract between the couple: the marriage would be valid for five years, after which either party could initiate divorce proceedings. During that period, he would be expected to receive his Green Card, and she would have a husband to care for her children and to be a companion.

But after five years they did not divorce. He told his friends later that he found her a nice person.

To earn a living overseas, the Chinese relied on their brains and their hands. Marriage was probably the only other available means.

Of course, marriage was only a means of last resort.

She was from Beijing, where she had been a technician in a factory. At the age of twenty-five she went as a privately financed student studying chemistry to a college in the Northeast. In the first year she was lonely. She wrote nearly every day to her boyfriend in Beijing and asked him to hurry up and come over. But his visa application was denied three times. In the second year her pitifully small scholarship was terminated, and she was not only lonely but also poor. So she began to work in a Chinese restaurant. She worked four days a week and earned enough to pay her rent. Meanwhile, she fell behind in her schoolwork. At the end of her second year, she felt she could no longer endure the hardship. She could see only two options: stay in America and work illegally, or drop out of school and return to China. She did not desire either option. Finally she chose a third one: get married.

She married a Vietnamese American. He was a refugee who had come to America after the Vietnam War and now owned a small grocery store just off-campus. His wife had died two years before.

No matter how one looked at it, all her problems, from her livelihood to a Green Card, were solved at once.

Several months later, her boyfriend in Beijing received the last letter from her, asking for forgiveness. The young man thought his sweetheart had become a fickle woman who caved in to the temptation of money.

In using marriage as a means to an end, Chinese women enjoyed a far greater advantage than Chinese men. Many Western men held a traditional romantic fixation on Asian women, thinking them beautiful and sexy. And they also naively believed that women of the East were tender and docile.

Thus there appeared spouse-seeking advertisements in Chinese newspapers in America: "White American genuinely seeks beautiful and sincere Chinese woman as friend and wife. Age should be between twenty-five and forty-five. Some English proficiency required."

Chinese women also initiated advertisements seeking husbands: "Chinese lady, thirty-three, with attractive appearance, gentle disposition, and a good heart, seeks a sincere and reliable man with U.S. citizenship or the Card as a companion: friendship first and marriage later."

Many Chinese women, soon after they started studying in a foreign country, would disappear from the campus. Further inquiries would most likely lead to the discovery that they had married a foreign husband. They were mocked as studying for the "Mrs." degree.

In this game of Green-Card marriage, sometimes men and women enjoyed equal opportunities.

After the June Fourth Incident, both the Canadian and the American governments gave Green Card privileges to many Chinese students under the pretext of protecting them. Unexpectedly, those Green Cards quickly created a paper-marriage market between the protected and the unprotected: the protected man or woman owned a Card and accepted bids, whereas the unprotected man or woman desired a Card and made offers. I found out that the going price in 1993 for a paper marriage was between $15,000 and $25,000. Besides, it was said by participants, because we were all from the mainland and had all received some education, the sale price was clearly marked; there was no deception, whether the customer was a man or a woman.

CHAPTER 7

Emotional Attachment to China

FLUCTUATING PATRIOTIC SENTIMENT

Chinese students who had lived abroad for a long time could dress in a different style, acquire different manners and living habits, use a different language, obtain a name different from that given by their parents, and even alter their nationality, but just as they could not alter the color of their skin, they could not change their consciousness of being Chinese.

In this generation of Chinese students, such consciousness was not simply something acquired since birth but was cast deeply into their psyches by a lifetime of upheaval and suffering. China, no matter how remote in distance and time, or whether it incited fury or love, would always be the land that would raise surging waves of emotion in the heart.

She was twenty-nine, a graduate of the foreign-language department of a key university in Beijing. She had gone to America in 1987, to study advertising at a college near Boston. After being there only a short while, she declared, "I really want to be an American!" She did not mean the Green-Card kind of American, but an American who spoke unaccented English, was courteous and respectful of others, and enjoyed life to the best of her ability. She spoke English fluently and was capable of using the latest fashionable words and phrases. She also acquired American manners, such as hugging to show affection. She liked to tell others that she had met some rich Americans, visited their homes, and learned the yuppie lifestyle. But she became upset one day when several American colleagues talked disparagingly about China during lunch. "I was furious," she said. "What do they know about China?!"

A visiting scholar more than fifty years old who was studying international relations at the University of Michigan told me the following episode. One day during lunch he was heating some salted fish in the microwave oven in the office, and the strong fish smell soon filled the room. His American colleagues, pinching their noses, said, "Smells good. What is it?" In embarrassment, he said hurriedly, "Japanese salted fish! Japanese salted fish!" He explained that he had lied because he did not wish any foreigner to have a bad impression about China, not even Chinese food, even though at that time he had terrible misgivings about China and was in no hurry to return to China to show his patriotism.

Ordinarily, patriotic sentiment had little opportunity to surface, because life was filled with the pressures of schoolwork, earning a living, and loneliness. But when reacting to events in which China was heavily involved, that emotion would suddenly erupt.

At about six o'clock in the evening on September 23, 1993, news began to spread that China had lost its bid to host the 2000 Summer Olympics. Impassioned comments immediately appeared in the Chinese-student e-mail network at the University of Michigan:

One student wrote, "Just heard that the last roll call was Sydney 45, Beijing 43."

Another one wrote, "I don't want to see this. Why didn't Beijing make it? It's because some Western countries are scared to death of a strong China!"

Someone continued, "This is a slap in the face of the 1.2 billion Chinese and 50 million overseas Chinese! Chinese all over the world, unite! No matter what kind of competition or the location of the contest, the twenty-first century will be ours!"

Someone else wrote, "I feel more strongly than ever that I will return to China, to contribute all I have to build a better China."

There were many other such examples.

In the spring of 1983 the Clean Up Spiritual Pollution Campaign began in China. The Chinese students at many American universities wrote collectively to the Chinese government, expressing their concern.

In early 1987 Hu Yaobang resigned from his post as secretary-general of the Chinese Communist Party. The Chinese students again wrote to express their concern.

On June 4, 1989, the Tiananmen Square Incident erupted. Chinese students all over the world, regardless of whether they had any interest in China's politics, all reacted strongly.

In the summer of 1992 a disastrous flood struck several southern provinces and cities in China. Chinese students in America and other countries organized a network for raising relief funds; many students donated their hard-earned money to help people in the affected area.

It was hard to believe that life abroad in fact could easily nurture an emotional attachment to China. Often, being abroad was far more effective than the education in patriotism one received in China. Even those who had felt little patriotism while in China gradually developed an emotional attachment to their homeland. And, like many other overseas Chinese, the older they got, the stronger the attachment. The reason was quite simple: the status of overseas Chinese was closely tied to China's image in the world. But the patriotic enthusiasm of Chinese students, like mercury in a thermometer, could go up or down. The fluctuation was actually regulated by some fairly simple rules.

First, the more abstract the motherland, the easier it was to love. As the motherland became more real, it became harder to love.

After one had lived abroad for a few years, the motherland somehow became sanctified and a supporting life force: a belief, a place to belong to, a meaning for life. But these abstract images of a sacred motherland would quickly evaporate when the motherland became a reality, such as when one applied for a new passport or for passport renewal at the consulate office, or when one wrote to one's old work unit for a certain supporting document.

A thirty-five-year-old Ph.D. candidate studying automation at the University of Michigan expressed this profound ambivalence well. He had come to America in 1986 as a visiting scholar. A year later he was awarded a scholarship, and he wished to change his status to "student" so as to continue his study in America. He first wrote to his old work unit, requesting instruction. The work unit ignored his letter. But after he had completed all the paperwork on this side of the Pacific Ocean, the work unit suddenly expressed its disapproval and reported his case to the National Education Commission. The work unit penalized him, and the Commission circulated a notice criticizing him. Later, his wife, who worked in the same unit, met with all kinds of obstruction when she applied for permission to visit him. He became agitated whenever he talked about the episode. His summary of the experience was "Motherland is at its best when you have nothing to do with it."

The second rule was that the farther away the motherland was, the easier it was to love; once it got too close, it became awfully hard to love.

After living abroad for a long time, one's impressions of the motherland gradually became cleansed: the unpleasant experiences of the past slowly faded, while old scenes gradually transformed into pleasant memories. But when high-spirited students returned to their motherland after living abroad for a long time, they were quickly reminded of the state of the nation by the unique professional manner of Chinese frontier guards and customs and health inspectors. The heightened enthusiasm of many students was chilled even before they left the airport. After a flight of dozens of hours, the first thing these tired students had to do, regardless of whether they were returning to work or for a short family visit, was to pay $15 to $30, or ¥150 to ¥180 of *renminbi* (the fee in Beijing, Shanghai, and some cities in Guangdong seemed to be different) for an on-the-spot AIDS blood test. The so-called test required having one's finger pricked, and the result was available within ten minutes. Its speed made one doubt whether the dollars or the *renminbi* were well spent. What really seemed unfair was that foreigners and Green Card holders were exempt from this treatment; they could walk into China without any test.

A forty-year-old Ph.D. student, after studying economics in a college in New York for ten years, was emotionally very stirred to be returning to China. He did not expect that, immediately after landing, the motherland would want his money and his blood. His enthusiasm was chilled. He vowed then never to return again.

Third, the rise and fall of patriotic sentiment was directly related to how well the Chinese were doing in America.

A thirty-nine-year-old chemistry student at a college in Mississippi once complained that he did not like America, especially the particular small town he lived in, because nothing ever happened there, and the weather was simply too hot. He said he would go back to China; there, whatever he would do would be meaningful. Besides, his daughter was almost seven years old, and her education would be a real problem. The schools in America were cause for concern, as kids became sexually active at a tender age, and teenage girls even became pregnant. At that time he was in his third year of thesis writing, and he did not want to graduate, because he could not find work. After another year and a half, he found a job with a small company in a nearby city. He no longer mentioned to acquaintances his wish to return. Instead, he would ask them, "How are things? Have you applied for a Green Card yet? We're working on it."

Different job prospects after graduation and adaptability to American society resulted in different patriotic sentiments. Generally speaking, the sentiment was stronger in visiting scholars than in degree students; stronger in humanities students than in natural-science students; stronger in science students than in engineering students; stronger in those with low English proficiency than in those with a good command of English; stronger in those without work than in those with work; stronger in men than in women; and stronger in older people than in younger people. Of course, these are just my personal impressions, and they should absolutely not be taken as a result of statistical data analysis.

For these reasons, this generation of students had often been criticized for being overly practical, almost to the point of selfishness.

Certainly, these students, who were Chinese by birth, probably would never be able to eradicate their consciousness of being Chinese. But under the prolonged nurturing of Western education and culture, most had already accepted the concept of a contractual relationship between an individual and the state about privileges and obligations. The traditional patriotism of the East, which called for unconditional sacrifice of the individual for the state, had gradually lost its appeal.

THE DARK SHADOW OF HISTORY

He was among the first of the privately financed students. After he went to America in 1981, he obtained a master's degree from a college in New York and then worked in the Asian department of an investment bank in Boston. His annual salary that first year was $48,000, and it eventually surpassed $70,000. In 1984 he bought a house in a suburb of Boston for more than $300,000. Every morning, dressed in suit and tie, he drove a Toyota Crown to the city to work. At five o'clock in the evening he drove home. By any measure, he was leading the life of a typical middle-class American. But he did not have the relaxed attitude and calmness of the American middle class.

While carrying on a conversation, he would walk to the door of the room he was in, open it abruptly, and look outside. Then he would mumble, "I thought there was somebody outside." On the road, if someone behind him tooted their horn, he would tense up and say anxiously, "Somebody's following me." Sometimes when he had an argument with his girlfriend over some trivial matter, he would reproach her and say, inexplicably, "Why do you want to hurt me?"

The sentence that most easily slipped into his conversation with others was "I'll get revenge for that." When saying that, he was really thinking about people from his past in China: the police in the station in the western district of Beijing where he and his family once lived, the security cadres of the public safety commission, and the women on the local residence committee. He had been gone from China for ten years, but he had not forgotten them.

He could not forget his years during the Cultural Revolution before he came to America. Every holiday, he and his two elder brothers had to report to the police station or the public safety commission to be lectured on discipline. During festivals, they were not allowed outside, not even to watch the fireworks. His parents, who were both physicists and had studied in America in their youth, were imprisoned as suspected spies. The children were labeled "bad children" because they received no parental discipline. Finally one elder brother was sentenced to death and executed on the charge of being a counterrevolutionary because he had stolen a few overcoats. His other elder brother was sent to labor reform camp because he got into a fight. At that time, he was spared from the proletarian dictatorship, but anybody could give him a stern lecture any time, any place. Or even hit him.

A thirty-year-old Ph.D. candidate studying political science at the University of Michigan said that at first he was surprised by the intense hatred harbored by some mainland Chinese students toward the society in which they had once lived. "I never would have thought they carried that much hate. Sometimes I also verbally attacked this or that person, but my fiery words were simply expressions of discontent. But some of these mainland students really hate—they gnash their teeth." He paused, and then sighed, "Perhaps it's because of differences in what families have experienced." He was from a family of CCP cadres, and his father had joined the revolution in Yan'an.[1]

It was true. The wounds left in the minds of some Chinese by a history of accusations, denunciations, and persecutions would not heal easily.

He was a Chinese who hated the Chinese with all his being. He often said that the Chinese, himself included, were the basest ethnic group. They were lazy, gluttonous, greedy, and filthy, like pigs.

He was only a bit over thirty, but seemed already down and out. Nobody knew when he had come to America. Perhaps he first went to Europe to study and then came to New York. In New York, besides working, he would drink and chase women. Not Chinese women, but Korean or Vietnamese women.

He never talked about his days in China. Once, after some heavy drinking, he was asked why he did not go back to visit his parents; after all, he had been away for ten years. He said that they had both died long ago. Then he was asked, "What about your brothers and sisters?" He shot back, "What for? They're only after big-ticket merchandise, or another opportunity to show their righteous loyalty to the Communist Party by denouncing another member of their family."

What was harbored in some Chinese was not only hatred. The dark shadow of history would reveal itself by other means. The unusual political environment in China in the last several decades had caused some Chinese students to become overly political; they lost the honesty required for being human, and they believed that the ends justified the means.

He, thirty-eight years old, had come from China to study in a Ph.D. program in electrical engineering at a Midwestern university and became very active in politics after the June Fourth Incident. He organized rallies and gave speeches and quickly became a leader in the protest movement at his American university. Furthermore, at every protest gathering he would ask others to photograph him, showing his energetic and fearless spirit. Only afterward did other students understand that the reason for his actions was to accumulate evidence to support his application for political asylum. Perhaps concerned that he had insufficient evidence, he wrote letters attacking the Chinese Communist Party to his work unit in China and to the work units of his parents and sibling. Finally, the Chinese police visited his parents, trying to figure out what had happened. When the frightened parents wrote to him, he was elated: this was hard evidence that his relatives in China were targeted for political persecution by the government.

Still others seemed to believe that once they left China, they had left behind moral constraints. They would do disgraceful things, shamelessly. In my discussions with Americans about the behavior of some Chinese students, they frequently responded by saying, "Oh! I know something much more terrible than that!"

He was said to be the least-trustworthy Chinese student. Whenever his name was mentioned among the people who knew him, they would shake their heads and say, "I've never seen any Chinese student that bad."

He was of middle stature, wore glasses, had a scholarly manner, and looked fairly guileless. But he could not tell the truth. One day he would tell you that he had never married, another day he would tell someone else that he was contemplating divorce, and the third day he would announce that his wife was coming from China.

He had come in 1987. First he studied in Texas but dropped out because he repeatedly failed his courses. He then went to San Francisco to attend a community college so as to keep his student status.

He was not at all stupid. When shopping in a supermarket, he often did not pay. He loved to give on-site demonstrations: he selected his merchandise, covertly removed the trademark and the magnetic coding film, and walked out of the store. Thus he had much merchandise at home, some useful and some not, from toothpaste and soap to bicycle tires. He also devised a method of making free calls from public telephones: he drilled a hole in a coin and pulled a thread through the hole. After depositing the coin and completing the call, he would pull the thread and recover his coin. One investment, multiple returns.

He not only cut the corners of capitalism, but also swindled his fellow Chinese students. After he had exhausted his pool of victims among the old-timers, he targeted the newcomers. Once, in a post office, he asked a recent arrival to cash his personal check for $100, claiming he needed the money to buy a money order for his parents in China. He said the post office would not accept his check because he had forgotten to bring an identification card. The student helped. The check, however, bounced, since the account had been closed for a long time. A few days later the newcomer, confronting him at his home and demanding the money, said, "I sweated for that money—it was not easy money." He said, "I have no money. I've already declared bankruptcy. You can sue me." Then he called the police to remove the newcomer on the charge of illegal forced entry of his residence.

Although he had a notoriously bad name, he seemed to lead a worry-free life. When chided by others, he always had a ready answer: "Who cares? This is America!"

According to one of his classmates, in China he had been respectful toward all the teachers, diligent about attending his political studies classes, and a well-behaved student.

The absence of rudimentary ethical concerns in some Chinese students reflected a distorted human nature.

The omnipotent political system and deeply ingrained traditional Confucianism had woven a seamless fabric of political control and personal moral confines in Chinese society. Beginning in elementary school, the teacher would begin to frighten the children daily by saying, "You'll have to write your own history—don't let that history stain your dossier." From college and on into the workplace, people around one were penalized, criticized, and destroyed because they were said to have committed political mistakes or to have conducted themselves questionably. That kind of life put one in a constant state of fear and trepidation, resulting in suppression of desire and self-denial. The highest imperative in life was "Don't ever make a mistake."

Once they were overseas, the students felt political control disappear. Their moral consciousness, which had been colored by ideology because of its fusion with political control, also disappeared. In addition, traditional Chinese culture did not include a religious element of the kind in Western culture, and hence it was difficult for the Chinese to acquire the kind of sacred respect and fear that transcended social reality. Hence, some people let loose their long-suppressed human nature without moral restraint. Like people who had always been well-behaved out of fear of damnation, they engaged in any wanton act when informed that hell did not exist.

Like people who have been abused or have suppressed deeply cherished desires in childhood and have become psychopaths in adulthood, the Chinese, who endured several decades of torment, could not shake loose overnight the aftermath of their past experiences. History cast a dark shadow on all of our spirits; no one escaped.

In recent years many books have been written by Chinese and published in America and Western Europe, and in them the authors describe their sufferings, real or imagined. What is deplorable is that they show a near total absence of introspection. Some writers unburden their grievances to gain the sympathy of foreign readers, not unlike when Xianglin's wife said to everybody, "I was really foolish, really."[2] Some take the route of sensationalism through exaggeration and exploit the opportunity provided by the clash of ideologies of China and the West. The tone of these books is like a child's tattling, but now to a foreigner: "Look how they bullied me!" These books are perhaps another manifestation of the "history syndrome" of the Chinese.

LU GANG'S DISTORTED NOTION OF INDIVIDUALISM

On the afternoon of November 1, 1991, in a classroom on the third floor of the physics building at the University of Iowa, several professors and graduate students were discussing a topic in astrophysics. Among them were Professors Christopher Goertz and Robert Smith and Chinese student Shan Linhua.

At about 3:30, twenty-eight-year-old Chinese student Lu Gang, who had been participating in the discussion all along, walked out of the room and then returned. Before anybody could react to what was happening, Lu Gang pulled out a gun, aimed, and fired at Professor Goertz, his thesis adviser. Goertz fell. Lu then calmly aimed and fired at Professor Smith, who was seated next to Professor Goertz. He, too, collapsed. After that Lu turned his gun at his Chinese classmate Shan Linhua and fired another shot.

While the rest of the students were too stunned and frightened to do anything, Lu hurriedly left the classroom. He went to the departmental office on the second floor. There he shot the chairman, Professor Dwight Nicholson.

As if to savor his own masterpiece for the second time, Lu Gang returned to the classroom on the third floor. There he saw that Professor Smith, who was lying in a pool of blood, was still breathing, and other professors and students were trying to revive him. Lu calmly asked everybody to leave and then fired the fatal shot at Professor Smith.

He had not yet finished. Lu walked out of the physics building and entered the administration building nearby. There he found and shot Ms. Anne Clery, assistant vice president in charge of academic affairs. A secretary who witnessed this screamed and was also shot.

At last another shot was fired: Lu shot himself in the head. The campus became quiet again.

At 3:40 in the afternoon the police siren could be heard approaching the scene of the crime. Five dead were carried out: Goertz, Smith, Shan Linhua, Nicholson, and Lu Gang. The next day Ms. Cleary died in the intensive-care ward of the hospital. The secretary was seriously wounded but survived.

Lu Gang had meticulously planned for a long time to carry out these killings. He had purchased the gun some time before and had practiced shooting at a local gun club. All of his targets, except for the secretary, were carefully chosen, intended victims.

What was the motive? Incredibly simple: Lu Gang, who had only recently received his Ph.D. in physics, felt that he had been unfairly treated by the department and the university administration in the nomination for an award for the best dissertation.

According to the suicide note that he had intended to mail to several American news organizations, he and his thesis adviser, Professor Goertz, had not been on good terms. Lu Gang had graduated from the physics department of Peking University in 1985 and had gone to America to study in 1986 after passing the screening examination administered by the Chinese American physicist T. D. Lee. Academically it had been smooth sailing all the way. He had always had excellent grades, and he passed his Ph.D. qualifying examination with a record-high score, which remained unbroken at the time of the killing. But Lu Gang believed that Professor Goertz purposely made things difficult for him in his thesis defense examination, in his attempt to publish his thesis, and in Professor Goertz's letter of recommendation for him in his job applications. This was why, he believed, he had failed his oral examination, could not publish his thesis, could not find work after graduation, and, finally, had lost the opportunity to win a thesis award.

What incited his fury and jealousy was his Chinese classmate Shan Linhua, who had been in Professor Goertz's good graces. The twenty-seven-year-old Shan had graduated from the University of Science and Technology in Hefei, China. He had come to the University of Iowa a year after Lu but received his Ph.D. before him. Furthermore, he was appointed to a postdoctoral position at the university immediately after graduation. And for Lu, the hardest thing to bear was that Shan's thesis had been nominated for the thesis award that he so strongly coveted.

From Lu Gang's viewpoint, Professor Smith was partial to Shan because he was simply trying to expand his own turf; Professor Nicholson not only unfairly nominated Shan for the thesis award but also had always administered the departmental academic affairs inequitably; and Ms. Cleary, being a part of the academic bureaucracy, had failed to respond to Lu's repeated attempts to expose the unfair treatment leveled at him, and had shielded and supported Nicholson and Goertz.

These incidents made Lu feel that he was justified in using "unusual means" to seek justice for himself.

This case of homicide in the peaceful, charming college town of only some sixty thousand inhabitants shocked the Chinese students.

In fact, Lu Gang was not the first Chinese student who committed murder with a firearm. In October 1990 Bai Xiaodong, a thirty-year-old Chinese student from Peking University who was studying at the University of California, Los Angeles, shot two American neighbors. But the shooting was apparently related to his mental instability. He was constantly under the delusion that he was being followed, watched, and sexually harassed by a homosexual organization. Criminal charges were dropped on the grounds of mental instability, and he was sent to a psychiatric hospital for treatment.

Lu Gang was different. He was sober. He killed all his victims calmly; a cold-blooded killer, the district attorney called him.

The immediate reaction of the Chinese students at the university was interesting. Their first worry was whether the case would tarnish their image on campus: "How will the white professors view us tomorrow?" They assumed that Lu Gang's personal behavior would be connected to the image of the entire Chinese nation. Later, many Chinese students who were interviewed about the case claimed that Lu was "bad," "a loner," and "had no friends at all"; they seemed anxious to distance themselves from him. Only a few American students who had known him were courageous enough to say, "He was not a bad guy."[3]

In fact, Lu Gang's homicide was the act of an individual, not of an ethnic group. The American media, in reporting the event, treated it as a campus crime and did not stress his Chinese background.

The means and motive of the homicide, however, were very American. In America, rampage killings with a gun could be seen several times a year on television. The motive usually was personal discontent. Furthermore, Lu's targets included not only Americans but also his fellow countryman; the crime apparently did not carry a racial overtone.

Nevertheless, Lu was a student from mainland China. Some people naturally analyzed his abnormal mentality in terms of his past social background. Chinese American writer Nie Hualing said that Lu Gang's obsession with "destroying everything at any price ... originated from the evil legacy of the Cultural Revolution in the mainland. The Cultural Revolution encouraged and created hate between one person and another."[4] Later there were also reports in China that concluded that Lu's behavior was related to China's history education, since it had always stressed the importance of "oppression-counterattack."[5] These analyses were not without merit. But there were many Chinese students in America who had been participants in the Cultural Revolution and were subjected to the indoctrination of the Communists, whereas Lu Gang was the only one who went about killing people.

The most conspicuous trait in Lu Gang's character was his extreme selfishness. The impression of his classmates was that he "was very calculating and would never get himself into a situation of holding the short end of a stick," "was extremely selfish," and "was self-centered and would never consider other people's feelings." A student who shared an apartment with him recalled that during the heat of the summer Lu would sleep in the living room and leave the refrigerator door open all night without any concern about whether other people's food would spoil.

It is more appropriate to describe Lu Gang's mental state as originating from contorted individualism than from extreme individualism. In Western culture, individualism as a value is the foundation of capitalistic society. Society advocates the right of individuals to pursue and to defend their self-interest; it also holds individuals responsible for their own acts. In China, individualism, having been criticized countless times on ideological grounds, has been deemed to connote selfishness, the philosophy of looking after oneself alone.

Beginning in the eighties, the consciousness of self in the Chinese people began to rise rapidly after ideological constraints were relaxed. Long-suppressed selfish desires, being a part of human nature, also began to grow rapidly in some people. But the notion of individual responsibility could not be built overnight. This uneven development led to a contorted individualism in which behavior was dictated by an overwhelming greed and the absence of courage to bear responsibility for one's conduct. People who failed blamed others, the family, society. We could see such enmity in Lu Gang's suicide note and in the last words he wrote to his second-eldest sister.

He first fixed the blame for his failures on personal gripes of Professor Goertz. He then attacked other professors and students in the department, the department chair, and the university. Then he extended his criticism to America as a whole. He wrote, "Although one does not have to worry about food and clothing in America, I am really penniless when compared to the very wealthy people at the top," and "Many Chinese American physicists who are not really doing well in America would return to China to toot their own horns." After blaming America, he blamed the country that sponsored his study to begin with because it "hoodwinked young people into studying pure science." The most surprising complaint was the one he leveled at his parents. Although possessing a doctorate in physics, he blamed his parents, two factory workers in China, for "providing no help in my studies in the past" and "having no financial resources to send me to study in America"; his plight today "was partially the fault of my parents."

There was only one person that he did not blame: himself.

It was precisely this mentality that made him incapable of bearing real failure. Like other mass murders in American society, the homicide committed by Lu Gang was not a display of the strength of his character, but of its fragility.

But Lu Gang did study in America for several years. After the killing, he bore the responsibility of his act by killing himself; he ended this tragedy of contorted individualism the American way.

THE MESS OF THE OVERSEAS DEMOCRACY MOVEMENT

In the summer of 1982, a Chinese student in Canada named Wang Bingzhang, who parted his hair in the middle, went to Columbia University in New York City. There, he proposed to several Chinese students that they form an overseas organization opposing the Chinese government. After some discussion, they decided to form an organization headed by Wang.

On November 11, 1982, Wang held a press conference in room 524 of the New York Hilton Hotel. During the conference he stated that, to pursue the realization of democracy in China, he was giving up his medical career, joining the democracy movement, and starting a new magazine, *China Spring*. The overseas democracy movement, with a variety of political leanings, thus made its debut.

Toward the end of 1983, Wang declared the formation of the Democratic Alliance of China. The Chinese government quickly declared it a reactionary organization.

In the first several years, Wang did get some publicity for himself, but the Alliance found almost no market among Chinese students. A student who was over forty and was studying at Harvard University at that time recalled that few people had attended Wang's speech at Harvard and that he had been unable to raise funds. Another student, a twenty-four-year-old at the University of California at Berkeley, said the same thing had happened there. When Wang was speaking, the students hissed, and some charged the podium, took over the microphone, and started a debate. The two sides nearly got into a fistfight toward the end. The scene was reminiscent of two factions battling during the Cultural Revolution.

In fact, even those who took part in bringing out *China Spring* and joined the Democratic Alliance had no confidence and trust in the democracy movement led by Wang Bingzhang. Within a year after his first press conference, several of the students who started *China Spring* with him had left. In December 1987 Wang's chairmanship in the Democratic Alliance was lost to Hu Ping, a graduate of Peking University and a visiting scholar at Harvard.

Soon afterward infighting erupted in the Alliance. In January 1989 Wang was recalled from his position as a member of the standing committee on the grounds that he had repeatedly violated the charter by pursuing personal gain. Refusing to give in, he withdrew all of the funds in *China Spring*'s bank account, more than $78,000, and declared on April 2, 1989, that he was forming the Chinese Democratic Party.

Just when the overseas democracy movement was turning from a pool of trouble to a farce, the June Fourth Incident erupted. After the incident, many reform champions and democracy-movement leaders in China were exiled. On September 24, 1989, the announcement of the formation of the China Democratic Front in Paris gave the overseas democracy movement a shot in the arm. At the same time, the shock of the June Fourth Incident caused many Chinese students to relax their guard against democracy-movement organizations.

But very quickly the reputation of the movement fell to a new low. The leaders of the Democratic Front, after acting out their part as if following a screen script, squabbled and dispersed; these warriors wrote articles and organized conferences but performed no specific deeds. The number of leaders increased while the number of followers dwindled.

To gain some impetus, the Democratic Alliance and the Democratic Front decided to join forces. After a lengthy discussion, they agreed to hold a joint meeting in September 1993. But the planned union of ideologies unexpectedly became a real union of fights. Filling the position of chairman, vice-chairman, and other similar posts caused fierce infighting in each group and cross-party fights between the two. During the final voting, some gave impassioned speeches, some walked out in a fury, and some wailed bitterly. The meeting was so chaotic that it was barely able to adjourn in an orderly manner.

Today very few people take the overseas democracy movement seriously. Like the term "reform specialist," the term "democracy-movement figure" carries a disparaging connotation among Chinese students. But the fact that it did become such a mess, as a phenomenon in political culture, is well worth analysis.

Some people said that the movement could not become a mass movement because it lacked presentable leadership. None of the leaders could be supported, but it would be all right if there were a leader like so and so.

Some people found fault with the ethical standards of the democracy-movement figures. They fought for power and privileges, sought a legitimate excuse in their applications for political asylum, or pocketed money donated for the support of the students in Tiananmen Square. Wang Bingzhang, for the purpose of obtaining a work permit, allegedly forged documents and assumed a false name, and then was caught red-handed by the U.S. Immigration and Naturalization Service. After he was exposed, he reportedly declared that he had done these things so it would be easier for him to carry out work for the democracy movement.

These criticisms of the movement might have had some validity, but they missed the crucial point. Some participants often flaunted the banner of pursuing the politics for a democratic China and assumed the role of rebel against one ideology so as to ingratiate themselves with another ideology. But in reality, this generation of people raised under communism had limited knowledge of democracy; they had a smattering of understanding of the theories of some Western thinkers, and they skillfully used the word as a slogan after repeated recitation. But their basic conception of politics and the operational skills in their practice were the same revolutionary principles and denunciation techniques that they had learned at a younger age.

First, democracy had become a new ideology; it was not just a belief, but a goal. Like the revolution in the past, democracy became an absolute standard by which all rights and wrongs would have to be measured. Anyone who ventured even a slight disagreement on this guiding principle would attract verbal and written abuses of an intensity reminiscent of those during the Cultural Revolution. If the criticisms were insufficient to overpower the dissident, the attack would become personal, but with political overtones.

Next, in its form of development, the movement could not free itself from the influence of the teachings of the Communist Party on the formation of a revolutionary organization. To start the movement, the first step was to form a party; the next was to convene the First Great Conference, and then a Second Great Conference, for the purpose of electing a chairman, a standing committee, and so forth. The participants fought tooth and nail to be the leader, as if they feared that the history of democracy in China at a future date would fail to record their deeds. Meanwhile, nobody was willing to analyze seriously the current status of China's various classes, to ask how China's society might be transformed over the next fifty years, and to ponder whether new democratic politics should have some new organizational forms.

Finally, the operation of the movement seemed to aim at initiating a mammoth revolutionary struggle. In a gathering, "overthrow," "defeat," and other familiar buzzwords were shouted out with zest. In moments of agitation, some people even cried out lofty slogans such as "Establish military arms for the revolution; create a military base for the revolution." Of course, nobody had yet signed up for returning to China to take up guerrilla warfare. After they vented the lofty words, they usually made an all-out effort to get a Green Card and did something like open a neighborhood grocery store.

In its fundamentals, the movement was a kind of "replay" of the Cultural Revolution. To the people who engaged in the movement, democracy, like revolution, was a social miracle. Its realization, like the success of a revolution, would create a brand-new society, and to believe in democracy was identical to believing in revolution—all problems in human society could be solved by certain radical political means.

Among the various overseas organizations, the All-America Autonomous Federation of Chinese Students and Scholars, formed on September 24, 1989, in Chicago by Chinese students from 203 American colleges and universities, was one organization that held a weak ideological position and a strong collective group interest.

In spite of its strong political tilt, the Autonomous Federation, being an interest group, by comparison did not often involve itself directly in ideological disputes. In addition, although it lacked a rigorous organizational form, it had a relatively strong population base. Since its founding, the Federation had taken up many activities on behalf of the practical interests of Chinese students, including lobbying the U.S. Congress. In addition, it had elected successive leadership personnel according to its charter.

But some leaders in the Federation did not appear satisfied that it remained purely an interest group. Often they used the name of the organization to speak ostentatiously about their own personal political beliefs in political disputes saturated with ideological flavor.

Probably nobody can speak with certainty about the future of the politics of democracy in China. It is possible that various interest groups will appear in China and that the conflict between different groups will be resolved by negotiation. Perhaps that is the foundation of democracy. Similar to the way conflicting religious beliefs cause wars, conflicts in ideology will inevitably lead to revolution. Since the inception of human civilization, humanity has gradually matured, so that it should be able to find means other than revolution to advance social progress and reforms.

NATIONALISM IN THE WHIRLPOOL OF IDEOLOGY

It should be a simple matter for overseas Chinese students to have patriotic sentiments. But in a world full of ideological conflict and disputes rooted in political interest, to be patriotic can become quite complicated. An interesting example was the annual argument, before 1994, between China and the United States on China's status as a most favored nation.

In May 1990 I attended a hearing of the Asian Pacific Committee of the U.S. House of Representatives on the extension of China's MFN status. This kind of hearing was open to the public; anyone who wished to could attend.

Four people testified: a former U.S. ambassador to China, the then deputy chairman of the National Committee on U.S.-China Relations, a representative from the Hong Kong business community, and finally a Chinese student who was studying at Harvard.

The two Americans and the businessman from Hong Kong all expressed their support or conditional support for an extension of MFN status. Regrettably, it was the Chinese student who firmly opposed the extension and advocated economic sanctions against China.

Quite a few Chinese students held such a view. Not only did they testify in Congressional hearings, but they also wrote letters to the American president, published articles, and gave speeches. All were done with great passion.

It was said that they did this to advocate democracy and human rights. Their logic was that the Chinese government was a bad government, undemocratic and callous about human rights, and to extend the MFN status would only strengthen that government, whereas economic sanctions would cause it to collapse. Then democracy would appear sooner in China and the conditions for human rights would improve rapidly.

The overseas democracy movement apparently did not consider the livelihood of several hundred million ordinary Chinese people, and it also ignored the decisive significance of economic development on social progress in China. Democracy and human rights once more became a political utopia that demanded sacrifices from a nation, a state, and every individual (especially others).

When an extreme opinion becomes an abstract principle that supersedes all other considerations, events develop into absurdities.

In 1990 an intellectual well known in China gave a seminar at the University of Michigan on China's future. This scholar, with a reputed deep concern for the country and the Chinese people, said that there would be another bloodletting in China and from that pool of blood would rise a pure and clean China.

These words sent cold shivers down my spine. I thought, What kind of purity and cleanliness in China was worth the Chinese' shedding their blood one more time? Had they not shed enough blood during the last hundred and some years? It was fortunate that not all the overseas Chinese students were so patriotic.

Before President Clinton decided on the issue, a group of Chinese students who had repeatedly expressed their concern about democracy and human rights in China wrote to the American president to petition for an unconditional extension of MFN status to China. Their reason was that the current economic reform in China was building a solid foundation for the future development of democracy and human rights in Chinese society. The American policy of extending the status would further help China to become a more open society, and the trend of this development was congruent with the interests of the Chinese and American people.

The position of most Chinese students, the so-called silent majority, was quite clear. In my interviews, their answer to the question was nearly unanimous: "Of course MFN status should be extended." When asked why, they answered, "It would benefit China's development." Some respondents were deeply disturbed by the fact that some Chinese students traded the interest of the Chinese people for their own personal gain in fame and profit; others expressed doubts about whether Western countries were genuinely concerned about democracy and human rights in China.

On May 26, 1994, President Clinton announced the renewal of MFN status for China, and he also stated that henceforth he would no longer link human-rights conditions in China to the bilateral trade relationship. The annual debate over China's MFN status, which had started in 1989, was finally brought to a close. Some people claimed that it was "a sad day for China's democracy fighters."

Just a few days before President Clinton's announcement, five Chinese students went on a hunger strike outside the White House, demanding that the U.S. government terminate China's MFN status. Upon hearing the president's decision, they felt put out. They withdrew from their post outside the White House and declared that the new site of their hunger strike would be the Chinese Embassy.

Western society certainly adored democracy and human rights. But in an international dispute or in a problem in which national interest was involved, these concepts became heavily colored with ideology, and their significance varied according to each country's own national interest.

In October 1993, Russian president Boris Yeltsin, after violating the Russian Constitution by dissolving the Parliament, laid siege and fired on the Parliament with tank artillery. This shocking event killed more than a hundred people and wounded several hundred others. When Yeltsin attacked the Parliament, President Clinton of the United States, Prime Minister John Major of Britain, and other Western heads of state all immediately expressed their firm support of Yeltsin.

The reaction of these leaders to Yeltsin's armed attack on the Parliament was more shocking to the Chinese students than was the attack itself, because they still retained a fresh memory of the June Fourth Incident. A thirty-year-old student who had left China after 1989 said furiously, "All crows are black no matter where they are! There's not a single patch of clean soil in the world!"

The different reactions from the Western countries to the Russian Parliament incident and to China's June Fourth Incident had their own logic. First, the people who occupied the Parliament were communists, and communists apparently were not to be included under the protection of human rights. Second, the policy of Yeltsin, who loudly proclaimed his support of democracy, was consistent with the national interest of the Western countries.

In the last half-century, politics in the postwar world have been consistently determined by ideology. The sharp opposition between capitalism and socialism not only divided the globe into the Eastern and the Western camps but also relentlessly placed humanity at the brink of war. Following the reform in China and the disintegration of the Soviet Union, ideology as a primary component in world politics began to fade. At the same time, nationalism became stronger by the day.

Today, to varying degrees, ideology still affects world politics and influences people's thinking when they have to formulate criteria for their decisions. It is also used from time to time as a pretext to cover up the scrambling for advantages over other nations. But behind the conflict of ideology is the overt or covert surging tide of nationalism. This affected the dispute over MFN status between China and the United States and led to the opposition of Western countries, under the pretext of human rights, to China's hosting of the 2000 Summer Olympics. For China, this may remain true for the Hong Kong problem, the Taiwan problem, and the Tibet problem.

Whether one likes it or not, nationalism perhaps will become the tide that guides world politics in the twenty-first century.

THE CHINESE ESPIONAGE CLOUD

On the evening of May 19, 1994, Connie Chung, Chinese American anchor at CBS, one of the three major television networks in America, broadcast a news item about Chinese espionage in America. The coverage began like this:

> Every day planeloads of Chinese students arrive legally in the United States—ordinary people. But to the Chinese government, some of them may be future spies, who a few years down the road will be activated to steal America's military and technology secrets, whether they want to or not.

This biased coverage immediately angered many Chinese students.

A Chinese student wrote in the Chinese student network that what this CBS news coverage wanted to tell the American audience was this: The Chinese in America are all potential spies, no matter how ordinary or peaceful they are. What angered the Chinese students was that the irresponsible report had not only seriously damaged the American public image of Chinese students but also could directly affect their lives and future employment. Just think: Who would be willing to hire a potential Chinese spy?

Organized by the All-America Autonomous Federation of Chinese Students and Scholars, some Chinese students started a large-scale protest movement. Their voice of discontent finally reached CBS headquarters in New York City.

Five months later, on October 18, 1994, Mr. Eric Ober, the chief executive officer of CBS, and representatives of the Chinese students met at CBS headquarters and began formal negotiations. The result was that on October 20, Mr. Ober, on behalf of CBS, wrote a letter of apology to the Chinese students and other Chinese in America. The letter said,

> We are fully aware that most Chinese, Chinese Americans, and other Asian Americans are just like any other people: legitimate and law-abiding students, visiting scholars, immigrants and citizens, whether they are here for a long time or for a brief visit. If our report did not reflect that awareness, we apologize for that.

It also stated that CBS "will make a serious effort to clarify this" on the upcoming Friday evening news.[6]

The CBS evening news of October 21 was again anchored by Connie Chung. In the news coverage she broadcast the following explanatory statement:

> In a program in May, we reported some documented evidence showing that the Beijing government is recruiting espionage personnel among the Chinese who were coming to America. It was not our intention to leave the impression that there were more than a small number of such individuals among the many tens of thousands of Chinese students, visitors, and immigrants who come to the United States every year. If we left an incorrect impression, we regret it.

Actually, what happened at CBS was not a chance occurrence. At the time of the CBS broadcast, a book about Chinese espionage activities in the United States, *Chinese Intelligence Operations*, was published on May 23, 1994. Nicholas Eftimiades, who claimed to be an intelligence officer of the CIA, was the author. He stated that Chinese espionage activity in America was more rampant than in any other country; not only were the 11,500 diplomats and trade officials possibly engaging in spy activities, but the 15,000 Chinese students who came to America every year and hundreds of thousands of Chinese Americans were all possibly deeply burrowed Chinese spies.

This Chinese espionage story, nearly a carbon copy of the CBS one, carried with it not only racial prejudice but also a strong ideological bias. Chinese students, after all, came from Red China.

It is interesting to note that while some Americans felt that every Chinese was a potential spy, some Chinese students felt that they were being watched by American intelligence agencies.

A thirty-six-year-old privately financed student who had come to America in 1986 and had settled down in Seattle said that he had always felt his telephone was bugged; he could hear a humming sound whenever he used the phone.

A forty-two-year-old government-financed student firmly believed that he and his wife were being watched even in their bedroom. His evidence was that one day, while lying in bed, he jokingly said to his wife that their schoolmate, who was leaving for China the next day for a visit, carried a suitcase of secrets. The following day, that student was stopped at the luggage inspection counter and all of his belongings were thoroughly searched.

Although those stories had no substantiating evidence, the following story about the encounters of a well-known visiting scholar is true.

A visiting scholar, more than sixty years old, was invited in 1989 to lecture at a university in the Midwest. Soon after his arrival, an FBI agent knocked on his door. The agent was very friendly; he showed his concern about the well-being of the visitor and asked if there were any problems. He continued to call every few days. Later he also volunteered to teach the elderly man how to drive and claimed that he would take care of Green Card business for him in the future.

A year later this visiting scholar transferred to a university in the south and freed himself from the pestering. But soon another FBI agent came. This agent was even more interesting. He first went through a sincere self-criticism, saying that he had been reprimanded by his superior for neglecting to look after the visitor. Now he would be more active in carrying out his duties, and that was the reason for his visit.

It was no surprise that China and the United States were spying on each other. But the "catch-a-spy" game was also played among Chinese students themselves. In moments of political argument, some people freely accused the opposition of being spies for the Chinese government or the CIA. This game reached a peak during the infighting in the Democratic Alliance of China; rumors flew and suspicion was widespread. But we did not hear whether any spy was actually exposed.

THE DIFFERENT DISPOSITIONS OF STUDENTS FROM THE OPPOSITE SIDES OF THE TAIWAN STRAIT

Because of decades-long hostility and political estrangement, the Chinese on the two sides of the Taiwan Strait seemed to have lived on two different planets. They could look at each other from a distance, but they could not communicate. Before the seventies, although they shared the same nationality and language, people from the mainland and people from Taiwan rarely met. A chance encounter at some international diplomatic function would always end in a protest withdrawal of one side.

The Chinese government's resumption of sending students abroad in 1978 made it possible for Chinese on the two sides to meet in a third location. In the initial stage of that contact, both sides were curious, suspicious, and guarded.

A student about forty years old went from mainland China to America in 1982. He said that when he first arrived in Cleveland to study at a university there, he was met at the airport and driven away, mistakenly, by the Taiwanese Student Association of that university. Upon reaching his living quarters, he found that he was surrounded by students from Taiwan. He was so nervous that he dared not utter a word, thinking, "This is terrible—I'm trapped in a spy's den!"

A thirty-eight-year-old student from Taiwan studying in New York City said that when she first heard of mainland students on campus, her roommate, also from Taiwan, hurried out to have a look. She returned after a while and told her excitedly, "I've seen them! They look just like us!"

During the more than three decades of political propaganda across the Taiwan Strait after 1949, the mainland Chinese were "the mainland fellow countrymen who lived in the abyss of suffering" and the people in Taiwan "the Taiwan fellow countrymen who yearned for liberation."[7] But in America the students from the different sides quickly discovered the same familiar Chinese characteristics in each other. It was not difficult to identify with the other side. Furthermore, although there were differences in lifestyle and political environment, the two sides had similar emotional experiences from which they could draw lessons.

On campus, students from the mainland and Taiwan got along well and conflicts were rare. Not only were friendships built between individuals, but students participated in social functions sponsored by the other side's student organization. There was neither civil war nor a war with a united front. The principal friction between the two sides, if noteworthy at all, was between the mainland students who were working in Chinese restaurants and the Taiwanese owners of those restaurants.

But having lived in different social systems and political cultures, the two student groups had different dispositions.

Some students from Taiwan said the mainland students had an "overbearing disposition,"[8] and some mainland students answered back sarcastically that the students from Taiwan had an "island mentality."[9]

Many mainland students, having gone through violent political storms and witnessed turbulent upheavals, freely indulged themselves, thinking that they would rewrite history. As soon as they left China, they set goals of making it big in the world outside before returning to see their families at home. If they could not create a new democratic era, they would at least liberate the several hundred million Chinese from their straitjackets; if not that, at the very least they would create a new IBM and amass a large fortune.

By comparison, most Taiwanese students came from middle-class families. Having grown up in a relatively stable society, their purpose in life was much more practical: studying for a degree, finding a job. Even owning a grocery store or a video-rental store would be quite satisfactory.

If you asked mainland students why they were staying in America, the answer would not be the higher standard of living but democracy and the opportunities for personal growth. Once I asked a Taiwanese student, just over twenty, that question. His answer was that America was so big that it had many interesting places for sightseeing, and the air was clean. Pounding on his chest, he said, "It's so comfortable here!" When asked how would he survive, he answered without hesitation, "Work in a supermarket, paint houses . . ."

The storm-hardened mainland students were generally more eloquent and fond of debate. Even when they were talking nonsense, they would deliver it in an overpowering manner. A thirty-three-year-old visiting scholar told me the story of one of his verbal battles. He said that when he was interviewed by American professors, he would start by saying that since he had been given only thirty minutes, he would talk first. Then he would talk nonstop for half an hour. "They were all impressed by my self-assurance," he remarked with pride. Taiwanese students, perhaps because of insufficient opportunities for practice, spoke awkwardly during a discussion or a debate. In my interviews, many people mentioned the same impression. An American graduate student said she found that the mainland students loved to talk but rarely listened.

As if to rebel against the concept of collectivism, the mainland students often liked to be on their own after their arrival in America. When I first arrived, more than one person advised me not to get involved with any group of Chinese students. Quarrels abounded in them, and once one got involved, it was hard to get out. Taiwanese students seemed to have no such concerns; they congregated as if needing to look after one another.

I once had a dinner engagement with an American, and she invited her roommate, a Chinese American, to come along. The roommate said that her cousin had just arrived from Taiwan and was studying at the university, too. Thus we all went to a Chinese restaurant together. But seven or eight other Taiwan students also came. It turned out that they had studied in the same department at different times in a university in the city of Tainan. Now they got together in America, shared a big house, had community meals, and engaged in group social activities.

The destruction of traditional moral confines in their homeland had resulted in the mainland students' having more daring spirits and taking risks. They had fewer self-imposed moral constraints. For small personal gains, they would tell lies as well as the truth, and do bad deeds as well as good ones, in the U.S. capitol or on campus.

By comparison, the students from Taiwan were far better behaved. They appeared to be frank, good natured, respectful of others, and modest. The most serious offense they ever committed was chasing after girls.

The notable fearless spirit of the mainland students often belied a lack of even the rudiments of proper upbringing and courtesy. Once, a well-known American China scholar gave a lecture at the University of Michigan, followed by a question-and-answer period. A mainland student, probably thinking that he was the most qualified person to ask questions because of the subject matter, first attacked the visitor's speech and then gave his own opinion, with zeal and assurance. He talked more than ten minutes, as if he were the lecturer. His boorishness stunned the audience. Another mainland student attending the lecture said afterward that he had been very embarrassed by his countryman.

With regard to upbringing and courtesy, there was no doubt that Taiwanese students were better mannered. Movie screenings can serve as an example. At such a gathering organized by mainland students, the scene was as chaotic as you would see at the field meeting in a peasant village, in which one would hear kids yelling for their moms and might also witness a ferocious power struggle.[10] The result was that often one did not know when the movie would begin. A gathering organized by Taiwanese students, however, would always be orderly.

But the group that displayed the most civilized upbringing was the Hong Kong Students Association. At movie screenings students stood at the door welcoming the guests and passing out synopses, and the film, of course, was most likely a kungfu movie.

CHAPTER 8

To Return or to Stay

THE OVERNIGHT CONVERSION OF MORE THAN FIFTY THOUSAND STUDENTS TO IMMIGRANTS

On October 9, 1992, the U.S. government announced a new law, the Chinese Student Protection Act. The legislation became a law after it was passed by both the Senate and the House of Representatives and signed by President Bush. Before its enactment, President Bush had repeatedly vetoed similar legislation, but finally, yielding to pressure from Congress and the coming presidential election, he signed it.

The legislation was connected to the earlier Presidential Administrative Order of April 11, 1990, issued after the June Fourth Incident of 1989. That order stated that Chinese students, visiting scholars, and other Chinese who had been in the United States in the period between June 5, 1989, and April 11, 1990, could stay until July 1, 1993. The 1992 Protection Act stipulated that if the president could not provide proof before July 1, 1993, that the people covered under the earlier administrative order could return to the People's Republic of China without being persecuted by the Chinese government, the American government would permit them to apply for a Green Card for the right to be permanent residents in the United States.

A year later Bill Clinton became the occupant of the White House. Apparently, he had no intention of going against the Act. On June 30, 1993, the U.S. Immigration and Naturalization Service announced the implementation details of the Act. The day after, the Act became law.

Within the first few days after the law became effective, the four district offices of the Immigration and Naturalization Service received more than 40,000 applications. After a month, the number exceeded 50,000. At the one-year deadline, the number exceeded 57,000. Thus, almost overnight, more than 50,000 Chinese students in America were made "overseas Chinese."[1]

Several other Western countries, including Canada, Australia, and New Zealand, passed similar legislation in that period. It was thus possible for many Chinese students to remain overseas.

These events originated with the June Fourth Incident. At that time, probably nobody would have thought that the "beneficiaries" of the incident would be Chinese students overseas. The kind of Green Card they received has been dubbed the "June Fourth Green Card."

The Chinese government protested when the U.S. Congress passed the Protection Act. The government spokesman pointed out that the excuse used by Congress—that students returning to China would be "unsafe" and subjected to "political persecution"—was groundless. The spokesman also said, "In fact, in the last half of 1992, many students returned from America and, without a single exception, received proper reception and treatment, and thousands of students, after returning to China for family visits, went back to America without a hitch."[2] What the Chinese government said was factual. In the summer of 1994—that is, about a year after the Protection Act became valid—the Office of Human Rights and Humanitarian Affairs of the U.S. State Department issued a report titled "Memorandum on the State of the Nation and the Asylum Application." The report acknowledged that the argument used by some Chinese students in their applications for asylum—that if they returned to China, they would be subjected to political persecution because of their antigovernment democratic activities—was not credible. The report first quoted an announcement by an organization called Asia Watch. That organization stated that to date there had not been a single case showing that returned students had been subjected to political persecution because of their active participation in overseas democratic rallies. The report quoted the text of a telegram sent by the American consul general in Shanghai in which he said that his talks with 120 Chinese students who were applying for J-1 and F-1 visas to return to the United States revealed no evidence that they had encountered obstruction from the Chinese government.[3]

In terms of bilateral relations, the U.S. Congress and administration clearly violated the series of understandings and agreements between the two countries on the exchange of students. Among them were the "Agreement on the Mutual Exchange of Students and Scholars between the People's Republic of China and the United States of America" signed by both countries, and the "Sino-American Educational Conference News Bulletin" jointly issued by China's National Education Commission and the U.S. Information Agency. In passing the law, the American government appeared to have moral justice on its side. But that moral justice was colored with ideology.

What was the attitude of the Chinese students when the two governments were locked in a battle of words? After all, application for a Green Card was not compulsory.

The choice of most Chinese students was clear and firm: to remain in America.

In the period between the spring and fall of 1993, when the Protection Act was still being debated in both the Senate and the House, some Chinese students, led by the All-America Autonomous Federation of Chinese Students and Scholars, launched a massive and effective campaign. They testified in Congress, claiming they would be persecuted if they were to return to China; they organized rallies, calling on the American public to be concerned with China's human rights; and they wrote letters, made telephone calls, and sent faxes to members of Congress requesting immediate passage of the Protection Act. The final passage of the Act was a testimonial to the fact that this generation of people who were hardened by the Great Proletarian Cultural Revolution should be treated with respect. The Federation, because of its all-out effort in promoting passage of the Act, won the label "The Green-Card Party."

The restlessness and anxiety of some Chinese students at that time were reflected vividly in discussions by the Chinese students on the e-mail network.

One student wrote, "In this critical moment of lobbying for the legislation, we can no longer just sit here and wait! Please call these Congressional members and request that they pass the legislation without any revisions! I will use my own money to reimburse you for your telephone calls."

Another one wrote, "Now is the time to take action for the passage of the legislation! Why is nobody organizing us? We cannot just sit and wait for the cake to fall from the sky, or to weep bitterly for the lost golden chance."

Still another wrote, "Everybody, act! Spend some money and time to write, call, fax! Do the arithmetic: you can get a Green Card for $20 when the act is passed, or you can hire a lawyer to do it for $3,000. Twenty is less than three thousand—everybody knows that."

On July 1, 1993, the day the U.S. Immigration and Naturalization Service began to accept applications for the Green Card based on the Protection Act, the response of the Chinese students was overwhelmingly enthusiastic. Many of them had everything already prepared: they had completed the application form, taken the physical examination, obtained identification photos, and had their fingerprints taken. Early in the morning they mailed the applications. Some cleverer ones sent the application by express mail to beat the rush. Since the Immigration Service reviewed the applications in order of receipt, an early mailing would mean early processing; a delay of just a few hours might mean falling behind several thousand or even several tens of thousands of other applications and a delay in getting the Green Card of several months. Word also circulated that there were only 45,000 slots left in the annual immigrant quota for that year and that when that was used up, the applicants would have to wait for next year's quota. In the first few days, the four regional offices of the Immigration Service received more than 10,000 applications per day. Then it became several thousand and then several hundred per day. A month later, the number dwindled to just over ten per day, and two months later to only a handful per day.

During the lobbying, some Chinese students, taking full advantage of a rare opportunity associated with the June Fourth Incident, played an American political game with Chinese characteristics. But claiming to risk persecution upon returning to China was a dishonest pretext, as the first thing many students did after receiving their Green Cards was to return to China for a family visit. As to human rights and democracy, they were words used to catch the attention of the naive and biased Americans. Many Americans also understood the maneuver of using a political reason for the purpose of immigrating to America. On July 11, 1993, shortly after the Protection Act became effective, I returned to America after visiting my family in China. At the customs inspection station, I heard the barbed comment of an inspection officer: "Oh, you Chinese can go back to China now."

Despite the political overtones of the whole episode, the great majority of the Chinese students who opted to remain in America did so not for political reasons alone. Some stayed for better personal growth, some for a better life.

In fact, even without the Protection Act, many students would have stayed by other means. Some government-sponsored students could change their visa status in accordance with the Presidential Administrative Order of 1990 so that they were exempt from regulations that required students to return to China for two years before becoming eligible for immigrant status; many privately financed students could find employment after graduation and then apply for a Green Card after receiving their work permits; other routes included political asylum, paper marriage, or simply going underground.

In America, the questions you would hear among the Chinese students greeting one another were "When are you going to graduate?" "Found a job yet?" and "Bought a house yet?" No one asked, "When are you going back?" If you told others that you were returning, they would be surprised and would assume that you could not survive in America anymore.

According to the statistics of the Chinese government, from 1978 to 1994 about 70,000 students, roughly one-third of the 200,000 who went abroad, returned. But the actual rate of returnees from America was far lower. According to an estimate by Rone Tempest of the *Los Angeles Times*, the rate was between 5 percent and 10 percent.[4]

To remain overseas was the choice of most Chinese students. They had their own reasons for that choice. But the exodus of students brought China its own sorrows.

THE REASON FOR NOT RETURNING

Many Chinese students remained abroad. This outcome was perhaps not expected by the Chinese government when it resumed sending students to study overseas. The June Fourth Incident in 1989 triggered this outcome, but in fact the trend to remain abroad had begun earlier.

According to the statistics of the U.S. Immigration and Naturalization Service, 6,238 Chinese students changed their status to "immigrant" between 1982 and 1987. Among them were 265 government-financed students.[5] There were two reasons for the small size of this group. First, the immigration law requires holders of J-1 visas to return to their country for a minimum of two years before they can become eligible for other types of visas. Second, most of them had yet to complete their studies.

In early 1989, when I was still in China, a recently returned Ph.D. student told me privately, "It looks as if most students are not coming back." I thought he was exaggerating to cause alarm. But he firmly believed his conclusion and commented sadly, "China is too poor. It's like a poor mother who can't feed her own children." After I went abroad, I realized that he was right. China, like all other developing countries, was inevitably disadvantaged in the international competition for talent in the twentieth century.

Objectively speaking, the Chinese government had made valiant efforts to get its overseas students back. In the early eighties the government each year sent goodwill delegations to American campuses during Chinese New Year, bringing song and dance to the students. Of course, sometimes the festivities included a report by Li Yanjie.[6]

In the nineties the goodwill delegation was replaced by the recruiting delegation. The first recruiting delegation, organized by the Service Center for Overseas Chinese Students, was sent in June 1989. The participants included the Zhongxing Company, the Capital Steel Company, Shenzhen Special Economic Zone, and the City of Xiamen.[7] Later, the recruiting effort was expanded to cover the United States, Europe, Canada, Japan, and Australia.

The Chinese personnel system, notorious for its stiffness, also showed some rare flexibility. In finding work for students, the guiding principles were to "let the students choose their own fields," "let both sides choose their own match," and "give the students the freedom to come and go." In 1985 the government began to create mobility centers for postdoctoral scientific research to ensure the mobility of the returned students. There were 278 such centers by the end of 1992.[8]

In pay and living conditions, the returned students were also treated with increasing favors, at least in terms of the number of special programs devised for them. Returned students who encountered problems with job rank, housing, or, if married, spouses having two different work locations were given special care, although the solutions were not perfectly satisfactory to everybody. In October 1992 the government announced a special privilege for returned students: purchasing a domestic automobile tax-free.[9]

Even more interesting was that the government adopted a more tolerant attitude with respect to politics. After the June Fourth Incident, the Administrative Office of the Office of the Premier issued a memorandum, Administrative Document No. 44 (1992), to appeal to students "to complete their studies abroad, to return to China, and to build a career in their motherland." It also stated that

> the students, without exception, will not be held accountable for their attacks, in words or in deeds, on the government while they were abroad. [Even] those who joined an antigovernment organization and participated in activities to injure the national security, honor, and interest will be welcome to return to work without exception if they withdraw from these organizations and do not participate in any further antigovernment activities that violate China's Constitution and law.[10]

But no matter how hard the government tried, the generally inferior living conditions and a political system that allowed less individual freedom could not be changed overnight.

"I can't go back. The teaching life would be just too harsh," a thirty-four-year-old assistant professor in a business school in Pennsylvania said. He was from Tianjin, had come to America in 1983, and earned a Ph.D. in economics at Columbia University. After graduation he found work that paid an annual salary of $50,000. Most people would not hesitate in a choice between an annual salary of $50,000 as a professor in America and a monthly salary of ¥500 to ¥600[11] in China, not to mention the fact that he was well aware of the harsh life of a teacher in China, as both of his parents taught at Tianjin Normal College.

For some students there were other reasons for staying.

A forty-year-old who received his Ph.D. from the University of Michigan in computer science summed it up in this way: "The Chinese government treats you the best when it can least control you." Two years after his graduation, he still had not found a job. He earned a living doing piece-work software design for some small computer companies and had never given a thought to returning to China. His logic was drawn from his personal experience in China. After he had completed all the paperwork for studying abroad as a privately financed student, he had asked repeatedly for the "favor" of approval from his work unit. The leadership objected vehemently, issued an announcement criticizing him, and finally expelled him.

Later, after he finished his degree and received his Green Card, the leadership changed its stance to let bygones be bygones. On a visit to America, they visited him and even brought him a present.

Lovable China certainly had some unlovable traits. But there was irony for the overseas Chinese students. One of the reasons they had been sent to foreign countries to study was that there was a need to change the social conditions in China. These very conditions, however, had unexpectedly become the reason that they chose not to return.

Some people commented that this generation of Chinese students, when compared to previous ones, lacked idealism and dedication, and had forgotten the motherland.

It was true that traditional patriotic sentiments had lost their appeal for these students, as most students had accepted the Western idea of individual freedom: the individual's right to choose supersedes all obligations, and national interest is not a sufficient reason to justify personal sacrifice. Perhaps few students would admit that they had no patriotic sentiments, but most people would rather choose their own ways to express those sentiments. It would be all right to do something for the country, but not when the act would entail personal sacrifice.

The study-and-then-stay phenomenon will perhaps last for some time. This is not a trend that can be turned around by attempts to "educate" the students overseas. But neither should one feel that the situation is deplorable. In this world that is ever shrinking due to the rapid development of science and technology, it is hard to say that China has "lost" (in the originally intended meaning of the word) its elite. Perhaps those students who opted to remain overseas will make their contributions to China's development in the future.

HARD TO LEAVE, HARD TO RETURN

Only a few took the journey back to China. The reason was that its path was not lined with beautiful flowers.

More than a hundred years ago, the Qing court abruptly recalled all its teenage students from America. During their return journey, although they felt sad, they indulged in the dream that the motherland would warmly embrace them with outstretched arms. But when they landed in Shanghai, they were met not by a cheering crowd, or their families and friends. Instead, like criminals who had been stripped of their citizenship, they were escorted by soldiers and confined in a "college" where each student was given a soiled bedroll and two wooden boards for a bed. There they were detained and not allowed to go out or to meet their families. The "living quarters were moldy and the humid air seeped through the cracks between the bricks and rose to fill the room."[12] After enduring detention for some time, they were sent to work in various places without having been asked first about their specialty or preference.

When compared to the misfortunes of those teenage students, returned students in the nineties seemed to have no reason to complain. But for most students, it was hard to leave as well as to return, although for different reasons. As soon as they returned, they felt that they were guilty of some wrongdoing, and it was hard to gain understanding from others.

A visiting scholar who had been abroad many times said his latest return to China was in May 1992. After a year of advanced study in America, he returned with his wife and son and entered the country in Guangzhou. An inspector of the Frontier Defense Office examined their passports and said, perhaps out of goodwill, "Your whole family has left. Why bother to come back?"

At work, life was even harder. His colleagues in the institute would ask as soon as they saw him, "Why are you back?" He felt that he could not make others understand the reason for his return. So he gave the same answer to every inquirer: "I have no talent. I couldn't survive in America."[13] *After repeating this excuse for more than two weeks, he was spared further pestering.*

After the return, the first trial was daily material life. The gap in living standards between Western countries and China made it hard at first for returned students to readjust to life in China.

A thirty-eight-year-old man with a Ph.D. in literature, who had returned to China in 1988, had been assigned to work in the Institute of Social Sciences. The institute took special care of him by giving him a one-room apartment. One night during a windstorm half of the windows in the apartment were blown away. Unable to sleep any more because it was too cold, he wrapped himself in a blanket and waited for the dawn. He was sad; the lofty idealism to which he had clung tightly before his return seemed to have blown away, too. At that time, his monthly salary was ¥96, and the postage for mailing his manuscript to a foreign journal for publication was ¥26.[14] *"That's equivalent to the milk and fruit money for my daughter for a whole month," he said wryly. "To trade the health of your child for a scholarly exchange is absurd."*

But frankly speaking, he was lucky to have gotten that one-room apartment.

A story circulating around Beijing went like this: A well-known university in Beijing was ready to welcome a returning student but could not provide housing. Finally the problem was brought to the attention of the vice-president in charge of housing, who said he could not get housing for the prospective returnee even if his life were at stake. Besides, he wouldn't dare to hand housing over to the returning student even if he had any. Doing so would so enrage other people on the waiting list that they would certainly kill him sooner or later.

Of course there were some relatively fortunate ones.

A man with a Ph.D. in language returned to his old institute in the late eighties from Canada. He, his wife, and their three-year-old child lived in the guesthouse of the institute after their arrival. Finally his mentor, an elderly man of impeccable reputation, after walking tirelessly with his cane from one office to another to negotiate housing for his student, got a two-room apartment for him. The elderly man was hoping to retain his best student at the institute so that there would be a successor to handle his work.

Among the numerous material difficulties faced by the returned students, the most serious was housing. China had an acute housing shortage, and an overall reform in housing policy had yet to begin. Under these circumstances, it was not fair for anyone to receive special treatment simply because he or she had studied abroad for a few years. But without housing the returned students would have found a country but not a home. Most students, while abroad, whether they had been doing very well or barely surviving, had a stable place to live. They had to think twice about their intention to return if they sensed that, once back, they would be homeless.

One student, upon hearing the government's offer to allow returned student to purchase domestic automobiles tax-free, said, "I don't want a car, and I can't afford a car. I just want an apartment."

Besides material hardship, there was intellectual hardship. To a large extent the modernization of a society depends not only on the presence of glittering buildings but also on the speed and breadth of information exchange. In this regard, many cities in China, even with their skyscrapers, were no different from remote and inaccessible rural areas. Some returned students felt suffocated.

A thirty-nine-year-old student with a Ph.D. in economics had returned to China in 1989. He said that he now felt deeply pained when he read foreign journals in the library. Although these journals were no longer current issues, the topics of the articles in them were new to him.

The speed of advances in science and technology was even faster than that in humanities. Returned students in these fields faced a grim challenge.

A thirty-four-year-old man with a Ph.D. from Stanford specialized in parallel processing in computer design. In 1991 he returned to China and worked for two years in a postdoctoral center. In those two years, he felt isolated because nobody in the whole university understood what he was doing. He could find hardly anyone to talk to. Four years later, in 1995, he went abroad for a second time. He noticed that he could hardly talk to his former teachers and classmates because he had never heard of the topics of their research. Those students who had not been on a par with him in the past now could easily give him a lesson or two.

Not everyone could bear such emotional suffering.

A twenty-eight-year-old man with a Ph.D. in physics from MIT returned to China in 1988. After working in a research institute for more than a year, he still could not start any serious research because of problems in funding and supporting facilities. Finally, he simply joined the institute's bridge team. He played bridge day and night and, upon returning to his dormitory, just dropped on his bed and slept. The good thing was that he had no time left for thinking.

Then there were the many special unwritten dogmas that were hard to adjust to. These dogmas were the traditions observed by the academics. One could sense them but could not point a finger at them. They were like taboos in politics, only more untouchable.

A thirty-seven-year-old man with a Ph.D. in sociology from Harvard said that after his return he felt as though he were taken to task for whatever he did. He said, "It's like explosions in a minefield, but I don't really know when and where I stepped on them." In his research, he chose realistic topics, constructed models, and analyzed data for substantiation, instead of following the old yet still-fashionable method of using purely theoretical analysis. His approach was jeered as heresy. After the results were published and attracted wide public attention, during job-performance reviews his work was criticized as unscholarly.

He believed that the principal cause of such dogmas was that these institutions functioned like the purchasing department of a bureaucracy; they processed paperwork for the purpose of maintaining the generally accepted authority and the existing order of a field. He felt that the older generation had aged prematurely, the younger generation had learned rapidly, and the middle-aged group, being hardened by the biased education of the fifties and by successive political movements, criticized others with abandon.

It was inevitable that sharp conflicts would arise in the future between the different generations in academia. Under the shadow of these dogmas, returned students who managed to do some serious work would be earmarked as heretics. Although dogmas exist in academia in every country, under the current system in China, those who violate them can become outcasts and hence accomplish nothing.

The Chinese government had repeatedly called on its overseas students to return, work, and contribute to China's development. The students who returned in the mid-eighties had already shown their influence; among them were government ministers and university presidents, and many more were leaders in various disciplines. But China's acute need of specialized talent in government and in economic development could not have been satisfied even if all students had returned.

It was not an easy matter for an overseas Chinese student to find a job in China. Before my own return I wrote letters to several government organizations and received no reply. Later I wrote to the Service Center for Overseas Chinese Students and asked them to find contacts for me. The reply came quickly, together with a form. I completed the form and mailed it back. Again, that was the end of it. I called the center some time later and was told that I had to return to China first and try to find a job on my own.

Even if a returned student could locate a job effortlessly, he would find the environment in the workplace quite complex. In a society that was run by seniority and rigid rules and regulations, whether a person with a skill could survive and make use of that skill was not at all assured. A thirty-seven-year-old returnee with a Ph.D. in sociology from a reputable university in the Midwest finally found a teaching job in a key university in Beijing after numerous failed attempts. However, he did not expect that he would be asked to teach freshman English.

The bottom line is that the sole factor that could attract the students to return to China was opportunity for growth. Those who were willing to return, regardless of their aspirations, did so for the purpose of accomplishing something. Although the returnees tend to have an uppity attitude, they should be treated well because China needs them. We must come to grips with the fact that China has plenty of people but few talents.

If the Chinese government fails to act effectively to attract overseas Chinese students, and if Chinese society fails to provide opportunities for career growth for the returned students, it is inevitable that Chinese talent will be harvested by other countries. In recent years the automobile giants near Detroit have conducted a large-scale effort to recruit and train Chinese college graduates, reputedly in preparation for a massive entrance into the automobile market in China in the future.

The problems faced by the returned students in fact are the problems that are endemic throughout Chinese society. These problems can be solved only with rapid economic growth. The development of a market economy will create more individual freedom and hence relax the stiff social system. At the same time, competition in business will lead to competition for talent, which Chinese society will begin to recognize as valuable. Only then can there be real improvement in work and living conditions for returned students. The trend of economic development in China points to this prospect.

But that journey may take a long time. Meanwhile, the working life, talent, and knowledge of many returned students may be wasted; this is one of the principal reasons that overseas Chinese students have been reluctant to return.

Then should the students simply wait overseas for China's economic climate to change? We can answer the question by asking why the students were sent abroad to study to begin with. The mission of the students was to promote changes in China, not to wait overseas for those changes to occur.

Like the stories of many of their predecessors, the story of the return of this generation of students may not have a happy ending. But also like that of their predecessors, the story will be interesting and full of meaning.

Let us return to Yung Wing, whom we discussed briefly in chapter 1. We can draw enlightenment from his experience after he returned to China.

THE LIFE OF YUNG WING: A TRAGEDY? A FAILURE?

On November 13, 1854, the twenty-six-year-old Yung Wing, freshly graduated from Yale, boarded a ship in New York to return to China after being away for eight years. He carried a dream with him: to allow the next generation of Chinese youth an opportunity for a Western education as he had had, for he believed that therein lay the hope of revitalizing China. In his memoir he said the education he received in the West had brought about tremendous changes in him, in thoughts and in actions; upon arrival in China he felt he was in another world. But his love for the country and the people, drawn from his sympathy for their suffering caused by ignorance and poverty, only became stronger.

Yet Chinese society cruelly dashed his dream.

In the summer of 1855 Yung Wing landed in Guangzhou, Guandong, where he lived for six months. There he witnessed a massacre. It was the time of the Taiping Rebellion, and some people in Guangdong took part in the uprising.[15] Ye Mingsheng, the viceroy of the Huguang District, carried out a bloody repression. In that summer alone, more than 70,000 people were executed, including many innocent people. Yung Wing's residence was not far from the execution ground. He gave the following eyewitness account of the holocaust:

> The ground was perfectly drenched with human blood. On both sides of the driveway were to be seen headless human trunks, piled up in heaps, waiting to be taken away for burial.... But no provision had been made to find a place large enough to bury all the bodies. There they were, left exposed to a burning sun. The temperature stood from morning to night in midsummer steadily at 90° Fahrenheit, and sometimes higher. The atmosphere within a radius of two thousand yards of

> the execution ground was heavily charged with the poisonous and pestilential vapor.[16]

Facing such a horrifying scene, Yung Wing was deeply disturbed. The violent act of the Qing court led him to sympathize with the rebels. He considered joining the Taiping uprising.

In the fall of 1859 Yung Wing had an opportunity to visit the provinces south of the Yangzi River that were under the control of the Taiping Heavenly Kingdom, to see for himself whether the Taiping army truly represented hope for China. In Nanjing he met Hong Ren'gan, the younger brother of Hong Xiuquan and the most knowledgeable person in the Taiping camp. Yung Wing presented seven proposals for reforms in the military, government, financial system, and education, and expressed his willingness to serve if the Taipings were interested in his suggestions. A few days later, when he was told that it was not yet possible to carry out his ideas, he was presented with a small parcel in which was wrapped a wooden seal engraved with the word "righteousness" (*yi*):[17] he had been made a noble of the fourth rank. Not knowing whether to laugh or to weep at this development, which was irrelevant to his aspirations, he began to question if the Taipings would be able to succeed.

After the trip to Nanjing, he turned to the tea-trading business. His plan was to amass a fortune and then carry out his plan with his own money.

In 1863, just when his tea business was booming, he was summoned by Zeng Guofan, who had risen to power because of his success in defeating the Taiping army. During the interview, Zeng asked him what task China should take on that was both possible and the most beneficial. Knowing that Zeng was considering building a factory, Yung Wing proposed a factory that could manufacture machines. Zeng entrusted to him the full authority necessary to build such a factory: planning, purchasing, and assembly.[18] The Jiangnan Manufacturing Bureau (the predecessor of the Jiangnan Shipyard Bureau) was one of the first factories in China.

But Yung constantly bore in mind his dream of sending students abroad for a Western education, believing that this would be the most beneficial thing for China. After returning from his purchasing trip for the machinery factory, Yung spoke with Zeng several times about his wish to send students to America. Years passed.

In 1871 a joint memorial on the study-abroad project, written by Zeng and several other ministers, finally reached the Qing court. Upon hearing this news, Yung was unable to sleep for many nights. Soon the Qing court approved the plan. His dream of many years finally became a reality. Beginning in 1872, four groups of teenagers totaling 120 students crossed the ocean and went to America to study.

But a political storm crushed his lifetime effort overnight. In 1881 the Qing court recalled all the teenage students, abruptly terminating their studies. After the collapse of this educational plan, Yung Wing successively proposed plans for banking and railroad construction, but none was adopted, for one reason or another. He said, with deep disappointment, "All my attempts proved abortive.... This ended my last effort to help China."[19]

By then it was 1898, and the Reform Movement began to bud.[20] The disappointed Yung Wing once more gravitated toward political movements. For a while his residence in Beijing became the meeting place for the leadership of the Reform Movement. He thus became a criminal wanted by the Qing court after the collapse of the Hundred Days of Reform.[21] He fled to Hong Kong by way of Shanghai and eventually returned to America, where he spent his final years.[22] He never returned to China.[23]

Viewing Yung Wing's life from a personal angle, we can conclude that it was a tragedy. He brought his dream to China, fought for its realization, and finally witnessed its demise. Of course, the tragic ending was related to the particularly difficult path that he chose. A fellow student, Wong Foon, accompanied him to America but made different choices. From America he went to Edinburgh to study medicine. After returning to China, he practiced medicine in the South and led a stable and well-off life.

But from a historical viewpoint, Yung Wing was anything but a failure, because to a certain degree he changed the history of China. Relying on his own efforts, he promoted two major events in China's recent history: the introduction of a modern machinery industry and the dispatching of Chinese students to study abroad. The latter had an especially important long-range impact on the direction of development in modern China.

Yung Wing once said that one must be a dreamer in order to accomplish something. To realize his dream, he was also a realist. Yung Wing dreamed of transforming China when he returned from America. But he held no illusions that he could miraculously complete that transformation overnight. Western education impregnated his mind with a strong spirit of pragmatism, and behind each dream was a concrete plan to build a factory, dispatch students abroad, create a banking system, or construct railroads. He recognized that his dreams might not be completely realizable, but their implementation would promote progress in China, step by step.

In addition, he deeply appreciated the fact that dreaming alone would not make dreams become reality. He did not have the aloof mentality that so permeated other Chinese intellectuals. He tried a variety of ways to realize his dreams, from business to lobbying. The acquaintance he made with Zeng Guofan provided him with a historical opportunity that he used effectively for his two major achievements.

His witnessing of the massacre in Guangdong propelled him to consider revolution as an alternative and extreme political action as a viable means for a speedy transformation of Chinese society; he placed high hopes on the Taiping Heavenly Kingdom.

He was disappointed by the Taiping group after his visit to the Taiping capital in Nanjing. His disappointment, however, led him to a deeper understanding of revolution. He said, "Rebellions and revolutions in China are not new or rare historical occurrences. During China's recorded history there have been at least twenty-four dynasties and as many attendant rebellions or revolutions."[24]

He also pointed out that the Taiping Rebellion had an enigmatic, dual character like that of a sphinx. A revolution could implement justice, and it could destroy. Revolution also could break out abruptly and vanish just as abruptly. It might leave little trace in history, as was the case of the Taiping Heavenly Kingdom.[25] Because of his distrust of revolution, Yung Wing firmly believed that his plan of sending students abroad to study was the true hope for China. He chose a path other than revolution.

An interesting historical phenomenon is the fact that few of those 120 returned students took part in the revolution led by Sun Yat-sen. Most of them became specialists in various fields. Thirty-nine became engineers in railroads, telecommunications, and mining; eighteen served in the navy; fifteen served in the Ministry of Foreign Affairs and other government offices; ten worked in the fields of education and health services; two worked in journalism; two in Chinese Customs; and seven in business.[26]

In subsequent years few people from the largest group—those who had returned from America—took part in the series of political revolutions. Most were scientists, engineers, scholars, or professors. It was the contributions of these returned students that formed the foundation of China's progress today.

SENDING STUDENTS ABROAD: A MEANS FOR ECONOMIC AND SOCIAL DEVELOPMENT

On May 25, 1995, after being abroad for nearly six years, I left America and returned to China, again by Northwest Airlines, taking the same direct route between Detroit and Beijing.

The return was as hurried as the departure, leaving no time for me to feel sentimental. After document-sorting, packing, selling furniture, cleaning up, closing and transferring bank accounts, saying goodbye, turning in keys, and so forth, I sat quietly in my empty room and realized that there were only three more hours before flight time. Then, when I walked for the last time along the path from my office to my living quarters as I had done so many times before, a sentiment toward the small city of Ann Arbor, where I had lived for so many years, welled up in me.

But I knew I could not stay there. This was not my destination. As the American poet Robert Frost said,

> The woods are lovely, dark and deep,
> But I have promises to keep,
> And miles to go before I sleep,
> And miles to go before I sleep.

My destination was China.

Before my return many people asked me, "Why are you going back?" The question was at once strange and reasonable—strange that today a Chinese would feel curious about another Chinese person's return to China, but reasonable because there was little attraction to returning. Interestingly, it was mostly Chinese who asked the question; obviously they had the question in their minds, too. From an American viewpoint, returning or staying would be equally natural.

During the flight over the Pacific Ocean, I thought about this question: Why was I returning? I found it hard to answer. For me it was an emotion that could not be described clearly; it was like a promise that I needed to keep.

An American scholar surveyed Chinese students on the subject of returning to China. The results showed that the reasons for staying in America were quite specific: lower living standards in China, the inflexible personnel system, poor facilities for scientific research, and limited opportunities for personal growth. These reasons were easy to understand. But the reason some chose to return was primarily an abstract patriotic sentiment. The American scholar was deeply puzzled by this result, since patriotic sentiment is a rather stale concept in American society.

He was puzzled, perhaps because he had overlooked a simple fact: China in modern times has been a weak country, and that weakness has saved patriotic sentiment from going out of fashion among Chinese.

For more than one hundred years, the Chinese had been caught by their dream of their country's becoming strong. This dream had been dashed many times but had survived changes of leadership, shifting of political power, the rise and fall of political parties, and social turmoil. To achieve that dream, the nation tried all conceivable means, including reform, rebellion, revolution, and civil war. Generation after generation had been willing to endure family fragmentation, to bear heavy burdens, to toil, and even to give their lives. No price was too high to pay. Among these efforts was the dispatching of students to study abroad.

For China, sending students abroad was not a simple gesture of cultural exchange but, rather, the shouldering of a burden in its determination to further the country's development. This was a reality that the students had to face.

This was a very Chinese way of thinking. It seemed as if the students not only had to bear the heavy burden entrusted by history, but they also had to be willing to make personal sacrifices. History showed, however, that it was precisely this Chinese sentiment that sustained the spirits of the nation. The sentiment allowed China, after enduring more than a hundred years of humiliating weakness and poverty, to see a ray of light at the dawn of the twenty-first century.

Chinese of the future may have new vistas to gaze on. But the current generation of Chinese students who went abroad to study must face the landscape of today.

TRANSLATOR'S ENDNOTE

A Personal Reflection on the Power of History

> Most of us are citizens by reason of the simple serendipitous fact of our birth here.
>
> —JUDGE JAMES A. PARKER

While reading the Chinese edition of Qian Ning's *Chinese Students Encounter America*, I was awed by the imprint of China's civilization on the social phenomenon known as "studying in America" in the last 150 years of Chinese history. I left mainland China with my family for Taiwan in 1949 at age sixteen and came to America to study in 1956. This endnote, which is about my life before I came to America, expresses my veneration for the power of history and hence explains why I translated this book.

I was born in Anhui, China, in 1933 and grew up in Nanjing (Nanking), then China's capital. One of my earliest memories is of being sheltered during the Nanjing Massacre, which took place when I was four. My parents, two older sisters, and I (my younger brother was not yet born) took refuge at Jinling Women's College, which was run by American missionaries. In the last four of the eight years of Japanese occupation, from 1937 to 1945, my family lived next to a Japanese civilian family. Having read very little of the history of conflict between China and Japan, I did not feel threatened by or hostile toward them. I studied Japanese in 1944 and 1945, as required by the Japanese occupier.

My grandmother came from a peasant family and was uneducated. Her feet were bound until the 1911 Nationalist Revolution. My grandfather taught himself to read and write and later became an herbal pharmacist. They scrimped to send my father, their eldest son, to Jinling University. But their second son, my uncle, was influenced by a wealthy distant cousin of his and became an opium addict at a young age. My mother had a few years of schooling, and could read more than she could write.

August 15, 1945, was a memorable day. On the way home after school, I heard Emperor Hirohito announce through loudspeakers that Japan would surrender unconditionally to the Allies. Although I did not comprehend the significance of the announcement, I had an inkling that this was important enough for me to run all the way home to my mother and tell her what I had heard.

The next two years were a happy time for me. The atmosphere of Japanese occupation and American bombing and leaflet dropping was replaced by the busy activities of the returning Chinese government and its American military advisers. The Americans rode in jeeps and, in wintertime, wore smart-looking leather jackets rather than a cotton-padded robe such as I wore. I saw movies featuring Johnny Weissmuller, Dorothy Lamour, and the hilarious pair Laurel and Hardy.

I knew the government was battling the Communists in the north, but I had never felt concerned. I did become familiar with some impressive-sounding American names, however: Albert Wedemeyer, Patrick Hurley, and George Marshall, the American mediators who were trying unsuccessfully to bring a negotiated settlement between the Nationalists and Communists.

Then inflation caused by financing the war against the Communists raged with gale force. One day in 1948 my father, who was employed by the Postal Savings and Remittances Bank (he also was a partner in a private bank and a textile factory), dug a small trench under the canopy of a sycamore tree in our front yard and buried a steel pipe two feet long by about four inches in diameter, with caps on both ends. Later he explained to me that the government would soon issue a new currency, "gold yuan," at the rate of one new yuan to three million old yuan. All privately held gold would have to be turned in to the central bank. The pipe contained gold bars that my father tried to hide from the government. (I have not seen the steel pipe since; I wonder if it and its contents are still there.) But soon the "gold yuan," too, became worthless, and goods and services were again purchased with silver dollars minted at the turn of the nineteenth century.

As the Communists continued their southward advance in the fall of 1948, my family packed up our cotton-padded bedrolls, pots, and pans to prepare for a 1,000-mile flight to the south. The eight-month stop-and-go trip was an exciting adventure for me. I rode on a train for the first time, and traveled through the battlegrounds of valorous generals who had lived at the end of the Eastern Han dynasty (25–220 C.E.). But on our journey we stayed in dark houses with mud walls and thatched roofs similar to the ones owned by the peasants. We were sometimes street vendors, selling our clothing and cookware to lighten our load. My first sale brought in three dollars for a pair of flannel pajamas. The thrill of hearing the ringing silver overpowered my embarrassment at having to squat on the sidewalk as a peddler.

One summer morning in Guangzhou in 1949, before the Communist takeover of the mainland, we fled on the last ship to Taiwan on which my father's employer had reserved bunks to evacuate its employees and their families. I felt sad as I said goodbye to the one-room apartment we had lived in for the previous two months. In contrast to the mud huts we had become accustomed to, it was bright and airy, with a high ceiling; it had been a bedroom in a stone house in Guangzhou's old French Concession.

Hurriedly we unloaded our belongings from a truck to a sampan on a sandy bank of the Huangpu River to reach the ocean-faring ship, which was anchored in deep water. Halfway to the ship, which was about as far from the bank as the Statue of Liberty is from Ellis Island, a gunman in another sampan approached us and diverted our boat to a remote marsh. The three bandits searched our belongings for about eight hours, leisurely picnicking on my family's stock of canned ham from America and on biscuits, candies, and my father's favorite cigarettes (Three Five brand) from England. These items were precious; China's canned-food industry was practically nonexistent at that time. What the bandits could not consume on the spot, they took with them. Finally, at dark, we were released and given $20 for travel money. All the while, I was thinking about the marsh bandits of the Song dynasty (960–1279) who were romanticized in the adventure stories of which I was fond.

At the time of the robbery, my two elder sisters were no longer with the family. Two months earlier, my eldest sister, who had introduced me to literature translated from English and Russian, had been nudged into a hasty marriage. On the morning after her wedding, I saw her, in tears, recede out of sight forever as the train carrying the family off to Guangzhou pulled away from the station. The logic of the wedding was the same as that of selling the pots and pans we had brought from Nanjing: to lighten the family load. Two weeks before that wedding, my second-eldest sister had run away to escape a similar fate. (Years later she rejoined the family in Taiwan. My eldest sister later committed suicide because her spirit had been broken by the discovery that her husband already had a wife from a "cradle marriage"; her body had been broken by the famine resulting from the Great Leap Forward. In Taiwan my father was laid off from the dissolved bank and, ever resourceful, supported the family by nightly winnings at poker. He died of a stroke when he was sixty, and my mother died soon after of loneliness.)

It took an hour to row to the ship after the bandits released us. I was worried that the ship would not wait for us and I would not be able to go to Taiwan, the island known to me by its folk hero Zheng Chenggong, who, history says, fought off the Dutch in the Ming dynasty (1368–1644). But the ship was still there, and I was happy again.

In Taiwan I completed high school and college. One of the most exciting events of college was to see some of my classmates leave for Korea to work for the American military as interpreters in interrogations of the POWs from the Resist-America, Aid-Korea Volunteer Army of the People's Republic of China. I, too, wanted to join but was discouraged by my parents. These classmates returned with seemingly limitless American dollars to spend. They talked mostly among themselves, drank openly, laughed loudly, and spoke of visiting prostitutes. Their un-Chinese behavior puzzled me. None of them talked about the POWs, and no student in the college seemed to be interested in that subject either.

In 1956 I came to America and have remained ever since; my brother came a few years later. I studied engineering in graduate school, worked at odd jobs, got married, found work doing research in physics, became the father of two children, and retired in 1994.

In December 1997 I visited the Academy of Sciences and Tsinghua University in Beijing and chanced to read *Chinese Students Encounter America.* I felt like Emily Webb in *Our Town*, who, after her death, was given the opportunity to see what had happened in her life.

It is easy for me and other international students from poor or warring countries to recognize elements of our own lives in the stories documented in *Chinese Students Encounter America*: freedom from the threat of war, the serenity and majesty of the open spaces, bewildering material abundance, the dizzying choices available in everyday life, the pressure of schoolwork and survival, the brutality of the culture of acquisitiveness. Where we differ is in the lives we left behind: Chinese students who came to America in the eighties and nineties had lived in China during Land Reform and the Cultural Revolution—a life my family would have lived had we, on that fateful day in Guangzhou, failed to get out of China. Had the bandits delayed us longer, had the ship left without us, then the name of my father, who owned farmland in Anhui, would certainly have been listed in Taiwan's newspapers among the landlords killed during Land Reform; I myself might have arrived one day in the early eighties on an American campus as a middle-aged visiting scholar from the People's Republic of China, speaking halting English; my children might have been among the boisterous students demonstrating in Tiananmen Square in 1989, or among the screaming Red Guards who beat their school principals, broke Ming-dynasty vases, and smashed Western violins more than a decade earlier. But China's millennia-old civilization, which passed on to modern Chinese the twin legacies of unyielding poverty at home and weakness among nations, and unmet longing for prosperity and equality, would have eventually swept my children to campuses in Berkeley, Ann Arbor, or Madison as they swept me to America from Taiwan.

We act out our roles according to the script of history, wherever, whenever, and whoever we happen to be. The script can change only after old forces are spent and new forces are born. Both the dissipation of the old and the creation of the new requires an open education for the young.

T. K. CHU
Princeton, New Jersey
June 30, 2000

APPENDIX I

Correspondence on Remission of the Boxer Indemnity

LIANG CHENG'S LETTER TO THE BOARD OF GOVERNORS, CHINA'S MINISTRY OF FOREIGN AFFAIRS (WAIWUBU)

[Received May 13, 1905]

[Letter no. 66. Subject:] The prospect of reducing the indemnity payment to America is good. Please consider declaring that the remitted money would be used for establishing schools and sending students to study abroad. Please send instructions.

I assume the Board has received letter no. 65, dated the twenty-ninth day, second moon [the thirty-first year of Guangxu (April 8, 1905)].

I have already reported my past attempts to recover the American indemnity. It now appears that the fund, excluding the legitimate claims by American business people and missionaries, actually exceeds $22 million. Ever since John Hay presented on my behalf [to the president?] the proposal of a reduction, I have also been lobbying, and there has been a significant change in attitude among high-level officials. Even Leslie Shaw, the unyielding secretary of the treasury, no longer objects outright to the remission. Based on these observations, a reduction appears possible.

The American minister Rockhill has been sympathetic toward the remission. I decided to confer with him before he leaves for China. The purpose was to ascertain a plan for the reduction, thus forestalling any future misunderstanding when he discusses the matter with you. I also felt that the meeting would

The correspondence in appendix 1 did not appear in the Chinese edition of this book.

prepare me for a more detailed discussion with Secretary Hay when he returns from his vacation. Then nothing will be overlooked. Thus in the last several days I have held discussions with Rockhill and the State Department concerning the method of remission.

According to Rockhill, the American president, knowing that China has already determined the method to raise the money from its citizens, had wondered whether the money, if returned by the United States, would go back to the citizens or would be used for other purposes. I told him that America's act of returning the indemnity money, which it does not rightfully own, would greatly enhance America's reputation for justice among nations, and China cannot make an advance declaration on the use of the money since it is our internal affair. Rockhill countered that the president does not intend to interfere but would like to know roughly how the money will be used, so he can word appropriately his request to Congress for authorization of a reduction.

China today is closely watched by the surrounding Powers and they will react to our policy. If we do not act out of the ordinary, they cannot concoct any treacherous scheme against us. We should mark what the American president said, regardless of whether he intends to interfere or not, so that the American government will not have excuses to hold up the money. In this regard, we should make a clear and righteous declaration to convince them. Therefore it seems appropriate to declare to the American government: Please return the indemnity so that it can be used for establishing schools and sending students abroad. The American government will be pleased to gain a reputation of being just and to bear witness to the development of talent through education. Even if there are a few dissenters in America, most of the country will welcome this lofty goal, and the $22 million will not all end up in other people's hands. To use for educational purposes the money that is already allocated for indemnity would create benefit from damage, and gain from loss. Besides, the act would heighten China's morale, lay a foundation for the nation's resurgence, and lift us from humiliation. Its benefit would be enormous. Furthermore, $22 million is a large sum, but if it were redistributed back to the provinces, it would become insignificant and there might be little benefit to the country. For these reasons, instead of seeing the funds fatten a few pockets or cause disputes in negotiations with the American government, it is better to spend the money on our critical needs—the development of talent.

I have given careful consideration to the matter before arriving at this conclusion. I realize that the eminent members of the Board have far greater vision and wisdom, are capable of drawing up a far-sighted plan, and will not reject minute considerations. Thus, I present my recommendations for your consideration and await your instructions, which I will transmit to the U.S. State Department. Let us hope the U.S. Congress discusses the remission in its fall session. The sooner the matter is concluded, the sooner China can plan for its future. If you could state clearly to Minister Rockhill our goal in the use of the money when he calls on you in Beijing, he can serve as a liaison, enhancing our chances for success. Please let me know if this plan is appropriate. I wish all eminent members of the Board good health.

SOURCE: *Qinghua Daxue shiliao bianxuan* (Selected source materials on the history of Tsinghua University), vol. 1 (Beijing: Qinghua Daxue Chubanshe, 1991), 76–77.

CORRESPONDENCE BETWEEN WILLIAM ROCKHILL AND THEODORE ROOSEVELT

July 12, 1905

Dear Mr. President:

You will remember that one of the questions which Mr. Hay had often in mind and greatly at heart in connection with Chinese affairs was the eventual return to China of a portion of the indemnity granted us in 1900, which we had found to be greatly in excess of the amount needed for the settlement of our equitable claims growing out of the Boxer troubles.

During the last two years Mr. Hay frequently spoke to me on this matter, and he always concluded his remarks by the statement that some means must be found by which we could perform this act of simple justice.

I feel it therefore a duty that I owe you, as well as one which I owe the memory of Mr. Hay, to bring this matter to your attention, trusting that in your wisdom you may be able to determine up some method by which this much desired end can be consummated.

On December 6th of last year, at the request of Mr. Hay, I wrote a draft of a message to Congress covering this question. Although I fancy that this was submitted to you at the time I enclose herewith a copy. In the last paragraph I suggested that 50 percent of the amount of the payments which may hereafter fall due the United States by China should be refunded, but even this reduction will leave us an amount greatly in excess of our claims and expenses; 75 percent refund would not, in my mind, be too great, for the private claims of our citizens, all of which have been settled at the present time, amounted to little more than two millions of dollars, and from what information I can gather the expenses of the military force which we sent to China and the extraordinary expenses of our Navy, cannot possibly have exceeded five millions. On the other hand China will have paid us by 1939, when the whole indemnity will be paid off, fifty odd millions of dollars, as principal and interest.

Although Mr. Hay never stated to the Chinese Minister at Washington that it was our intention to refund any portion of this indemnity to China, he did not hesitate to let him understand that our government was considering the subject of an eventual rearrangement of the matter. I was therefore not surprised when I returned to China to be questioned concerning it by the President of the Foreign Office, the Prince of Ch'ing, and by the Viceroy of this province who is the most influential statesman in the Empire. Others in high position have also spoken about it to me, and all have emphatically declared that in their opinion any amount of this indemnity returned to China by the United States should be solely devoted to educational purposes. I have no doubt myself that this wish of theirs would be carried out, for it is quite evident that all the high officials in this country are convinced that they and the people must have education on modern lines, which alone can insure them independent existence. With the present very restricted revenues of the country they are left absolutely groping in the dark for some means to follow out what they rightly preceive [*sic*] to be the foremost need of the country.

I do not forget that Professor Jenks, who has also been seeking to secure the refunding to China of a portion of this indemnity, wishes to see it applied to the creation of a Gold Reserve Fund to be used, when China adopts her new national currency, for maintaining the parity between gold and silver. In a memorandum which I had the honor to submit to you in the early part of this year, I gave my reason for believing that this scheme was impracticable. I am equally convinced that there is no such impracticability to securing the application by the Chinese Government of this refund to educational purposes. Very probably it would even ask the participation of the United States in the management of this educational fund.

I have called this matter directly to your attention, for there is no record in the Department of State that it was ever taken up officially there, the whole subject was discussed time and time again by Mr. Hay and myself but nothing was written on the matter, this must be my excuse for importuning you with it.

Should ultimately means be found for refunding a portion of this indemnity to China, provision should be made that it will be by annual installments. By this method we would retain our full interest in the indemnity and our right, under the provisions of the Final Protocol of September 7, 1901, to take part in the general management of the question by the Signatory Powers. We would thus remain in position to exercise a beneficial and restraining influence whenever necessary, both on China and the beneficiary Powers.

Your obedient, faithful servant,
[W. W. Rockhill]

Enclosure:
Draft of Message to Congress.

Honorable Theodore Roosevelt,
President of the United States,
Washington, D.C., U.S.A.

The White House,
Washington.
Confidential

Oyster Bay, N.Y.,
August 22, 1905

My dear Mr. Minister:

I have all along been intending to make that recommendation very strongly in my message. I only hesitate on account of the action of the Chinese government, or its inaction, in the matter of the boycott and in the matter of this Hankow railway concession. I may do it anyhow, but I wish you would in the strongest way impress upon the Chinese Government that the chance of my getting favorable action by Congress will be greatly interfered with by the failure of the Chinese to do justice themselves in such important matters as the boycott and the Hankow concession. In the boycott matter I wish you would see our consuls at Shanghai and elsewhere and make a full report to me on the whole project, sending me a synopsis by cable. Meet the men at Shanghai whom the San Francisco Chamber of Commerce want you to meet; but of course you can not join them with you in the investigation. I intend to do the Chinese justice and am taking a far stiffer tone with my own people than any President has ever yet taken, both about immigration, about this indemnity, and so forth. In return it is absolutely necessary for you to take a stiff tone with the Chinese where they are clearly doing wrong. Unless I misread them entirely they despise weakness even more than they prize justice, and we must make it evident both that we intend to do what is right and that we do not intend for a moment to suffer what is wrong.

Sincerely yours,
Theodore Roosevelt

Hon. W. W. Rockhill,
The American Minister,
Peking, China

SOURCE: "Rockhill Papers," Houghton Library, Harvard University.

APPENDIX 2

The Number of Students Studying Abroad, 1978–1988

Year	*Newspapers, Magazines*	China Encyclopedia Almanac[a]	China Education Almanac[b]
1978	480 (pu)[c]		
1979			
November	2,230 (pu)[d]		
December	2,700 (pu)[e]	2,700–3,400 (pu, cum)	1,750 (pu)
1980	5,192 (pu)[f]	2,124 (pu); 3,000–4,000 (pr)	2,124 (pu)
1981		3,416 (pu); 4,000–5,000 (pr, cum)	2,922 (pu)
1982			
March	6,000 (pr, cum)[g]		
June	12,000 (pu, cum)[h]		
December		3,410 (pu); 900 (pr)	2,326 (pu)
1983	18,500 (pu, cum); 7,000 (pr, cum);[i] 25,500 (total)[j]	2,001 (pu)	2,633 (pu)
1984			
June	26,000 (pu, cum); 7,000 (pr, cum)[k]		
December		2,938 (pu)	3,073 (pu)
1985			
July	29,000 (pu, cum); 7,800 (pr, cum)[l]		
December	38,000 (total)[m]	4,888 (pu)	4,888 (pu)

continued on next page

Year	*Newspapers, Magazines*	China Encyclopedia Almanac[a]	China Education Almanac[b]
1986	6,380 (pu);[n] 41,000 (total); 10,000 (pr, cum)[o]		
1987			
June	40,000 (pu, cum); 10,000 (pr, cum)		
December	3,000 (pu, g); 5,000 (pu, w)[p]	4,703 (pu, g); 6,569 (pu, w)	
1988	64,000 (pu, cum); 10,000 (pr, cum)[q]		12,527 (pu)

cum = cumulative; g = government-financed; pr = privately financed; pu = publicly financed; w = work-unit financed

[a] *Zhongguo baike nianjian* (China encyclopedia almanac) (Beijing: Zhongguo Dabaike Quanshu Chubanshe, 1980–1989).

[b] *Zhongguo jiaoyu nianjian* (China education almanac) (Beijing: Renmin Jiaoyu Chubanshe, 1980–1985, 1989).

[c] *Renmin ribao* (People's daily), January 4, 1979.

[d] *Beijing zhoubao* (Beijing weekly), no. 47 (1979): 5.

[e] Xinhua News Agency, December 22, 1979.

[f] Ibid., November 7, 1980.

[g] *Zifei chuguo liuxue ruogan wenti de jueding* (Resolutions on the problems arising from studying abroad with private financial means) (Chinese Communist Party document, March 31, 1982).

[h] Xinhua News Agency, August 22, 1982.

[i] *Renmin ribao*, December 10, 1983.

[j] *Beijing zhoubao*, no. 3 (1984): 11.

[k] *Renmin ribao*, November 23, 1984.

[l] *Renmin ribao haiwaiban* (People's daily, overseas edition), July 25, 1985.

[m] Xinhua News Agency, July 8, 1986.

[n] *Zhongguo nianjian* (China almanac) (Beijing: Zhongguo Nianjianshe, 1987), 456.

[o] *Zhongguo jiaoyubao* (China educational news), October 27, 1987.

[p] *Renmin ribao*, April 6, 1988.

[q] Ibid., November 24, 1988.

APPENDIX 3

Vacillations of Study-Abroad Policy in the 1980s

The implementation of the study-abroad policy vacillated in the 1980s. Its stringent or liberal execution could be read as a barometer forecasting the gathering or dissipation of a political storm. At the same time, a changing political climate also influenced the policy.

In the early part of 1980, about one year after the official restoration of the study-abroad program, the Ministry of Education and the Bureau of Science and Technology of the Office of the Premier jointly convened the National Workshop on Students Studying Abroad. The meeting established that the policy was to emphasize "the training of teachers in institutions of higher learning and the study of natural sciences and technological aspects of natural sciences."

In the same year, politics in China underwent a historical transformation. In the momentous discussion on "Practice is the sole criterion with which to test truth," the "Whatever Wing" of the Chinese Communist Party lost its influence and gradually faded from the political scene.[1] Deng Xiaoping gained the controlling influence in politics. Hua Guofeng faded out, and Hu Yaobang and Zhao Ziyang emerged on the stage. Slogans advocating reform and opening up were formally declared.

In early November 1980 another National Workshop on Students Studying Abroad was convened. Going along with the prevailing wind, the participants proposed new guidelines "to assure quality and to strive for pluralism." A month later, on January 14, 1981, the Office of the Premier approved the "Interim Regulations on Studying Abroad with Private Financial Means" drafted by the Ministry of Education and six other ministries and departments. Thus, the government opened the door for studying abroad on private financial means for the numerous younger students who had been born and had grown up under the Red flag.[2]

The "Interim Regulations" applied to undergraduate and graduate students alike. Currently enrolled students could keep their names on their school's roster. Key staff members of institutions—such as research assistants, lecturers, engineers, physicians-in-charge, exemplary athletes, artists, and writers—were all brought into the government-financed plan.

One year later, in 1982, the political wind began to change. The first event that reflected the change was the modification of policy on studying abroad.

On March 31, the Chinese Communist Party issued the document "Resolutions on the Problems Arising from Studying Abroad with Private Financial Means." It first stated that studying abroad with private financial means was one way to foster talent. It then pointed out the numerous problems: some went abroad by illegitimate means; some graduate students interrupted their studies so that they could go abroad; some went abroad under false pretenses; some were deceived after they went abroad; some became reactionaries and escaped to Taiwan; some, while abroad, were drawn to Taiwan's intelligence circles to advocate "peaceful evolution" of the Taiwan-mainland relationship. The document proposed denial of the privilege of studying abroad on private financial means to students who were currently enrolled in undergraduate or graduate studies, or who were children of high-level government officials (deputy ministers or higher and all those in bureaus of foreign affairs).

To put into effect the spirit of that document, the Ministry of Education called for another workshop in the first half of June 1982. The new spirit was embodied in "Regulations on Studying Abroad with Private Financial Means," a document drafted by seven ministries, including the Ministries of Education, Public Safety, Foreign Affairs, and Labor and Human Resources. It was approved by the Office of the Premier on July 16. These regulations later appeared in newspapers under the headline "Further Clarification on the Limits of Studying Abroad with Private Financial Means."[3]

When compared with the earlier "Interim Regulations," the new regulations broadened the definition of studying abroad by private financial means to include "undergraduate studies, studies in technical colleges (including language schools before college enrollment), graduate studies, and other advanced studies." But new restrictions were added. First, age limits of thirty-five for undergraduate and graduate studies, and forty-five for advanced studies, were imposed. Second, currently enrolled undergraduate and graduate students were not eligible; high school graduates, after working for two years and securing governmental approval, could apply for admission to colleges abroad. Third, teachers, scientists, engineers, professionals, and graduate students who had completed their studies would no longer "belong to the category of studying abroad with private financial means."

One year later, the nationwide Clean Up Spiritual Pollution Campaign began. But soon afterward the political atmosphere in China began to relax again.

In the first half of 1984 the Chinese government completed an internal document on studying abroad in which it signaled a relaxation. The document first affirmed the work of the past several years. It then proposed that the guideline in the selection of government-financed students was to assure quality: "It is better to leave the quota unfilled than to become wasteful." The target groups were those studying for master's and doctoral degrees and those who continued for advanced studies. For students financed by private means, it boldly proposed much greater latitude.

To implement the new spirit of this revised policy, the Office of the Premier sponsored yet another workshop from November 23 through 29 of that year. Zhang Jinfu, a member of the State Council, proposed that the policy should "set free the mind, overcome leftist influence and the legacy of feudal society, reform the administrative system, increase the number of students, extend care and help to overseas students, and help returned students find employment." In doing so, "a new phase of the project of sending students to study abroad can begin."[4]

As a result of the meeting, on December 26, 1984, the Office of the Premier issued new "Interim Regulations on Studying Abroad with Private Financial Means." This version first removed all barriers set up in the 1982 regulations: all citizens, regardless of academic status, age, or employment status, could apply for studying abroad as undergraduate or graduate students or for advanced study. It also emphasized that currently enrolled students could keep their student status for one year, those currently employed would be granted leaves of absence for one year, and spouses and children of students studying abroad could apply for family visits. Exemplary staff members of an institution could go abroad as "privately financed, institution-sponsored" students. The essential elements of these interim regulations appeared in newspapers under the headline "New Regulations Announced by the Office of the Premier on Students Studying Abroad with Private Financial Means."[5]

On National Day [October 1] in 1984, Deng Xiaoping reviewed China's military forces in Tiananmen Square. The parading students of Peking University held out a banner reading, "How are you, Xiaoping!" China was joyfully celebrating almost a decade of reform and opening up.

Soon afterward, though, elation was replaced by complaints about inflation and the slow pace of political reform.

In 1986 the political atmosphere once more became charged. Again, the first indication of subtle change was the policy on students studying abroad.

On May 4, 1986, the Chinese government circulated an internal document, "Memorandum on the Problems Related to the Reform and Strengthening of the Policy Governing the Students Studying Abroad." The memorandum first stated that dispatching students to foreign countries through various means was in complete harmony with the opening-up policy and should be firmly supported in the future. But it then stated that the country must face numerous problems concerning selection criteria and administration: the dispatching plan did not fully satisfy the country's need in economic development, there was a mismatch between what students learned abroad and what skills China needed, and the students were weak in political studies. The memorandum proposed an emphasis on sending visiting scholars and doctoral students, an adjustment of the distribution of students to foreign countries so as to take advantage of the strength of the host country and to reduce the number of students sent to America, and implementation of a contractual agreement between the students wishing to go abroad and their work units. The government no longer encouraged family visits for visiting scholars.

Following tradition, the National Education Commission convened another workshop from May 7 through 13 in Beijing. In the meeting, Deputy Director He Dongchang reported on how to "improve the study-abroad policy so as to foster needed manpower for the Four Modernizations."[6]

The complete text of "Several Interim Regulations Governing Students Studying Abroad," which was written in the workshop, was later published in *People's Daily*.[7] The way it was published showed an unprecedented transparency, but these interim regulations indicated a tightening of policy.

Foremost, they restored in several ways the restrictions on studying abroad with private financial means. First, "To assure an orderly work atmosphere in institutions of higher learning and scientific research, staff members wishing to leave for foreign studies must obtain approvals from their work units," thus granting the work unit virtually unlimited control over the individual. Second, "Current-year college graduates who have already received work assignments from the government must accept their assignments to serve the country," and third, "Currently enrolled graduate students should complete their studies and in general should not disrupt their studies to go abroad with private financial means."

Another sign indicating a tightening of policy was the implementation of the "Agreement on Studying Abroad" for government-sponsored students (including those who were privately financed but sponsored by an institution—that is, those professionals and people who had completed their graduate studies). To receive permission to leave, the students had to agree with "the purpose, contents, duration, demand for the return to work, and rules governing the financial provisions to the students set forth by the government and their work units." The agreement also called for students' and work units' mutual recognition "of other rights, obligations, and responsibilities." This was an attempt to use an imposed contractual agreement to control the students.

Within six months after the workshop, a political storm blew over Beijing and swept the entire country. Toward the end of 1986, there were repeated student strikes. In early 1987 Hu Yaobang resigned.[8]

Between 1987 and 1989 the demand for political reform appeared again and policy decisions on economic reform faltered repeatedly. In the propaganda for supporting "the initial stage of socialism," the antiliberalization sentiment persisted. Amid the waves of "control and discipline," the calls for thorough reform also could be heard now and then.

Under this political tug-of-war, the policy on students studying abroad appeared to be shifting. Rumors flew.

In early 1988 a document designated as "Document No. (1987)-679, National Education Commission" was circulating among Chinese students in and outside China. Its two principal recommendations were a reduction of the number of students sent abroad, especially to the United States, and the setting of time limits for study abroad: two years for a master's degree and five years for a doctorate. Both the Associated Press and United Press International carried the news. The *New York Times* ran an article titled "China Plans to Let Fewer Students Go Abroad, Especially to the U.S."[9]

Students in China became alarmed, and those outside China wrote petitions. Thus, the government had to clarify the policy.

First, on April 5, 1988, Huang Xinbai, a member of the National Education Commission who was in charge of the study-abroad program, declared that sending students abroad was a long-range national policy; it had not changed and would not change; the report that the number of students going abroad would be drastically reduced was groundless.[10]

Then, on April 30, 1988, Premier Li Peng, in a meeting with delegates to the Fourth Sino-Japan Civilian Conference, said that China's policy of sending students abroad was part of the overall opening-up policy and would not change.[11] On June 4, He Dongchang, deputy commissioner of the National Education

Commission, substantiated the premier's statement. As to government-financed students who were already in the United States, the government should not and would not force compliance and would not pursue a policy hurting their feelings.[12]

Amidst the rumored imminent change in policy and the repeated official clarifications, a social crisis broke out in April 1989 that eventually led to the June Fourth Incident.[13]

Suddenly, the whole world was watching China closely: After such a violent storm, in what direction would this ship of state lead its 1.1 billion people? China's policy toward students studying abroad once more became the focal point of attention.

On July 26, 1989, a spokesman for the National Education Commission declared, while answering questions from a reporter, that China "will continue to send students abroad," and "under the general guideline of our policy of reform and opening up, China will continue to make the project work."[14] But the tone did not sound as firm as before.

After a brief moratorium Beijing's Bureau of Public Safety resumed accepting passport applications. But it also required a new exit card and proof of untainted behavior during the June Fourth Incident, to be signed by the Party secretary of the applicant's work unit or the local Bureau of Public Safety. At the same time, the National Education Commission implemented new restrictions on studying abroad with private financial means: undergraduate and graduate students could apply to study abroad after they had completed their studies, worked for five years, secured permission from their work unit, and registered with and gained approval from the provincial, regional (for China's autonomous regions), or city (for cities under the direct jurisdiction of the central government) education commission.[15]

Nevertheless, China's policy of sending students abroad stubbornly limped along.

Surprisingly, amidst the repeated pronouncements by China's leadership that the policy would not change, a more relaxed policy began to emerge: the exit card was abolished, passports were issued expeditiously, time limits on studying abroad were no longer mentioned, and official passports could be exchanged for unofficial ones.

In 1992 Deng Xiaoping toured the south and delivered speeches. China's economy, which had been sluggish for several years, came to life again and caught the world's attention.

At this time the government injected a new spirit into the study-abroad policy: "supporting the project of sending students to study abroad, encouraging them to return, and allowing them the freedom to come and go."[16] Word also emerged from the National Education Commission that "the government shall further relax its policy governing studying abroad with private financial means, improve the selection process for government-financed students, and implement steps making studying abroad easier for citizens."[17]

The new policy for studying abroad on government-financed means finally made its debut in January 1996. The National Education Commission abolished the old quota system regulated by the central government. The new policy called for work units to select participants on the basis of "individual application, review by experts, fair competition, and selection of the best qualified." An assistance fund was established in lieu of the old government fund. Students could now apply for support by signing an agreement; they would incur a penalty if they broke it. Thus, the policy incorporated competition into government-financed opportunities. It also changed the function of the work unit from controlling everyone to making contractual agreements with willing individuals.

APPENDIX 4

Students in the First Dispatch, December 1978

Name	*Chinese Affiliation*	*U.S. Institution*
Wang Zhimei	Biology, Peking U.	U. of Calif. (UC), Berkeley
Pan Weijun	Biology, Peking U.	UC Berkeley
Tai Yuandong	Biology, Peking U.	State U. of N.Y. (SUNY), Stony Brook
Yang Weisheng	Biology, Peking U.	SUNY Stony Brook
Lin Zonghan	Biology, Peking U.	UC Berkeley
Ma Jiming	Chemistry, Peking U.	Lehigh U.
Yin Longan	Math. Mechanics, Peking U.	New York U. (NYU)
Yan Dachun	Math. Mechanics, Peking U.	Johns Hopkins U.
Huang Yongnian	Math. Mechanics, Peking U.	Mass. Inst. of Technology (MIT)
Yue Zengyuan	Geophysics, Peking U.	MIT
Xu Zhuoqun	Computer Sci., Peking U.	SUNY (branch unknown)
Li Yanda	Automation, Tsinghua U.	MIT
Zhang Chuhan	Hydraulic Engineering, Tsinghua U.	UC Berkeley
Liu Baicheng	Mechanical Manufacturing, Tsinghua U.	U. of Wisconsin
Zheng Yanheng	Electronics, Tsinghua U.	(unknown)
Peng Jiehu	Radio Engineering, Tsinghua U.	Washington U.
Cui Guowen	Nonmetallic Material Specialty, Tsinghua U.	MIT

Name	*Chinese Affiliation*	*U.S. Institution*
Zhang Yuman	Engineering Physics, Tsinghua U.	UC Berkeley
Zhao Nanming	Engineering Physics, Tsinghua U.	UC Berkeley
Cao Xiaoping	Chemistry, Tsinghua U.	UC Berkeley
Dai Zongduo	Inst. of Mathematics, Chinese Academy of Sciences (CAS)	UC Berkeley
Pei Dingyi	Inst. of Mathematics, CAS	Princeton U.
Shen Xianjie	Inst. of Geology, CAS	Columbia U.
Zheng Yong	Beijing Industry U.	UC Berkeley
Wang Yiming	Beijing Industry U.	MIT
Jin Hanping	Inst. of Geological Mechanics	UC Berkeley
Zhu Xixing	Inst. of Electronics, CAS, Beijing	Columbia U.
Shi Yanyang	Inst. of Electronics, CAS, Beijing	Cornell U.
Wang Jinghua	Inst. of Mathematics, CAS, Beijing	NYU
Zhu Youlan	Computer Center, CAS, Beijing	NYU
Xu Jincheng	Beijing Inst. of Atomic Energy	Calif. State U. (branch unknown)
Li Zhuxia	Beijing Inst. of Atomic Energy	SUNY (branch unknown)
Tan Zhongwei	Computer Center, Beijing Automobile Manufacture	UC Los Angeles
Gong Rongshu	Beijing Inst. of Post and Telecommunication	MIT
Chen Junliang	Beijing Inst. of Post and Telecommunication	Calif. State U. (branch unknown)
Wu Rushan	National Bureau of Geology	MIT
Wu Yuantao	Fifth Research Inst., Ministry of Second Machinery	UC Berkeley
Yi Fusheng	(unknown)	Cornell U.
Tong Tanjun	Biochemistry, Beijing Medical College	Johns Hopkins U.
Liu Zhiwu	Acad. of Agricultural Sciences	UC Davis

Name	*Chinese Affiliation*	*U.S. Institution*
Wu Baozhen	Beijing Capital Hospital	Columbia U.
Wu Ning	Beijing Capital Hospital	Columbia U.
Shi Shuanghui	Inst. of Nuclear Physics, CAS, Shanghai	UC Berkeley
Gong Zuba	Shanghai Inst. of Biochemistry	UC Berkeley
Wu Deying	First Research Inst., Shanghai Bureau of Post and Telecommunication	Washington U.
Shen Luping	Inst. of Biochemistry, CAS, Shanghai	UC San Francisco
Wang Xukun	Inst. of Chemistry, Nankai U., Tianjin	UC Berkeley
Chen Weizhu	Inst. of Chemistry, Nankai U., Tianjin	Rohm and Haas Research Lab.
Chen Lu	Physics, Nankai U., Tianjin	U. of Arizona
Xu Xi'en	Chemical Engineering, Tianjin U.	U. of Pittsburgh

Notes

Unless stated otherwise, source notes are the author's, and substantive and descriptive notes are the translator's.

TRANSLATOR'S PREFACE

1. Foreword by Richard Leone, in Patrick Tyler, *A Great Wall: Six Presidents and China: An Investigative History* (New York: PublicAffairs, 1999). For example, the most numerous international student groups in 1998–99 were: at the University of California at Berkeley, Chinese (10.8 percent) and Koreans (9.4 percent); at the University of Wisconsin, Koreans (13.7 percent) and Chinese (11.9 percent); and at Princeton University, Chinese (15.9 percent) and Canadians (9.6 percent). More than 90 percent of the Chinese students were in graduate school, whereas students from other countries were more evenly distributed between graduate and undergraduate schools. (These numbers were supplied by the offices of international students at the respective universities.)

2. Qian Ning, *Liuxue Meiguo* (Studying in America) (Nanjing: Jiangsu Wenyi Chubanshe, 1996).

3. "Central Kingdom" (Zhongyang Daguo) is in contrast to "Middle Kingdom," the literal translation of "Zhongguo" (China).

4. "Western diplomats in Beijing are avid about the book, sending drivers to the bookstalls when fresh copies arrive.... The book is recommended reading for senior Chinese officials" (Rone Tempest, *Los Angeles Times,* March 1, 1997).

5. China's isolation—by its policy of self-reliance, by the American embargo on trade with China triggered by the Korean War, and by the Sino-Soviet rift that began in the late 1950s—limited its development and aggravated its

poverty. In an environment of rigid one-party rule, the venting of frustration over economic hardship and its suppression by the Chinese Communist Party pitted the Party against the people, the people against the Party, and the Party against the Party. In 1949 Land Reform targeted land owners; in 1950 and 1951 the Campaign against Counterrevolutionaries targeted Nationalist (Guomindang) spies; in 1951 the Three Antis Campaign targeted Party members; in 1952 the Five Antis Campaign targeted remnants of capitalistic industrialists and businessmen; in 1957 the Anti-Rightist Movement targeted intellectuals, following the brief Hundred Flowers Movement initiated by the Chinese Communist Party to encourage intellectuals to criticize the Party; later in 1957 the Great Leap Forward mobilized the peasants to boost grain production with gigantic water projects and steel production in backyard furnaces but in 1961–62 resulted in the starvation of tens of millions; in 1963 the Four Cleanups Campaign targeted commune administrators; and, finally, beginning in 1966 and ending shortly after Mao Zedong's death in 1976, the Cultural Revolution again targeted intellectuals and eventually evolved into the Criticize Lin Biao and Confucius Campaign.

6. According to traditional Confucian teaching, the five basic human relationships, between two persons, are ruler and minister, father and son, husband and wife, older brother and younger brother, and older friend and younger friend. (In practice, these relationships tend to inhibit the formation of relationships other than the two-person kind and the development of the concept of *self* as in an isolated individual.) They are hierarchic and imply a give-and-receive encounter and not the mutual give-and-take of human relations among equals. The campaigns carried out in the three decades after 1949 were intended to destroy the traditional hierarchic relationships and to replace them by a single one between the Party and an individual.

7. Prior to the mid-seventeenth century, China's population, though increasing slowly, had remained for the most part under 100 million. But by 1848 the population was 426 million and the per capita cultivated land had decreased from 1.3 to 0.45 acre (Kang Chao, *Man and Land in Chinese History* [Stanford, Calif.: Stanford University Press, 1986], 89). China's urban population had decreased from 21 percent of the total in 1220 to 6.9 percent in 1820 (ibid., 60). A more recent study indicates that the accelerated pressure on land from population growth may have begun in the early Ming dynasty (1368–1644) (Martin Heijdra, *The Socio-Economic Development of Rural China During the Ming*, in *The Cambridge History of China*, ed. D. Twitchett and F. W. Mote, vol. 8 [Cambridge, England: Cambridge University Press, 1998], 450). From 1500 to 1800, the life expectancy of those Chinese who had already reached the age of fourteen had decreased from about sixty-two to forty-eight years (ibid., 437). The factors that resulted in the Industrial Revolution in the West were a change in productive potential—due to a change in the stock of knowledge—

and a consequent change in organization to realize that potential (Douglass C. North, *Structure and Change in Economic History* [New York: W. W. Norton & Company, 1981], 17. These factors were absent in Qing dynasty China.

8. *Mengzi* (The Analects of Mencius), "Liang Hui wang" (King Hui of Liang), part 2, section 8.

9. The story of Yung Wing and the students who went to study in America in 1872–81 is described in chapters 1 and 8. A detailed account can be found in Yung Wing, *My Life in China and America* (New York: Henry Holt and Company, 1909), and Thomas E. LaFargue, *China's First Hundred—Educational Mission Students in the United States* (Pullman: Washington State University Press, 1942). A recent book on the subject is Shi Ni's *Guannian yu beiju* (Concept and tragedy) (Shanghai: Shanghai Renmin Chubanshe, 2000). In 1901, the year after the siege of the foreign compound in Beijing by the Boxers (see this preface, note 25), Viceroys Zhang Zhidong and Liu Kunyi wrote to Emperor Guangxu, "Even last summer there were still some high officials, both in and outside the capital, who claimed that the ocean people [Westerners] could not walk on land, and others who claimed that once the embassies and churches were destroyed, the ocean people would be eliminated" (*Guangxu zhengyao* [Records of the Guangxu reign] [Yonghezheng, Taibeixian, Taiwan: Wenhai Chubanshe, 1969], vol. 27 [1901]: 41).

10. That window of opportunity was cultivated by Burlingame; Xu Jiyu and Wenxiang in China's Ministry of Foreign Affairs (Zongli Yamen); Robert Hart, a British consul who later worked in China's Imperial Maritime Customs Service; and British minister to China Rutherford Alcock. Xu, after witnessing the easy victory of the British fleet while he was governor of Fujian during the First Opium War, began to study Western geography, history, and culture. He became a great admirer of the kingless America and George Washington. Burlingame, during his last days as U.S. minister, presented a copy of one of Gilbert Stuart's portraits of George Washington to Xu. Xu remarked that Washington had become "an example and guide to mankind. His merit thus becomes a link between the ancient worthies and the men of succeeding ages." Xu's words were inscribed on a granite block from Fujian placed at the three-hundred-foot level of the Washington Monument (Arthur Smith, *China and America Today* [New York: Fleming H. Revell Company, 1907], 209; Fred Drake, *China Charts the World* [Cambridge, Mass.: Harvard University Press, 1975], 188, 243). The more equal Sino-British relationship, however, did not materialize. The opening of the Suez Canal rekindled the desire among British merchants for trade advantages in China, and the renegotiated Treaty of Tianjin, which concluded the Second Opium War, was rejected by the British House of Commons (Jonathan Spence, *The Search for Modern China* [New York: W. W. Norton & Company, 1990], 20). Spence's work served as a basic source of information on contemporary China for this preface.

11. Paul H. Clyde, *United States Policy Toward China: Diplomatic and Public Documents* (Durham, N.C.: Duke University Press, 1940), 85.

12. *Tongzhichao chouban yiwu shimo* (Beginning-to-end [records] on dealings on barbarian affairs during Tongzhi's reign) (Taipei: Guofeng Chubanshe, 1963), 1896–97. In the same memorial Li Hongzhang wrote that the British minister, upon learning that China had planned to send students to America, expressed that China should feel free to send students to the fine academies in Britain.

13. The Chinese Educational Commission was located at 352 Collins Street. The teenage students studied in schools in the Connecticut River Valley area before entering college. The Connecticut Historical Society has kept newspaper clippings about the returned students. In 1996 the Chinese Students Memorial Society (www.120ChineseStudents.org) was founded in Connecticut with the intention of memorializing Yung Wing, the students, and the American host families they lived with. In 1998 Governor John G. Rowland of Connecticut recognized September 22, 1998, as Yung Wing and the Chinese Educational Commission Day in Connecticut. On May 5, 2000, Yale University unveiled a portrait of Yung Wing in its Grand Hall. In September 2000 a Yung Wing Memorial Fund for International Students was endowed at Yale.

14. In 1868 Ulysses S. Grant was elected the eighteenth president on the Republican ticket. In 1870 Congress ratified the Fifteenth Amendment, which gave all citizens the right to vote regardless of race. In 1872 Congress passed the Amnesty Act, which restored civil rights to the citizens of the South. In 1875 it enacted the Civil Rights Act, which gave equal rights to African Americans in public accommodations and juror duty. Nook Farm, a residential area in Lord's Hill where the Chinese Educational Commission's headquarters was situated, sheltered progressive thinkers who were influential in politics of the day. Among them were Harriet Beecher Stowe, who had written *Uncle Tom's Cabin* in 1851; Mark Twain, who had begun *Huckleberry Finn* by 1876; and Joseph Hawley, publisher, opponent of American slavery, educator, general in the Civil War, governor, and senator (Anita Marchant, *Yung Wing and the Chinese Educational Commission at Hartford* [M.A. thesis, Trinity College, 1999]).

15. LaFargue, *China's First Hundred* (1987 edition), 50.

16. The slogan of the Workingmen's Party of California in the 1880s was "The Chinese Must Go!" (This sentiment, although not its cause, was, ironically, similar to that expressed in 1900, nearly twenty years later, by the Boxers in China in regard to foreigners: "Revive the Qing [dynasty]; destroy the foreign.") The anti-Chinese political atmosphere eventually led to the passing of the Chinese Exclusion Act of 1882 (only Connecticut and Massachusetts, in whose schools most of the Chinese students studied, voted against the Act). In 1884 legislation also broadened the term "laborers" so that additional categories of workers were excluded. The legislation was repealed in 1943.

17. The State Department's answer to Yung Wing's application on behalf of the Chinese students was "There is no room provided for Chinese students" (Yung Wing, *My Life*, 207–9). No corroborative document on the refusal has been found.

18. Ibid., 211–15.

19. Chris Robyn, *Our Celestial Neighbors: The Chinese Mission in New England, 1872–1881*, unpublished ms. excerpted in idem, *Building the Bridge: The Chinese Educational Mission to the United States* (Master of Phil. diss., Chinese University of Hong Kong, 1996); Tsung-loo Kao, *Zhongguo liumei youtong yu Meiguo Masheng Ligong Xueyuan* (Chinese teenage students who went to study in America and MIT), *Zhuanji wenxue* (Biographical literature), vol. 75 (Taipei: Zhuanjiwenxue Chubanshe, 1999), 29.

20. Japanese pirates operating in China's coastal waters from the fourteenth through the sixteenth century were called by Ming Chinese *wokou*, "bandits of diminutive stature." In Qing China's declaration of the 1894 war against Japan, Japanese were named *woren*, "people of diminutive stature."

21. In connection with China's boycott of America and the passage of the Chinese Exclusion Act and other anti-Chinese legislation in the United States, Secretary of Commerce and Labor Victor Metcalf reported to the House of Representatives in 1906 that 116 Chinese students were admitted to America between 1903 and 1905 and twelve were denied entry (Clyde, *United States Policy*, 239).

22. In April or May 1898, Yano Fumi, Japan's minister to China, wrote to China's Ministry of Foreign Affairs, "My government plans to cultivate friendship with China. I realize that China urgently needs talented people. If [you] select and send students to study [in Japan], my country will pay the expenses." He later verbally proposed that two hundred students receive such support (Shu Xincheng, *Zhongguo jindai jiaoyu shiliao* [Source materials on the history of China's modern education] [Shanghai: Zhonghua Shuju, 1928], vol. 1: 219). On May 14, 1898, Yano wrote to Nishi Tokujiro, Japan's minister of foreign affairs, "If the Japanese-educated Chinese talents become dispersed in the old empire, it would be the best strategy for establishing Japan's power base in East Asia . . . , winning the trust of Japan among Chinese officials and citizens . . . , and expanding Japan's influence on the mainland without limit" (Kawamura Kazuo, *Chusinjidai no Yano Ryukei si* [Yano Ryukei in the Qing dynasty], cited in Huang Fuqing, *Qingmo liuri xuesheng* [Chinese students studying in Japan near the end of Qing dynasty] [Taipei: Institute of Modern History, Academia Sinica, 1975], 8).

23. Chen Xuexun, comp., *Zhongguo jindai jiaoyu dashiji* (Record of major events in China's modern education) (Shanghai: Jiaoyu Chubanshe, 1980), 163; *Xuebu zouzi qiyao* (Major memorials from the Department of Education), vol. 1. A Japanese source numbers the students at eight thousand (Tofuji Kaishu,

Chugokujin Nihon ryugakushu [A history of Chinese students in Japan], 16; cited in Huang, *Qingmo liuri xuesheng*, 24).

24. For a detailed account of the remission, which includes both American and Chinese source materials, see Michael Hunt, "The American Remission of the Boxer Indemnity: A Reappraisal," *Journal of Asian Studies* 31 (1972): 539–59.

25. In the late nineteenth century, China's repeated military defeats led to xenophobia and to fear that it was about to be carved up by foreign powers. The Boxers United in Righteousness was a cult group formed by peasants in Shandong in response to provocation by Western missionaries and their Chinese Christian converts. In June 1900 the Boxers killed Chinese Christian converts, four French and Belgian engineers, and two English missionaries. On June 17 foreign powers—mostly from Japan, Russia, Britain, the United States, and France—responded by seizing the forts at Dagu and advanced from the port city of Tianjin to Beijing to protect the foreign embassies, businesses, shops, and residences concentrated around Dongjiaomin Alley in the Legation Quarter. When news of the loss of Dagu reached Beijing two days later, the Boxers laid siege to the Quarter. The siege led to the invasion and occupation of Beijing in August 1900 by twenty thousand foreign troops. See Peter Fleming, *The Siege at Peking* (Oxford: Oxford University Press, 1984).

The indemnity set by the Boxer Protocol was 450 million taels ($334 million, or $724 million with accrued interest), to be paid in thirty-nine years. The total annual income of the Qing court was around 250 million taels ($185 million). The American share of the indemnity was 7.3 percent, or $24.4 million. Russia's share was the largest, at 29 percent, followed by Germany, France, Great Britain, Japan, the United States, Italy, and others.

26. British prime minister Lord Salisbury defined "sphere of influence" in 1900: "A sort of an 'ear mark' upon territory [in China] which in case of a break up England did not wish any other power to have" (Whitney Griswold, *The Far Eastern Policy* [New York: Harcourt, Brace and Company, 1938], 52).

27. Rockhill, in turn, had been urged by Alfred Hippisley, an Englishman who worked in the Chinese Imperial Maritime Customs Service (Clyde, *United States Policy*, 201–17). Hay's diplomatic note was sent to Great Britain, Russia, Germany, France, Italy, and Japan. The Open Door concept had actually first been floated by Great Britain to the American government in 1898 as a possible means to protect Britain's trade dominance in China. It was quietly abandoned after Britain recognized that the spheres of influence were there to stay (George F. Kennan, *American Diplomacy, 1900–1950* [Chicago: University of Chicago Press, 1951], 21–37).

28. Clyde, *United States Policy*, 215. But Rockhill and Hippisley had long held the idea of preserving China's territorial integrity. In his letter to Hippisley in 1899, Rockhill had written, "I would like to see it [the United States] make

a declaration ... [on] maintaining the integrity of the Empire" (Griswold, *The Far Eastern Policy,* 67), and later, in another letter, "I think for the time being we had better not broach it [China's territorial integrity] over here" (ibid., 75).

29. American historians tend to view the Open Door policy as a failure because it was poorly defined and thought out, it did not win clear endorsement by treaty powers, and Hay was not prepared to back up the policy with substance. Chinese historians view it more favorably, probably because China was in fact not partitioned by treaty powers. Lee Yunhan wrote, "Because of this well-known Open Door policy, the Powers temporarily adjusted their policy, and the tragedy of a carved-up China was avoided" (*Zhongguo jindaishi* [China's modern history] [Taipei: Sanmin Shuju, 1985], 135). Fu Qixue (Fu Sinian) criticized American historians' view that the Open Door policy was a failure as "biased and narrow [*pianxia*]" (*Zhongguo waijiaoshi* [China's diplomatic history] [Taipei: Sanmin Shuju, 1960], 139). In any event, it is difficult to envision how a partitioned China would have promoted America's interest in trade or eliminated conflicts among the treaty powers.

30. In answering Hippisley's letter complaining about the Dark Ages ethics of the occupying powers of Beijing in 1900, Rockhill wrote that he was "sick and tired of the whole business" and "It may be a long time before the United States gets into another muddle of this description" (Griswold, *The Far Eastern Policy,* 83). Rockhill wrote to Hay in 1901 about China, "I greatly feel that ... there is no life, energy or patriotism throughout the whole governing class. It looks to me very dark ahead for China" (Michael Hunt, *Frontier Defense and the Open Door* [New Haven: Yale University Press, 1973], 59).

31. An anti-Chinese atmosphere in America had persisted since the Chinese Exclusion Act in 1882. In 1888 U.S. president Grover Cleveland proclaimed that the Chinese were "an element ignorant of our constitution and laws ... and dangerous to our peace and welfare," and the Republican presidential candidate Benjamin Harrison spoke of his "duty to defend our civilization by excluding alien races whose ultimate assimilation with our people is neither possible nor desirable." In a somewhat similar vein, in 1793, when China enjoyed an inflow of silver from Britain in exchange for tea and crafts, Emperor Qianlong had written to King George III regarding Britain's desire to expand trade, "We have never valued ingenious articles, nor do we have the slightest need of your country's manufactures. Therefore, O king, as regards your request to send someone to remain at the capital, while it is not in harmony with the regulations of the Celestial Empire we also feel very much that it is of no advantage to your country" (J. L. Cranmer-Byng, ed., *An Embassy to China: Being the Journal kept by Lord Macartneys during His Embassy to the Emperor Ch'ien-lung, 1793–1794* [Hamden, Conn.: Archon Books, 1963], 340).

On the connection between the U.S. immigration policy and the Chinese boycott of American goods, see C. F. Remer, *A Study of Chinese Boycotts* (Baltimore: The Johns Hopkins Press, 1933), 29–35.

32. Much of this change was instigated by students who had returned from Japan.

33. Rockhill wrote to U.S. minister Charles Denby in Beijing in 1900 that the purpose of the Open Door policy was "not only for our trade, but for strengthening the Peking Government so that it can find no means of escaping the performance of all its obligations to the Treaty Powers" (Griswold, *The Far Eastern Policy*, 76).

34. In 1897 Liang was knighted by Queen Victoria. In 1898 he won a diplomatic argument with the Kaiser's court over whether China's Prince Chun, whom Liang had accompanied to Berlin to apologize for the killing of German subjects in Shandong, should kowtow to Wilhelm II as the German government had demanded (Walter Muir Whitehill, *Portrait of a Chinese Diplomat, Sir Chentung Liang Cheng* [Boston: Boston Athenaeum, 1974], 13). During his tenure as China's minister, he was known as a loyal alumnus at Andover, made an honorary member of Amherst's class of 1885, and awarded honorary degrees by Yale and Amherst.

35. Liang also spoke publicly against the indifference of the American government and courts to the violence committed against the Chinese in the country. In an address in Chicago, he said, "More Chinese subjects have been murdered by mobs in the United States during the last twenty-five years than all the Americans who have been murdered in China in similar riots. . . . In every instance where Americans have suffered from mobs, the authorities have made reparation for the losses, and rarely has the punishment of death failed to be inflicted upon the guilty offenders. On the other hand, I am sorry to say that I cannot recall a single instance where the penalty of death has been visited on any member of the mobs in the United States guilty of the death of Chinese, and in only two instances out of many has indemnity been paid for the losses sustained by the Chinese" (Smith, *China and America Today*, 165).

36. *New York Times*, June 23, 1907. The indemnity discussion began with China's request to make payments in silver, in lieu of gold as stipulated in the Boxer Protocol. The remission plan evolved after the request was rejected.

37. Liang Cheng's letter is translated in appendix 1.

38. Griswold, *The Far Eastern Policy*, 124. The correspondence between Rockhill and Roosevelt on the remission, from the "Rockhill Papers," now in the Houghton Library at Harvard University, is reproduced in appendix 1. A reading of Rockhill's letter to Roosevelt does not leave this reader with the impression that the president had asked Rockhill how the Chinese government would spend the money if it were returned by the United States, as reported

by Liang Cheng to China's Ministry of Foreign Affairs; it is possible that Rockhill learned of the question through Hay.

39. On March 12, 1907, Liang wrote to the Ministry of Foreign Affairs, "I have learned that Secretary of State Root . . . said the indemnity will ultimately be reduced. But the amount that has been collected so far is insufficient, and it will be another few years before any definite conclusion can be reached" (Lo Xiang-lin, *Liang Cheng di chushi Meiguo 1903–1907* [Liang Cheng: Chinese minister in Washington, 1903–1907] [Hong Kong: Institute of Chinese Culture, 1977], 150).

40. Ibid., 151.

41. *New York Times*, June 19, 1907.

42. During the floor debate on the remission, Edwin Denby (son of Charles Denby; see note 33, this preface), a representative from Michigan who had worked for the Chinese Imperial Maritime Customs Service between 1887 and 1894, stated that the Chinese "have absolutely no standing in this matter, except that we desire to show them that our civilization means justice as well as battle ships. But it's better to be just and even generous to our own people whose markets and establishments were ruined in China before we begin to be generous to a foreign power" (Hunt, "The American Remission," 547). The final amount claimed was about $12.5 million, with interest (Westel W. Willoughby, *Foreign Rights and Interests in China* [Baltimore: The Johns Hopkins Press, 1927], 1013).

43. Rockhill's intention to control the use of the money is indicated in his 1905 letter to Roosevelt (appendix 1). Two students who had returned to China in 1881 were involved in the negotiations: Liang Dunyan, China's foreign minister; and Tang Shaoyi, a special envoy sent in November 1908 to thank the United States for the remission. Another mission of Tang's trip—negotiation of a loan from the United States, with the remission money used as collateral—was foiled by Rockhill, who orchestrated with the State Department a publicity campaign for the educational plan and made it difficult for Tang to meet with Root to discuss the loan (Hunt, *Frontier Defense*, 174).

44. On June 20, 1907, the *New York Times* commented on the remission in an editorial titled "An Example to All the World," which concluded, "Again, and not for the first time, we have set an example to the nations, an example of importing into international relations those principles of right and justice and highmindedness that prevail between honorable men." Sarah Conger, wife of the U.S. minister to China and a survivor of the siege at Beijing, wrote to her niece on September 22, 1907, "The attitude of the United States . . . that caused her, without compulsion, to cancel the Boxer indemnity, is an attitude too deep, too broad, too high for word expression. . . . The attitude is not one of spontaneity; the seed was brought over in the *Mayflower*; it was planted in the virgin soil of liberty, where it rooted, and was watered with treasured

dewdrops; was nourished into being in Love's tenderness; was sustained in Truth's fortitude. This is the story of our country's attitude" (*Letters from China* [Chicago: A. C. McClurg & Co., 1909], 373).

45. Arthur H. Smith, *Chinese Characteristics* (New York: Fleming H. Revell Company, 1894 [orig. pub. Shanghai, 1890]), 316–30. Smith's conclusions were influenced by his observation of opium addiction, foot binding in women, female infanticide in poor families, and concubinage, in addition to polytheism, pantheism, and atheism, which he found repugnant to his Christian beliefs: "The most melancholy characteristic of the Chinese mind [is] its ready acceptance of a body without a soul, of a soul without a spirit, of a spirit without a life, of a cosmos without a cause, a Universe without a God" (ibid., 313). (Both Christianity and Confucianism espouse the love of others. In monotheistic Christianity, the ideal emanates from God's teaching as described in the Bible. In Confucianism, it emanates from a human consideration of compassion [*ren*] toward others, without instruction from God; concepts of *tian* [heaven, nature, universe] are human constructs.) Smith also regarded Confucianism as the cause of China's social ills but did not consider the effect of long-lasting poverty, labeling, for example, the frugal living habits of coolies who carried sedan chairs for Westerners as "irrational." Smith also wrote *Village Life in China* (New York: Fleming H. Revell Company, 1899).

In 1902 much of the U.S. investment of $19.2 million in China (2.5 percent of all foreign investment) was for missionary activity.

46. Smith, *China and America*, 213–16. Until the 1970s authors of Chinese books and articles on the remission, unaware of the "Rockhill Papers" (which were available to Griswold) and Liang Cheng's correspondence with China's Ministry of Foreign Affairs, had credited Smith for successfully prodding Roosevelt to remit the indemnity. The religious undercurrent of public support for the remission is also indicated in Sarah Conger's letter (see note 44, this preface).

47. *Guangxu zhengyao*, vol. 27 (1901), 20.

48. Smith, *China and America*, 214–15.

49. Because of the toppling of the Qing government in 1911, a fourth detachment of eleven students, made up of preparatory students who had passed the examination in 1910, was unable to make the trip until 1914 (Hu Guangbiao, *Zhongguo xiandaihua de licheng* [China's modernization odyssey] [Taipei: Zhuanji Wenxue Chubanshe, 1981], 78).

50. Women students were required to have "natural feet" (*tian zu*), as opposed to bound feet. Later, the program for women was usually the first suspended during periods of higher expense, such as World War I. Chinese women students began to study in the United States and Japan in 1905 (Lin Zixun, *Zhongguo liuxue jiaoyushi, 1847–1975* [A history of China's study-abroad education, 1847–1975] [Taipei: Hwa Kang Press, 1976], 73, 167, 273–74).

51. One of the students supported by the remission fund, Qian Xuesen, became a prominent rocket scientist at the California Institute of Technology in the late 1940s. During the McCarthy period, he was arrested and eventually deported to China on dubious charges of being a member of a Communist cell at Caltech. See Iris Chang, *Thread of the Silkworm* (New York: Basic Books, 1995).

52. LaFargue, *China's First Hundred*, 142.

53. China ceded Taiwan to Japan in the Treaty of Shimonoseki in 1895 after its defeat in the Sino-Japanese War; Japan returned Taiwan to China in 1945 after its defeat in World War II.

54. Lin, *Zhongguo liuxue jiaoyushi 1847–1975*, 532–34. On a per capita basis, this would be equivalent to about 50,000 students per year in the People's Republic of China.

55. In 1992 "fifty-three percent of Cabinet ministers in Taiwan have degrees from American universities . . . and there is always a higher proportion of American Ph.D.s in the Taiwan Cabinet than in the American Cabinet" (Nicholas Kristof, *New York Times*, January 4, 1992). "It is the engineers trained in the United States that have made the [Hsinchu Science] park, and Taiwan's high-tech industries, a success" (Edward A. Gargan, *New York Times*, July 19, 1994).

1. THE INTERMITTENT HISTORY

1. See Translator's Preface, note 25.

2. In the People's Republic of China in the late 1980s, the political climate prohibited free speech; open disagreement with government policies could result in an investigation of the speaker by the government.

3. Cadres are minor CCP functionaries. In China's socialistic economy, a person is employed in a "work unit" in which the secretary-general appointed by the CCP supervises all aspects of ideology, coordinates the work of government, and shares power with its administrative head. The structure is similar to that in a business corporation: the Party secretary-general is the chairman of the board and the administrative head is the chief executive officer.

4. The old man was upset probably because he considered it unjust that these people would be able to leave the country while he was left behind with his grievances unresolved.

5. Here "another facet" (*lingyi cengmian*) probably means that the idiosyncrasies of legal issues in China are quite distinct from those of passport applications for studying abroad.

6. On April 15, 1989, Hu Yaobang, who had supposedly resigned from the post of secretary-general of the Chinese Communist Party in 1987, died of a

heart attack. On April 17, students in Beijing held a mourning rally at Tiananmen Square, calling for political and economic reforms that Hu advocated before leaving office. In the weeks that followed, the demonstration—led by students well trained in the past by the Party in the techniques of applying and maintaining political pressure—grew in magnitude, intensity, and scope, and attracted student and nonstudent participants from many other cities. In a meeting in May between the students and the government to discuss the student demands, the students found the government arrogant and aloof, and the government found the students rude and incoherent (Spence, *The Search*, 739). On May 27, Chai Ling, commander-in-chief of the students' Defend Tiananmen Headquarters, after seeing the HK$27 million (about US$4 million) cash donated by supporters of the movement in Hong Kong and feeling the surge of the crowd, reneged on her earlier vote with the majority of the student leadership group to end the occupation of the Square. She declared publicly to her followers that the demonstration would continue, hoping privately that the government would be provoked to kill her followers and thereby trigger a revolution, and planned to leave the scene herself because she "wanted to live" (Tyler, *A Great Wall*, 354–56). On the night of June 3, 1989, the People's Liberation Army struck to clear the Square. Hundreds of people are believed to have been killed, and thousands were wounded.

In China it is customary to refer to an event of historical importance by the month and date of its occurrence, hence the "June Fourth Incident."

7. In the sixties and seventies, to advance Mao Zedong's idea of economic development through self-reliance, the Chinese government promoted the slogan "In industry, emulate Daqing; in agriculture, emulate Dazhai." Daqing (a rich oil field in Heilongjiang) and Dazhai (a commune in Shanxi) had exceeded their assigned production quotas for successive years.

8. *Renmin ribao* (People's daily), July 8, 1978.

9. Ibid., July 7, 1978.

10. Ibid., July 8, 1978.

11. Private conversation with Leonard Woodcock, February 24, 1991.

12. Private conversation with Michel Oksenberg, March 1990.

13. Edmund J. James, president of the University of Illinois, in a letter to President Theodore Roosevelt in 1906. (Translator's note: see Arthur Smith, *China and America*, 213–16; and this volume, Translator's Preface, note 46).

14. The Wangfu district (Wangfujing) is a bustling commercial district in Beijing.

15. *Renmin ribao*, July 8, 1978.

16. These students were in fact the first allowed to study abroad after the Cultural Revolution. Details will be discussed in chapter 4 (author).

17. In the early sixties, historian and writer Wu Han, reflecting a prevalent sentiment in China, wrote an allegorical play about the Ming dynasty court

official Hai Rui to criticize the incompetence of the CCP leadership, and Mao Zedong in particular. In 1966 the hard-line Shanghai faction of the Party headed by Jiang Qing (Mao's wife), supported by Mao, gained the upper hand over the Beijing group headed by Mayor Peng Zhen and launched the Great Proletarian Cultural Revolution to purge all anti-Party and anti-socialist culture. The decade-long movement wrought terror and disorder in China: intellectuals were sent to work in communes and factories; schools and colleges were closed; and students were enlisted as the vanguards of the movement, the Red Guards.

18. *Renmin ribao*, July 10, 1978.

19. Ibid., July 11, 1978.

20. *New York Times*, July 11, 1978.

21. *Deng Xiaoping wenxuan* (Selected works of Deng Xiaoping) (Beijing: Renmin Chubanshe, 1983), 37.

22. Ibid., 54.

23. *Renmin ribao*, December 27, 1978. According to a report in the *New York Times* on December 28, there were fifty-two people in this group. See chapter 4.

24. Yung Wing is discussed further in chapter 8.

25. The principal port of trade between China and the West in the eighteenth and nineteenth centuries was Guangzhou (Canton), in Guangdong. Thus the coastal area of Guangdong had the earliest contact with European and American merchants and missionaries.

26. In the eighteenth century, European and American traders found a receptive market in their countries for China's teas, silks, and handicrafts. But China showed little interest in what Europe and America had to offer: manufactured goods that resulted from the recent Industrial Revolution. The resulting trade imbalance caused a flow of silver from foreign countries to China. In the late eighteenth century, in order to find the silver to pay for the tea, British traders, who were selected by the British East India Company as purchasers of the opium derived from its crops in India, began to sell opium to China. A triangular trade web was woven with the complicity of Chinese merchants and officials. The flow of silver reversed. In 1839 the Chinese government confiscated 20,000 chests of British merchants' opium without compensation. Britain reacted by sending a fleet of sixteen warships and four thousand troops to attack China's coastal cities in an undeclared war in 1840. China lost. In the resulting Treaty of Nanking, the British obtained concessions from China, including the ceding of Hong Kong (which was returned to China in 1997).

27. Yung, *My Life*, 16.

28. After eight years of medical study in Scotland sponsored by a British missionary group, Wong Foon returned to China in 1857 and became a reputable surgeon in Guangzhou. Yung Wing's study at Yale was partially supported by the Ladies Association of Savanna, Georgia, through arrangements

made by the Rev. Brown. Wong Shing later worked as an interpreter on the Chinese Educational Commission in Hartford, Connecticut (Yung, *My Life*, 33–36).

29. Ibid., 41.

30. A viceroy was governor general of one or more provinces, in charge of administrative, judicial, military, and foreign affairs of the region. He could be recalled or transferred by the throne. Zeng Guofan was then the viceroy of Huguang District, which included the provinces of Hunan, Hubei, Guangdong, and Guangxi.

31. The name of the commission when translated in full is Educational Commission for the Selection and Supervision of Early Teen Youth to Study Abroad.

32. Such a waiver was signed by the father of Zhan Tianyou, a student (Xu Qiheng and Li Xibi, *Zhan Tianyou he Zhongguo de tielu* [Zhan Tianyou and China's railroad] [Shanghai: Renmin Chubanshe, 1978]) (author).

33. In 1912, the year after the founding of the Republic of China, Sun Yatsen, its first provisional president, sent a telegram to Yung Wing asking him to return to China to help develop the nation. Yung became ill and died at the age of eighty-four while planning his return trip to China. See the preface to Wang Qing's Chinese translation of Yung Wing's *My Life* (*Wo zai Zhongguo he zai Meiguo shenghuo de zhuiyi* [Beijing: Zhonghua Shuju, 1991]).

34. Cedar Hill Cemetery, 453 Fairfield Ave, Hartford, Connecticut; Yung Wing's grave is in section 12.

35. Wen Bingzhong, "Yige liumei youtong de huiyi" (Recollections of a teenage boy who went to study in America), a speech given on December 23, 1923, to Class D, Beijing Tax Institute, in Tsung-loo Kao [Gao Zonglu], comp., *Zhuanji wenxue* (Biographical literature) (Taipei: Zhuanjiwenxue Chubanshe, 1980) 37, no. 3. It was the ethnic hairstyle of the Manchus, who established the Qing dynasty, for males to shave their forehead and braid their hair into a long pigtail, or "queue." The Qing government required the practice of all males in China.

36. The Four Books are *The Great Learning* (Daxue), *The Doctrine of the Mean* (Zhongyong), *The Analects [of Confucius]* (Lunyu), and [*The Analects of*] *Mencius* (Mengzi). The Five Classics are *The Book of Songs* (Shijing), *The Book of History* (Shiji), *The Book of Changes* (Yijing), *The Book of Rites* (Liji), and *The Spring and Autumn Annals* (Chunqiu). By "numbing the mind," the author probably means that exclusive studying of these classics leads to blind belief in them and impedes inquiry and discovery.

37. A member of the Hanlin Academy. Members were admitted by passing examinations and usually were given civil-service appointments. Such appointments for the educated were no longer assured in the nineteenth century because of the limited number of government jobs.

38. In Chinese thought, ghosts are quite similar to gods, and are not necessarily disrespected. In *The Analects* (6: 20), Confucius said, "Respect gods and ghosts and keep them at a distance." The word "ghost" (*gui*) in "foreign ghost" (*yangguizi*) is, in certain contexts such as this, a crude label for a foreigner but does not carry a derogatory racial overtone; a Japanese would be a ghost of the East and a European or American a ghost of the West. Its popular usage may have come from *Investiture of the Gods* (Fengshen yanyi), a seventeenth-century book of science fiction and mythology by Xu Zonglin in which many gods and ghosts were foreign (Indian) in origin and were often deployed to human society by a mandate from Heaven to implement justice.

39. Minister was one rank lower than ambassador. At that time China had no ambassador to the United States.

40. Yung, *My Life*, 200, 205.

41. See Zhong Shuhe, Foreword to *You Meizhou riji* (Journal of an American journey), "Zouxiang shijie congshu" (Stride into the world series) (Changsha: Yuelu Book Co, 1985), about the early teenage Chinese students in America, 1872–81.

42. Yung, *My Life*, 205.

43. Six students refused to go back, according to one version of the story. See Wen Bingzhong, "Yige liumei youtong de huiyi" (author).

44. Liang Dunyan pitched for Yale's varsity baseball team, and many of the other Chinese students also played baseball. In 1881 while the students waited in San Francisco for a steamer to take them home, they accepted the challenge of the Oakland team for a game. The Chinese students won (LaFargue, *China's First Hundred*, 53). Liang also took part in negotiations with the United States on the remission of the Boxer indemnity fund. An account of the careers of the returned students can be found in LaFargue, *China's First Hundred*; and Shi Ni, *Guannian yu beiju*.

45. Seven of the students who returned from America in 1881 and served in China's naval fleets died in battles: four died in the Sino-French naval war in 1884, and three died in the Sino-Japanese War a decade later.

46. Yan Fu also translated, in the 1890s, John Stuart Mill's *On Liberty* and *A System of Logic*, Montesquieu's *The Spirit of the Laws*, Spencer's *The Study of Sociology*, and Adam Smith's *The Wealth of Nations*. These translated books started a trend, the Enlightenment Movement, among educated Chinese to study Western thought.

47. *Guangxu zhengyao* (Records of the Guangxu reign) (Yonghezheng, Taibeixian, Taiwan: Wenhai Chubanshe, 1969), vol. 13 (1887): 4–5 (author). Guangxu was the seventh emperor of the Qing dynasty.

48. There were nine civil-service ranks, the first being the highest. Two hundred taels equaled about $148.

49. *Guangxu zhengyao*, vol. 28 (1902): 40–41.

50. Zhang Zhidong, *Quanxue pian: Youxue dier* (Essays on the importance of education: Studying abroad being the second) (Yonghezheng, Taibeixian, Taiwan: Wenhai Chubanshe, 1968).

51. In the 1870s Li Hongzhang, continuing the earlier effort of Zeng Guofan, initiated foreign-style entrepreneurial, educational, and diplomatic efforts to modernize China. This was known as the Foreign Adaptation Movement (Yangwu Yundong).

52. In 1894 China and Japan, in a dispute over the Japanese seizure of the Korean royal palace, fought a sea battle on the Yellow Sea and a land battle in Seoul and Pyongyang. China was defeated. In the Treaty of Shimonoseki, which concluded the war, China acknowledged Korea as a protectorate of Japan, gave up four more treaty ports, ceded Formosa (Taiwan), the Pescadores, and the Liaodong region of southern Manchuria, and paid 200 million taels (about $148 million) of indemnity.

53. In 1898 Liang Qichao and Kang Youwei, two scholars of Chinese classics (Liang had also worked as a newspaper editor), proposed to Emperor Guangxu political reforms, known as the Wuxu Reforms (Wuxu Bianfa, *wuxu* being the Chinese calendar year for 1898), based on the concept "Chinese learning is the essence, and Western learning is for practical development" [Zhongxue wei ti, Xixue wei yong]. The reforms met an abrupt end when Cixi (Guangxu's aunt, the empress dowager), after being informed by the conservative faction of the court about the reforms, emerged from semiretirement, resumed power, detained Guangxu, and ordered the arrest and execution of Liang and Kang, along with their followers. Both fled the country.

54. The 1911 Revolution began on October 10, 1911, when revolutionaries, including members of the Revolutionary Alliance organized by Sun Yat-sen, launched a hastily arranged uprising in Wuchang against the Qing court after the Qing police discovered their hideout when a homemade bomb exploded accidentally on October 9. The uprising quickly gained the widespread support of mutinous troops, and the Qing dynasty was soon toppled. Sun returned from France to become the provisional president of the new Republic of China.

The New Culture Movement began on May 4, 1919, when citizens and students in Beijing protested in a public rally against the Treaty of Versailles, which, with the concurrence of Woodrow Wilson of the United States, David Lloyd George of Britain, and Georges Clemenceau of France, stipulated the transfer of Germany's rights in China's Shandong Province to Japan instead of returning them to China. This agreement ignored China's contribution to the Allied force in World War I: China had sent 96,000 laborers to France in 1917–18 to unload military cargo, build barracks and hospitals, dig trenches, clean battlefields, and handle ammunition in railway yards. (Of these laborers, 543 were lost at sea when their boats were sunk by German submarines in the Mediterranean, and about two thousand died in France.) The public protest began as a movement "to fight for China's rights internationally and to remove traitors to Japan domestically." It evolved into a broad cultural movement in which the Chinese questioned Western moral values (see note 46, this chapter, on the Enlightenment Movement), promoted writing in the vernacular cadences of ordinary speech (as opposed to the "classical," literary language), and analyzed China's own culture. (Because it was blocked by the Chinese students in Paris from leaving its hotel, the Chinese delegation did not sign the treaty.) See Spence, *The Search*, 288–94.

55. The program referred to here is the remission of the Boxer Indemnity, discussed in the Translator's Preface.

56. Xinchou (the Chinese calendar year for 1901) Tiaoyue.

57. The Boxer Indemnity is known in China as the "Genzi indemnity," Genzi being the year 1900 in the traditional Chinese calendar.

58. The Tsinghua School, located in Beijing, is now Tsinghua University.

59. *Jiaoyu zazhi* (The educational review) 3, no. 7 (1911): 12–13.

60. On the interruption of the study-abroad program, see note 49, Translator's Preface.

61. On the 1911 Revolution, see note 54, this chapter.

62. The quick collapse of the Qing dynasty in 1911 was caused by the mutiny of its troops. For the next fifteen years, different regions of the country were run by military commanders, or "warlords," who collected their own taxes and tariffs, conscripted their own soldiers, and made their own deals with foreign powers. The central government in Nanjing had little control over them.

63. See Translator's Preface, note 50.

64. The Northern Expedition began on July 1, 1926, in the southern city of Guangzhou, when Chiang Kai-shek led the National Revolutionary Army of 115,000 men on a northward campaign to quash the regional warlords and unify China.

65. On March 21, 1927, the General Labor Union in Shanghai, directed by the Chinese Communist Party, launched a general strike against the city's industrialists to show support for the approaching National Revolutionary Army of Chiang Kai-shek. On April 12, the Society for Common Progress, an antilabor group organized by the industrialists, attacked many union headquarters with the assistance of foreign-concessions authorities (whose investment and wealth depended on labor peace) and the National Revolutionary Army (who needed Shanghai's wealthy elements to bankroll its Northern Expedition).

66. The nucleus of the Chinese Communist Party was formed in 1920. In 1934 the Nationalists began a military encirclement of the Communist stronghold in Jiangxi. In October of that year the Communists broke through the blockade and escaped to eventual safety in Shaanxi. The 370-day, 6,000-mile trek in harsh terrain became known as the Long March.

67. On July 7, 1937, Japan, then already occupying the eastern part of

Hebei Province (in which Beijing is located) and China's northeastern provinces (Manchuria), claimed that one of its soldiers, missing from a roll call after a night maneuver with its base at the Marco Polo Bridge (Lugouqiao) ten miles west of Beijing, had been captured by Chinese troops. Japan ordered an attack—the firing of the first shot of World War II—on the Chinese troops at nearby Wanping.

Beijing (formerly romanized "Peking") was renamed Beiping (formerly romanized "Peiping") when the Republic of China chose Nanjing (formerly romanized "Nanking") as its capital in 1911. Beiping (Northern Peace) was renamed Beijing (Northern Capital) when it again became the capital of China under the People's Republic in 1949.

68. After China's war against Japan ended in 1945, fighting resumed between the Nationalists and Communists. The mediation by the United States through some of its most respected diplomats and military leaders—Albert Wedemeyer, Patrick Hurley, and George Marshall—failed to bring a peaceful settlement. In 1949 the Communists took control of the mainland and founded the People's Republic of China, and the Nationalists retreated to Taiwan.

69. *Renmin ribao*, August 25, 1955.

70. *Jiefang ribao* (Liberation daily), November 12, 1950.

71. *Renmin ribao*, August 23, 1955.

72. *Renmin ribao*, August 20, 1955.

73. Xinhua News Agency, wire news, December 16, 1955.

74. *American Foreign Policy, 1950–1955*, vol. 2 (Washington, D.C.: U.S. Department of State, 1957), 2517–19.

75. Between 1949 and 1969, 8,424 Chinese students were sent to the Soviet Union and 1,109 to Eastern European countries (Huang Shiqi, *Contemporary Educational Relationships with the Industrialized World: A Chinese View in China's Education and the Industrialized World*, ed. Ruth Hayhoe and Marianne Bastids [New York: M. E. Sharpe, 1987], 225) (author).

76. For about a decade after 1949 the Soviet Union provided military and industrial aid to China. A rift between the two countries, due to disagreements in ideology and in policy on development and national defense, began in the late fifties. The Soviet Union terminated its aid in 1960–61.

77. Only 206 students remained in the Soviet Union in the mid-sixties (Huang, *Contemporary Educational Relationships*, 225) (author).

78. The poem was written by Wang Bo (649–676), to commemorate his friend Du's departure for distant Sichuan to assume the post of sheriff.

2. THE ROAD TO STUDYING ABROAD

1. A "Request for Instruction" is a policy document drafted by a lower bureau for consideration and approval by a higher administrative official.

2. Leo A. Orleans, *Chinese Students in America: Policies, Issues and Numbers* (Washington, D.C.: National Academy Press, 1988), 39.

3. Some of the students who received F-1 visas also received financial support from private foundations in the United States. Since the Chinese Ministry of Education handled administration and processing, it seems appropriate that they were classified as government-sponsored students (author). An F-1 visa does not require that the student return to the home country before applying for immigrant status.

4. *Zhongguo jiaoyu nianjian* (China education almanac) (Beijing: Renmin Jiaoyu Chubanshe, 1981), 667.

5. *Renmin ribao, haiwaiban* (People's daily, overseas edition), January 26, 1989. Also, see *Wenhuibao* (Wenhui news), March 26, 1989.

6. The sweet dream is the hope to go abroad; the nightmare is the return to the same old reality when hope is destroyed by inability to obtain permission to leave, a passport, or a visa.

7. See chapter 1, note 66.

8. Full-time leave classes are for students who have received permission from their work unit to take a leave of absence for studying a foreign language.

9. At that time, ¥150 equaled about $40.

10. The sobbing woman was most likely in need of monetary help. In China, many people have spare time but no spare money, so they become onlookers without ability to offer help; in America, many people have spare money but no spare time, so they either offer money or leave.

11. *Tuofu*, in Chinese, means "thanks to you." Its pronunciation in the Cantonese dialect is closest to "TOEFL" in English. Cantonese is spoken by the Chinese in Hong Kong.

12. ¥200 was worth about $24 at the 1996 exchange rate.

13. *Qigong* is a martial art that also emphasizes meditation.

14. *The Journey to the West* (Xiyouji) is an adventure novel written in the 1590s about the pilgrimage of a Tang dynasty (618–907) monk, accompanied by his capable but mischievous monkey disciple, to India in search of Buddhist scriptures.

15. The I-20 form is a certificate of admission issued by American universities to foreign students for obtaining F-1 visas.

16. Xinhua News Agency, wire news, January 3, 1979; December 23, 1979.

17. Ibid., December 9, 1983; article by He Dongchang in *Renmin ribao*, September 21, 1984; Xinhua News Agency, wire news, November 28, 1984.

18. *Guangming ribao* (Guangming daily), November 24, 1988.

19. *Zhongguo jiaoyu nianjian* (1981), 667

20. *Renmin ribao, haiwaiban*, February 2, 1989.

21. *Wenhui bao*, March 26, 1989.

22. *Huashenbao* (Huashen news), January 16, 1990.

23. *Renmin ribao*, May 3, 1988.

24. *Wenhui bao*, March 26, 1986.

25. Housing is usually assigned by a person's work unit, with preference given to married couples. Unmarried workers sometimes share dormitory rooms or get no housing.

26. ¥20,000 was worth about $6,800 at the 1985 exchange rate.

27. A person approved for attending an international conference receives a fixed amount of foreign currency for expenses and is allowed to bring back to China, duty free, foreign goods within quota and not exceeding a specified monetary value.

28. In April 1957 Mao Zedong, with the reluctant support of the hardliners of the Chinese Communist Party, launched the Hundred Flowers Movement in a speech calling on the nation to criticize the Party. An outpouring of such criticism began on May 1, 1957, from all walks of life, but particularly from intellectuals. The movement lasted until July 7, when the hardliners, with Mao's backing, began a backlash known as the Anti-Rightist Movement, in which 300,000 intellectuals were labeled "rightists." Many were imprisoned, sentenced to hard labor, banished to remote frontiers, or driven to suicide after being humiliated and denounced in public rallies called "struggle sessions."

29. The U.S. administrative order, issued on account of the June Fourth Incident in China, stated that Chinese students, visiting scholars, and other Chinese who were in the United States in the period between June 5, 1989, and April 11, 1990, could stay until July 1, 1993. This order and the Chinese Student Protection Act of 1992 will be discussed in chapter 8.

30. The IAP-66 form is a certificate of admission issued by American universities to foreign students for obtaining J-1 visas.

31. A Neighborhood Committee informs residents of a designated neighborhood of government policies and looks after issues of public concern.

32. The broad sword, a traditional weapon, is sometimes used in martial arts.

33. *Renmin ribao*, January 4, 1979.

34. During an interview, I read these data in a supplementary document attached to a government propaganda publication (author).

35. Orleans, *Chinese Students*, 79; *Zhongguo jiaoyu nianjian* (1981), 667.

36. According to the CCP Central Committee's document "Resolutions on the Problems Arising from Studying Abroad with Privately Financed Means" (Zifei chuguo liuxue ruogan wenti de jueding; March 31, 1982), "Since 1979, about six thousand students have gone abroad through various privately financed means" (author).

37. *Zhongguo baike nianjian* (China encyclopedia almanac) (Beijing: Zhongguo Dabaikequanshu Chubanshe, 1980, 1981).

38. *Zhongguo jiaoyu nianjian* (1980–85); *Zhongguo baike nianjian* (1981); Orleans, *Chinese Students*, 79.

39. *Renmin ribao, haiwaiban*, January 4, 1989.

40. Ibid., November 18, 1989.

41. Ibid., October 7, 1989, October 27, 1992, January 16, 1993; Zhu Kaixuan, Deputy Director of the Chinese Education Commission, in answering a question during a press conference (*Shijie ribao* [World journal] [U.S.], March 16, 1995).

42. Gu Weiqun, "A Survey of Chinese Students and Scholars in America," in the annual report of the Chinese Political-Science Students and Scholars Association of America, 1990.

43. *Renmin ribao,* May 30, 1980.

44. Between 1981 and 1983, China had an economic upturn and a small trade surplus after several years of trade deficits. Concurrently, some artistic and cultural works, because of Western influence, were critical of the Chinese Communist Party. The political journals of the People's Liberation Army were the first to launch sharp criticism at this "spiritual pollution" from the West. They were joined by Deng Xiaoping and later by Hu Yaobang.

45. *Renmin ribao,* November 27, 1983.

46. Ibid., November 29, 1983.

47. Ibid., December 4, 1988.

48. *Renmin ribao, haiwaiban,* October 7, 1989.

49. A more detailed account of this circular dance is given in appendix 3.

50. The author probably means that a departing student is usually preoccupied with worries about missing his flight, misplacing his passport or ticket, or being detained at the last minute.

51. Many married couples live apart because they have work assignments at different places or have no housing.

52. ¥10,000 was worth about $2,700 in 1989.

53. The author probably means that a person usually develops a more acute sense of one's own country after one becomes an alien.

3. THE SHOCK OVERSEAS

1. "The red lanterns and the green wine" is a traditional expression used to describe the festive activities of the rich and powerful.

2. She was paraphrasing a popular Chinese sarcastic expression: "Oh, he/she thinks the moon in America [or another foreign country] is rounder than that in China." On a more scientific note, the burning of coal, which is a principal energy source in China, results in a hazy atmosphere. The perceived whiter clouds in America may be a result of its cleaner air and bluer sky.

3. See chap. 1, note 14.

4. The Great Hall of the People is a mammoth government building adjacent to Tiananmen Square that houses a huge auditorium and many smaller meeting rooms and banquet halls.

5. To get goods through the "back door" means to obtain them through means such as personal favoritism or bribery.

6. *Renminbi* is the currency of the People's Republic of China.

7. In a society in which everybody works for the government, bureaucratic power accomplishes more than monetary power does.

8. The bearded man got his history somewhat mixed up. Yuanmingyuan (Yuanming Garden), once the playground of the Qing court, was nearly completely burned down by the British and French troops in 1858 during the Sino-British and French War by order of Britain's Lord Elgin. Some feeble reconstruction took place after the burning. In 1900 the Eight-Country Allied Force damaged the Yiheyuan (Yihe Garden), the Summer Palace of the empress dowager and her court, and burned what was left of the Yuanmingyuan. It has not been rebuilt.

9. Zhuangzi (ca. 350–270 B.C.E.) founded a philosophy espousing humanity's absolute emancipation and peace. For an English rendition of his thoughts, see Thomas Merton, *The Way of Chuang-Tzu* (New York: New Directions, 1969). See also Burton Watson, trans., *The Complete Works of Zhuangzi* (New York: Columbia University Press, 1968).

10. *Jinpingmei* (lit., *The Plum in the Golden Vase*, but translated into English in 1939 by Clement Egerton under the title *The Golden Lotus*), an anonymous novel from the early 1600s, describes how the rich and powerful amused themselves with games and plots of greed and selfishness, which brought about their destruction. The unabridged version has been banned in China for centuries because of its explicit sexual episodes.

11. The student probably was unwilling to tarnish the image of his country. See also the episode of "Japanese salted fish" in chapter 8.

12. See chapter 1, note 53.

13. The author probably means that the ethos of America is different because it has been shaped and defined by factors not found in other countries. The natural factors are America's open space, arable land, climate, and natural resources; a major human factor was the fact that Europe, which provided America's early settlers, was the continent of the Renaissance, the Industrial Revolution, and the budding concept of modern democracy.

14. The concept of unification in thinking may have its roots in the teachings of Mencius. In *Analects of Mencius*, King Xiang of Liang asked how the country could be stabilized. Mencius replied, "[It will be] stabilized by being in unity" (*ding yu yi*) (*Mengzi*, "Liang Hui wang," part 1, sec. 2).

15. The Misty school of poetry (Menglongshi) was a movement popular among youth in the eighties. It reflected their feelings about the Cultural Revolution and emphasized vague and nonexplicit images.

16. For the meaning of "which side has a rounder moon," see this chapter, note 2.

4. DIFFERENT GENERATIONS, DIFFERENT TALENTS

1. The different generations here represent students who had different experiences as teenagers, e.g., during the founding of the People's Republic of China, the Cultural Revolution, and the post–Cultural Revolution years.

2. *New York Times*, December 28, 1978.

3. *Renmin ribao*, December 27, 1978.

4. *New York Times*, December 28, 1978. The names of students in the first dispatch are given in appendix 4.

5. See chapter 1, note 7.

6. The Red Capital was a men's clothing store in Beijing in the seventies.

7. Orleans, *Chinese Students*, 107.

8. American institutions sometimes assign a Chinese student who is more proficient in English to act as a local host or problem-solver for visiting scholars on short visits from China whose command of English is limited.

9. Orleans, *Chinese Students*, 97.

10. Xidan Wall, known as the "Democracy Wall," was a stretch of wall to the west of the former Forbidden City in Beijing on which, beginning in November 1978, posters (known as "big-character posters" because of the large writing used for easy reading at a distance) speaking out against the state and advocating democracy were pasted for passersby to read.

11. The next in rank were Purdue University, the University of Pittsburgh, Columbia University, the University of Minnesota, the University of Illinois, Cornell University, the University of California at Los Angeles, Ohio State University, and Stanford University. The school having the highest number of privately financed students was the City University of New York (Orleans, *Chinese Students*, 105–6) (author).

12. Words written in English in the letter are designated by roman type here.

13. During the Cultural Revolution some parents named their newborns Hong (Red) to commemorate the revolutionary spirit of the time.

14. Chen Ning Yang and T. D. Lee, two Chinese students who came to America in the forties, were co-winners of the 1957 Nobel Prize in physics.

15. However, some American universities offer mortgages at below-market interest rates to help their faculty and staff purchase homes.

16. On December 11, 1936, while Generalissimo Chiang Kai-shek was in Xi'an to round up support for his campaign against the Communists, General Zhang Xueliang, a subordinate, seized him and demanded a policy of inclusion, rather than annihilation, of the Communists, to form a united front against the encroaching Japanese. The follow-up negotiations, which included Zhou Enlai as the Communist representative, resulted in the release of Chiang and a tacit agreement to a united front. Thereafter, Mao Zedong's

Eighth Route Army in the Long March was recognized as the New Fourth Army.

17. A "golden doll" means a small fortune.

18. See chapter 2, note 29.

19. This is an allusion to striptease or sex shows.

20. Calvin Coolidge, in a speech to the American Society of Newspaper Editors, January 17, 1925.

5. THE OTHER SIDE OF THE BRIGHT MOON

1. In the various political campaigns of the first three decades of the People's Republic of China, targeted people were often sent to work in communes or factories "to learn from the masses," or to undergo "reeducation."

2. Growing bean sprouts requires frequent spraying and washing of the sprouts with water.

3. Mencius, 371–289 B.C.E., like Confucius (551–479 B.C.E.), was an educator who aspired to serve in government to practice his teachings. These passages are from *Mengzi*, "Gaozi," part 2, sec. 15.

4. Workers in a commune are divided into several production brigades, each of which is assigned a specified task. The team holds regularly scheduled meetings to discuss production-related issues, including airing and resolving grievances.

5. After the Chinese Communists attained power in 1949, the government seized cultivated land from landlords. The Land Reform process was generally carried out with violence against landlords, many of whom were killed.

6. During the Cultural Revolution, people could be charged with a "crime" in public gatherings such as a staff meeting in an institution or a neighborhood gathering. The accused, if unable to clear the charge, would be sent to a commune or factory to reform through labor. Sometimes the charge would result in a public rally (a "struggle session"), in which the accused would be denounced for his crime and paraded on a stage or in the streets wearing a tall hat on which was written his crime. Bodily injury, confiscation of personal property, and ransacking of the home of the accused could also result. The humiliation of this process drove some of the accused to commit suicide.

7. Mark Graham, "Millionaires' Row," *Asia* 30, no. G22 (August 21, 1993).

8. *New York Times*, August 19, 1991.

9. See chapter 3, note 15.

10. "Record of the Peach Blossom Spring" (Taohua yuan ji) by Tao Yuanming (Tao Qian, 365–427), tells the story of a fisherman in the Jin dynasty (265–420) who, having lost his way during a fishing trip along a river, comes across the Peach Blossom Spring. The residents there are descendants of peasants who had fled the war of unification of the Qin dynasty (221–206 B.C.E.) and who

know nothing of the passing of later dynasties. The fisherman, after returning to his village, decides to go back but can no longer find the spring.

11. The people in China's northeastern provinces of Liaoning, Jilin, and Heilongjiang are taller and heavier than Chinese in other regions.

12. Qian Zhongshu (1910–98), one of the twenty-four students in the third dispatch, funded by the remission of the Boxer Indemnity by the British government, studied at Oxford in 1935, and later at the University of Paris. In 1947 he published his only novel, *Weicheng* (Eng. trans., Jean Kelly and Nathan K. Mao, *Fortress Besieged* [Bloomingdale: Indiana University Press, 1979]). Today he enjoys a literary reputation in China perhaps unsurpassed by any other twentieth-century writer for his five-volume *Guanzhuibian* (selected essays trans. by Ronald Egan in *Limited Views: Essays on Ideas and Letters* [Cambridge, Mass.: Harvard University Asia Center, 1998]). In it he analyzes topics from the Chinese classics and history books and compares them with corresponding Western ideas and writings; topics include anthropology, sociology, literature, and politics.

Lu Xun (1881–1936), after giving up his medical study in Japan, returned to China to write about China's social ills. He is generally regarded as the trailblazer of modern Chinese literature.

13. On big-character posters, see chapter 4, note 10.

14. The ranking of professions in traditional Chinese society according to perceived social status is (from top to bottom): scholar, farmer, worker, businessman, soldier.

6. SOME MARRIAGES HOLD TOGETHER, MANY FALL APART

1. *South China Morning Post*, March 17, 1994.

2. Until a few decades ago, milk in China was not pasteurized and it was necessary to boil it before drinking, so people are accustomed to drinking milk hot. Heating cooking oil to a high temperature before stir-frying vegetables ensures rapid cooking so that freshness and flavor are retained.

3. *Sifangqian* literally means "private-chamber money." In traditional Chinese marriages it was money kept by a married woman, given by her parents, for her use, since she had little or no access to pocket money in her husband's household.

7. EMOTIONAL ATTACHMENT TO CHINA

1. Yan'an, in Shaanxi, was the base of the Chinese Communist Party after the Long March of 1934–1935, in which the Communists were pursued by the Nationalists.

2. Xianglin's wife is the principal character in "The New Year's Sacrifice" by Lu Xun, a story about the cruel treatment that Chinese society dealt to a poor and uneducated woman.

3. Liu Xuesheng, "What Kind of Person Was Lu Gang?" *'90s Hong Kong*, December 1991.

4. Nie Hualing, *Shijie ribao* (World journal; U.S.), November 3, 1991.

5. *Beijing qingnian bao* (Beijing youth news), May 7, 1992.

6. This quotation is translated from the Chinese translation of the original text.

7. These are slogans used by the Nationalist government in Taiwan from 1949 until the end of the eighties to advocate its declared policy of liberating the mainland and by the People's Republic of China to advocate its declared policy of liberating Taiwan.

8. *Baqi*, the mentality of an overlord, a tyrant, a bully.

9. *Daoqi*, a parochial and insular mentality, as in the comparison, in size, of an island to a continent.

10. A "field meeting" is a membership meeting in a commune.

8. TO RETURN OR TO STAY

1. Ethnic Chinese who are permanent residents or citizens of a foreign country are called "overseas Chinese" (*huaqiao*) in China.

2. *Renmin ribao, haiwaiban*, October 15, 1992.

3. *Shijie zhoukan* (World weekly) (U.S.), July 25, 1994.

4. Rone Tempest, *Los Angeles Times*, January 3, 1995.

5. *Statistical Yearbook of the Immigration and Naturalization Service* (Washington, D.C.: U.S. Department of Justice, 1982–1987). See also Orleans, *Chinese Students*, 39.

6. Li Yanjie, a well-known propagandist in the eighties, advocated morality to students.

7. *Renmin ribao, haiwaiban*, October 26, 1989.

8. Ibid., October 15, 1992.

9. Ibid., October 22, 1992.

10. Ibid., August 21, 1992.

11. About $130 to $160 (in 1989).

12. Letter from Huang Kaijia, one of the teenage students, dated January 28, 1882, to Mrs. Fannie Bertlett, an American. See Zhong Shuhe in chap. 1, note 41 (author).

13. The answer is a cue to the questioner that the speaker does not wish to discuss the subject.

14. About $25 and $7, respectively.

15. China, suffering from its defeat in the First Opium War (1839–42) and from having missed the Industrial Revolution earlier, was ripe for uprisings against the Qing court because of rapidly worsening poverty brought by population growth and its pressure on land use, lack of employment opportunities for the educated, outflow of silver due to trade imbalance, high taxation to pay for war indemnity, widespread opium addiction, and corruption at all levels of government. Among the uprisings, the one led by Hong Xiuquan attracted the most followers. Hong was born in a peasant family in 1814 but studied classics and yearned to become a government official. In 1850, after failing for the fourth time the qualifying civil-service examination, Hong, who in an earlier day had claimed to be the younger brother of Jesus because he had seen and conversed with God the Father and Jesus in a dream, declared himself King of the Heavenly Kingdom of Great Peace, or Taiping Heavenly Kingdom (Taiping Tianguo), in Guangxi. The Taiping force pushed northeastward and established its capital at Nanjing. It was defeated by the Xiang (Hunan) Army led by Zeng Guofan in 1864.

16. Yung, *My Life*, 53–54.

17. *Yi* also means "justice, loyalty."

18. The purchase order for materials for the factory was filled by Putnam Machine Co., Fitchburg, Massachusetts.

19. Yung, *My Life*, 238.

20. On the Reform Movement, see chapter 1, note 53.

21. Between June and September 1898, Emperor Guangxu issued a series of edicts on government reforms. The period is known as the Hundred Days of Reform. See also chapter 1, note 53.

22. It is not known how Yung Wing was able to return to America in 1902, since his U.S. citizenship was revoked in 1898. In that year Secretary of State John Sherman wrote to Minister Charles Denby in Beijing,

> Your dispatch No. 2880 of February 28th has been received. You therein report that Yung Wing ... submitted for your examination a certified copy of his naturalization certificate, together with several passports issued by this Department. He further stated that he had voted without objection at all elections since his naturalization in 1852, and claimed that after such recognition by the government of the United States, his status as a citizen could not be questioned.... A refusal to admit now his right to privileges which he has apparently exercised for many years on its face seems unjust and without warrant. Nevertheless, in view of the construction placed upon the naturalization laws of the United States by our highest courts, the Department does not feel that it can properly recognize him as a citizen of the United States. (Edmund Worthy, "Yung Wing in America," *Pacific Historical Review* 34 [August 1965]: 283).

The naturalization law pertaining to this case was the 1878 *In re Ah Yup* decision on the ineligibility of Chinese immigrants to become American citizens.

23. On Yung Wing's death, see chapter 1, note 33.

24. Yung, *My Life*, 113.

25. Yung Wing wrote, "The [Taiping] rebellion rose in the arena of China with an enigmatic character like that of the Sphinx, somewhat puzzling at the start" (*My Life*, 119), but he did not explain what the enigma was. Apparently, the rebellion's enigmatic character or "dual aspect" arose from (1) its origin as a supposedly Christian movement and (2) the eventual pillage, plunder, and indiscriminate destruction—without discipline or indication of religious restraining power—by the Taiping troops.

In 1864 Zeng Guofan wrote to the emperor on the recapture of Nanjing from the Taiping army: "Not one of the 100,000 rebels in Nanking surrendered themselves when the city was taken but in many cases gathered together and burned themselves and passed away without repentance. Such a formidable band of rebels has been rarely known from ancient time to the present" (Franz Michael and Chang Chung-li, *The Taiping Rebellion: History and Documents*, vol. 1 [University of Washington Press: Seattle, 1966], 174).

26. Three people met early death in America and thirteen more died in China. These numbers are according to Wang Huansheng, *Liuxue jiaoyu—Zhongguo liumei jiaoyu shiliao* (Studying abroad: A source book of the history of Chinese students studying in America), ed. Liu Zheng (Taipei: National Bureau of Translation and Editing [Taiwan], 1980). The total number, however, still does not add up to 120 (author).

APPENDIX 3: VACILLATIONS OF STUDY-ABROAD POLICY IN THE 1980S

1. After the death of Mao Zedong, Deng Xiaoping, emerging from banishment, advocated adding the pragmatic line "Practice is the sole criterion with which to test truth" to Mao Zedong's abstract ideological line "Seek truth from facts." After attaining power in 1976 following the death of Mao, Hua Guofeng, the chairman of the Chinese Communist Party handpicked by Mao, said that all the Chinese needed to do to guarantee a bright future was to obey "whatever" Chairman Mao had said and to ensure the continuation of "whatever" he had decided. Hua and his followers were labeled as the "Whatever Wing" (Fanshipai).

2. Students who were born after the founding of the People's Republic of China in 1949.

3. *Renmin ribao*, July 30, 1982.

4. Ibid., November 30, 1984.

5. Ibid., January 12, 1985.

6. Ibid., May 14, 1986. The Four Modernizations were in industry, national defense, science, and technology.

7. Ibid., June 16, 1987.

8. On December 5, 1986, students of the University of Science and Technology in Hefei organized a rally protesting manipulated elections (from a government-prepared slate of candidates) and advocating democratic reform. In the days that followed, students in other cities also protested. The Chinese Communist Party reacted swiftly by dismissing several prominent reform advocates and announced the resignation of Hu Yaobang, who had spoken in the past on the need for rapid reform.

9. *New York Times*, March 23, 1988.

10. *Renmin ribao*, April 6, 1988.

11. Ibid., May 3, 1988.

12. Zhongxingshe, wire news, June 4, 1988.

13. See chapter 1, footnote 6.

14. *Renmin ribao*, July 27, 1989.

15. Ibid., July 27, 1989.

16. Ibid., October 24, 1993.

17. Ibid., January 16, 1993; October 27, 1992.

INDEX